Mastering React Native

Leverage frontend development skills to build impressive iOS and Android applications with React Native

Eric Masiello
Jacob Friedmann

BIRMINGHAM - MUMBAI

Mastering React Native

Copyright © 2017 Packt Publishing

All rights reserved. No part of this book may be reproduced, stored in a retrieval system, or transmitted in any form or by any means, without the prior written permission of the publisher, except in the case of brief quotations embedded in critical articles or reviews.

Every effort has been made in the preparation of this book to ensure the accuracy of the information presented. However, the information contained in this book is sold without warranty, either express or implied. Neither the author(s), nor Packt Publishing, and its dealers and distributors will be held liable for any damages caused or alleged to be caused directly or indirectly by this book.

Packt Publishing has endeavored to provide trademark information about all of the companies and products mentioned in this book by the appropriate use of capitals. However, Packt Publishing cannot guarantee the accuracy of this information.

First published: January 2017

Production reference: 1060117

Published by Packt Publishing Ltd.
Livery Place
35 Livery Street
Birmingham
B3 2PB, UK.

ISBN 978-1-78588-578-5

www.packtpub.com

Credits

Authors

Eric Masiello
Jacob Friedmann

Reviewers

Patrick Puritscher

Commissioning Editor

Wilson Dsouza

Acquisition Editor

Denim Pinto

Content Development Editor

Divij Kotian

Technical Editor

Rutuja Vaze

Copy Editor

Safis Editing

Project Coordinator

Sheejal Shah

Proofreader

Safis Editing

Indexer

Rekha Nair

Graphics

Abhinash Sahu

Production Coordinator

Aparna Bhagat

Disclaimer

We are using the New York Times' API for illustrative purposes only. We do not recommend you publish your application to the app store using this API without first reading the Terms of Use (`https://developer.nytimes.com/tou`). For more information please consult the NYT's terms and conditions.

About the Authors

Eric Masiello is a lead software engineer for Vistaprint Digital. Formerly, Eric worked as a principal frontend engineer for the Advisory Board Company and built mobile apps for the Education Advisory Board. Eric has worked primarily as a frontend/UI developer for over 10 years and freelances as a website designer/developer at `http://www.synbydesign.com`. He has taught frontend topics at General Assembly in Washington, D.C. and was a technical reviewer for Mastering ReactJS, a video by Packt Publishing.

You can follow him here:

- `https://www.linkedin.com/in/ericmasiello`
- `https://twitter.com/ericmasiello`
- `http://synbydesign.com`

First and foremost, I must extend an enormous thank you to my beautiful, talented, and always-inspiring wife, Hyun. If not for her support, this book would honestly not exist. My deepest gratitude also goes out to my family: Mom, Dad, Brian, Juliana, Nicolas, Umma, and my sisters Hannah, Min, and Carroll. I'm truly blessed to have such a wonderful and supportive family. Shout out to all the inspiring people I've had the honor of working with over the years. I've learned so much from all of you. Thanks to Keith, Michael, Andrew, Scott, Shelley, Kelly, the inimitable Karthik, Jesse, Jaworski, Beth, Mat, Anbu, Ashwin, Kevin, Ann, all my PIC/RCS homies, the EAB dev/UI team, the entire ABC/EAB UX team, and finally my new Vistaprint Digital family. Thank you to all my close friends who have balanced me, challenged me, shared a drink, or just a laugh: Bryan, Alan, Chris, Kyril, Brandon, April, and the whole Expansion Broadcast + DC crew. Thank you to everyone at Packt for bringing me along on this amazing (and sleepless) journey. And finally, thanks to my coauthor Jacob for all the work he did in realizing this book and for agreeing to even write a book with someone he had known for all of two weeks.

Jacob Friedmann is a developer living in Seattle, WA. He has been working as a developer professionally for 5 years and is currently a principal software engineer at AddThis, an Oracle company. At AddThis, he works on large front and backend applications. He also builds mobile applications using React Native, including Audicy (`http://audicy.io`), which will soon be launched on the App Store. He has taught several classes, including frontend web development and JavaScript development through General Assembly in Washington D.C.

You can follow him here:

- `https://www.linkedin.com/in/jacob-friedmann`
- `https://twitter.com/JacobDFriedmann`

Writing a book (my first!) is hard, and I don't think I would have been able to do it without the support of my loving boyfriend, Matt. He weathered my frequent complaining in stride and kept me focused when I needed it most. For that, I am incredibly grateful. Huge thanks to all of my AddThis family who have always inspired me to keep learning and pushed me to do my best work. To all of my friends and family, who were patient with me when I became a recluse to finish this project, thank you. You are loved, and I promise not to do this again for a while! Finally, to Eric for pulling me along on this adventure. I definitely didn't know what I was getting myself into when I agreed to this, but I can't imagine having a more dedicated and capable partner.

About the Reviewer

Patrick Puritscher began developing websites at the age of 14 by teaching himself the necessary skills. Already using React.js, he started to develop with React Native, shortly after watching the initial presentation. He is also active in the community with his open source components and recently published an app for iOS, completely written with React Native. After graduating with his bachelor's degree, Patrick worked as the lead developer for multiple internally used web apps and a website with several million visits each month. It is his personal ambition to create software for people that makes their life easier, rather than making it more difficult with poor UX. Patrick has just started with his master's degree in Business Informatics.

You can follow him on:

https://twitter.com/whoispurii

http://patrickpuritscher.com

www.PacktPub.com

For support files and downloads related to your book, please visit `www.PacktPub.com`.

Did you know that Packt offers eBook versions of every book published, with PDF and ePub files available? You can upgrade to the eBook version at `www.PacktPub.com` and as a print book customer, you are entitled to a discount on the eBook copy. Get in touch with us at `service@packtpub.com` for more details.

At `www.PacktPub.com`, you can also read a collection of free technical articles, sign up for a range of free newsletters and receive exclusive discounts and offers on Packt books and eBooks.

`https://www.packtpub.com/mapt`

Get the most in-demand software skills with Mapt. Mapt gives you full access to all Packt books and video courses, as well as industry-leading tools to help you plan your personal development and advance your career.

Why subscribe?

- Fully searchable across every book published by Packt
- Copy and paste, print, and bookmark content
- On demand and accessible via a web browser

Customer Feedback

Thank you for purchasing this Packt book. We take our commitment to improving our content and products to meet your needs seriously—that's why your feedback is so valuable. Whatever your feelings about your purchase, please consider leaving a review on this book's Amazon page. Not only will this help us, more importantly it will also help others in the community to make an informed decision about the resources that they invest in to learn. You can also review for us on a regular basis by joining our reviewers' club. **If you're interested in joining, or would like to learn more about the benefits we offer, please contact us**: customerreviews@packtpub.com.

Table of Contents

Preface

React Native is a library for creating mobile applications using familiar web technologies without sacrificing performance or the *look and feel* typically associated with fully native applications. It is built on top of Facebook's open source JavaScript library, React, and indeed, iOS and Android applications created using the library are primarily written in JavaScript. Because one does not need to learn new languages, ecosystems, and best practices for each platform they work on, React Native is pushing the boundaries of what is possible for React developers.

In this book, we will look at the fundamental concepts of React and React Native, as well as the libraries and tools within the React Native ecosystem. We will also work towards the more practical goal of creating a complete React Native application. Finally, we'll dig into useful and complex React Native concepts such as animation, navigation, native modules, testing and performance analysis. Upon turning over the last page of this book, you'll be armed with the knowledge to create polished, sophisticated mobile applications using React Native.

What this book covers

Chapter 1, *Building a Foundation in React*, In order to work effectively in React Native, you must first understand React. This chapter explains the motivation behind React and teaches you how to *think* in React.

Chapter 2, *Saying Hello World in React Native*, contains two primary topics. First, we'll review how React Native works and compare it to other popular mobile development options. Then, we'll switch gears and focus on configuring your computer to build your first React Native project for iOS.

Chapter 3, *Styling and Layout in React Native*, React Native borrows many concepts from the web development world, including some of the best parts of Cascading Style Sheets (CSS). It also deliberately avoids some of CSS's less desirable qualities. This chapter explains how to style React Native apps and how to use Flexbox to layout components.

Chapter 4, *Starting our Project with React Native Components*, React Native includes many powerful components and APIs. This chapter demonstrates how to use many of these as we begin to build our news reader app, called Readly.

Chapter 5, *Flux and Redux*, ... The React community has largely eschewed the Model View Controller pattern in favor of a unidirectional data flow pattern called Flux. In this chapter, we'll help you *think* in Flux and explain how to leverage a popular Flux implementation known as Redux.

Chapter 6, *Integrating with the NYT API and Redux*, builds upon what we learned in this chapter. In order to bring our Readly app to life, we'll implement Redux and Redux middleware as a means of managing our data and communicating with the New York Times API.

Chapter 7, *Navigation & Advanced APIs*, Navigation in React Native has been a long journey resulting in an abundance of navigation options. But which should you choose? This chapter will make sense of these options. We'll then apply experimental navigation components along with other advanced React Native APIs to our project.

Chapter 8, *Animation and Gestures in React Native*, React Native offers two primary ways of creating fluid animations. This chapter will explain how to apply each of these along with touch gesture support to build out an on boarding experience for our Readly app.

Chapter 9, *Refactoring for Android*, React Native makes cross platform development simple. However, configuring your computer to actually build for Android is a bit less than simple. This chapter will walk you through, step by step, how to install and configure all the tools necessary for Android development. We'll then revisit our project, refactoring it to both work and feel like a first class Android app.

Chapter 10, *Using and Writing Native Modules*, One of the most amazing parts of React Native is that it doesn't limit you to the components and APIs that come packaged with the framework. If you want your app to do something else, you can either bridge custom native code to React Native or include other third-party libraries. This chapter adds additional capabilities to our project by exploring how to create custom native code written in Objective C for iOS and Java for Android.

Chapter 11, *Preparing for Production*, Discovering the root cause of bug or performance problem can be a real chore. In this chapter we'll introduce Jest, a testing framework along with other tools for uncovering pesky performance problems. Finally, we'll show you how to bundle your apps so you can ship them to the iOS and Android stores.

Chapter 12, *React Native Tools & Resources*, React Native is praised for its awesome developer experience and cross platform support. But can we take React Native even further? In this final chapter, we'll show off some tools that can improve upon how you build React Native apps. Then we'll explore a few React Native projects that allow us to extend platform support to the web, macOS, and even Windows.

What you need for this book

While we will add Android support to our project in later chapters, the majority of this book focuses on iOS development. In order to develop for iOS, you must have access to an Apple Mac computer capable of running Xcode 7 or later. Xcode is only necessary for building and testing React Native apps. You're welcome to edit your code in any editor or IDE of your choosing.

In addition to Xcode, React Native requires a few other tools. These include Homebrew, Node.js (6.5.0 or later), npm (3.10.3 or later), Watchman, the React Native CLI, and Google Chrome for debugging. We'll explain what all these tools are and how to install them in Chapter 2, *Saying Hello World in React Native*.

In Chapter 9, *Refactoring for Android*, we'll update our project so it can run on both platforms. Android has its own set of software requirements including the Java Development Kit (JDK 1.8 or later) and Android Studio. Once again, we'll walk you through how to install and configure these tools in Chapter 9, *Refactoring for Android*.

Finally, in Chapter 12, *React Native Tools & Resources*, we'll evaluate software that can aid your React Native workflow and allow you to build React Native apps for even more platforms. All of these installations are completely optional. However, it's worth noting that the React Native plugin for Universal Windows Platform will require a computer or virtual machine running Windows 10 and Visual Studio 2015 Community.

Who this book is for

It's expected the reader possess a strong understanding of JavaScript and is familiar with ECMAScript 2015 (ES2015 or ES6). Code samples in this book will heavily leverage ES2015 features such as classes, arrow functions, destructuring, and spreading. Familiarity with React, mobile development, HTML, and CSS will aid in your understanding but are not a requirement.

Conventions

In this book, you will find a number of text styles that distinguish between different kinds of information. Here are some examples of these styles and an explanation of their meaning.

Code words in text, database table names, folder names, filenames, file extensions, pathnames, dummy URLs, user input, and Twitter handles are shown as follows: "We can include other contexts through the use of the `include` directive."

A block of code is set as follows:

```
[default]
exten => s,1,Dial(Zap/1|30)
exten => s,2,Voicemail(u100)
exten => s,102,Voicemail(b100)
exten => i,1,Voicemail(s0)
```

When we wish to draw your attention to a particular part of a code block, the relevant lines or items are set in bold:

```
[default]
exten => s,1,Dial(Zap/1|30)
exten => s,2,Voicemail(u100)
exten => s,102,Voicemail(b100)
exten => i,1,Voicemail(s0)
```

Any command-line input or output is written as follows:

```
cp /usr/src/asterisk-addons/configs/cdr_mysql.conf.sample
  /etc/asterisk/cdr_mysql.conf
```

New terms and **important words** are shown in bold. Words that you see on the screen, for example, in menus or dialog boxes, appear in the text like this: "Clicking the **Next** button moves you to the next screen."

Warnings or important notes appear in a box like this.

Tips and tricks appear like this.

Reader feedback

Feedback from our readers is always welcome. Let us know what you think about this book-what you liked or disliked. Reader feedback is important for us as it helps us develop titles that you will really get the most out of. To send us general feedback, simply e-mail feedback@packtpub.com, and mention the book's title in the subject of your message. If there is a topic that you have expertise in and you are interested in either writing or contributing to a book, see our author guide at www.packtpub.com/authors.

Customer support

Now that you are the proud owner of a Packt book, we have a number of things to help you to get the most from your purchase.

Downloading the example code

You can download the example code files for this book from your account at http://www.packtpub.com. If you purchased this book elsewhere, you can visit http://www.packtpub.com/support and register to have the files e-mailed directly to you.

You can download the code files by following these steps:

1. Log in or register to our website using your e-mail address and password.
2. Hover the mouse pointer on the **SUPPORT** tab at the top.
3. Click on **Code Downloads & Errata**.
4. Enter the name of the book in the **Search** box.
5. Select the book for which you're looking to download the code files.
6. Choose from the drop-down menu where you purchased this book from.
7. Click on **Code Download**.

Once the file is downloaded, please make sure that you unzip or extract the folder using the latest version of:

- WinRAR / 7-Zip for Windows
- Zipeg / iZip / UnRarX for Mac
- 7-Zip / PeaZip for Linux

The code bundle for the book is also hosted on GitHub at
`https://github.com/PacktPublishing/Mastering-React-Native`. We also have other code
bundles from our rich catalog of books and videos available at `https://github.com/Packt`
`Publishing/`. Check them out!

Errata

Although we have taken every care to ensure the accuracy of our content, mistakes do
happen. If you find a mistake in one of our books-maybe a mistake in the text or the code-
we would be grateful if you could report this to us. By doing so, you can save other readers
from frustration and help us improve subsequent versions of this book. If you find any
errata, please report them by visiting `http://www.packtpub.com/submit-errata`, selecting
your book, clicking on the **Errata Submission Form** link, and entering the details of your
errata. Once your errata are verified, your submission will be accepted and the errata will
be uploaded to our website or added to any list of existing errata under the Errata section of
that title.

To view the previously submitted errata, go to `https://www.packtpub.com/books/conten`
`t/support` and enter the name of the book in the search field. The required information will
appear under the **Errata** section.

Piracy

Piracy of copyrighted material on the Internet is an ongoing problem across all media. At
Packt, we take the protection of our copyright and licenses very seriously. If you come
across any illegal copies of our works in any form on the Internet, please provide us with
the location address or website name immediately so that we can pursue a remedy.

Please contact us at `copyright@packtpub.com` with a link to the suspected pirated
material.

We appreciate your help in protecting our authors and our ability to bring you valuable
content.

Questions

If you have a problem with any aspect of this book, you can contact us
at `questions@packtpub.com`, and we will do our best to address the problem.

1
Building a Foundation in React

There is a common trope within the frontend web development community that boils down to *new day, new framework*. It is a comment on the velocity at which this profession is changing and evolving. The rapid pace can be exhausting, but it is also exciting because of what it represents. The domain of frontend developers seems to be ever expanding–from simple web pages to web applications, mobile applications, and beyond–and with that, the number of smart people contributing ideas and code to the collective knowledge bank is also expanding.

With all of that said, any sane person must pick and choose which developments to tune into. When React.js emerged on to the open source scene in May 2013 from the inner-sanctum of Facebook, it would have been easy to brush this library off as just another frontend library. That, however, would have been a mistake. It could be said that React was the most significant and influential open source development in frontend technology in recent memory. Its growth beyond the web and its application in the realm of mobile development through React Native is both a testament to its popularity and a boon to its potential utility.

React Native is a library for creating native mobile applications using familiar web technologies that is built on top of React. What this means is that in order to understand React Native, we must first explore React. In this chapter, we'll examine the fundamentals of React. First, we'll talk briefly about the circumstances that led to React being created. We'll also cover these React concepts:

- JSX, a JavaScript/HTML hybrid that we use to describe React components
- React components
- Component composition
- Component properties, or props
- Handling events
- Component state

- The React component lifecycle
- Alternate component forms

 A note to the reader: this chapter focuses on React for the web, the original purpose of the library. This provides important context for the remainder of the book. If you already know React for the web, then it is probably safe to skip this chapter and proceed to `Chapter 2`, *Saying Hello World in React Native*.

Library versus framework

When people describe React, they often eschew the description of framework–a description often used for something such as Backbone or Angular–in favor of library. The reason for this more lightweight description is that React is not a complete solution for application development. It is often relegated to only a view-layer solution, and that characterization is mostly correct. React has some mechanisms for maintaining internal state, but it has no opinion about or solutions for data flow and management, server communication, routing, or other common frontend application concerns.

React, therefore, is often coupled with some other library or libraries to create a fully fleshed out application. The most common pairing is with an application architecture that is also the brainchild of the wizards at Facebook called **Flux**. Flux is not a library in and of itself; it is a set of design patterns that have been implemented by many different libraries, which will be discussed in more depth in Chapter 5, *Flux and Redux*.

Motivation for React

React and the community, libraries, and patterns that surround it are very much a reaction (pun intended) to some of the most frustrating and prevalent issues that plague JavaScript applications as they grow in size and complexity. JavaScript was not designed for creating large applications; it was designed, famously, in just 10 days as a scripting language to add a modicum of interactivity to lifeless web pages.

Chief among these concerns is the unpredictability that comes with shared mutable state. Historically, passing around JavaScript objects that represent the application's state to different views and controllers has been common practice. The ease with which those objects can be mutated by a rogue view, wisdom notwithstanding, can lead to hard-to-diagnose bugs, especially as applications and teams grow.

The foundational building block in a React application is the component, which is a declarative description of some visual feature on the page, such as a form or a menu. The declarative nature of components promotes predictability: given some set of external inputs (properties), the output is well defined and deterministic.

React also aims to combat one of the hurdles to writing efficient applications: the **Document Object Model (DOM)** is notoriously slow. If changes to the DOM are relatively infrequent, this may not be a problem, but in a complex application the time it takes to alter and redraw the DOM can add up. This is especially true for applications that take a declarative approach as React does, which necessitates re-rendering whenever the application's state changes.

The solution proposed by the React framework is to keep a representation of the DOM in memory, called a virtual DOM, and make all alterations there. Once the alterations have been made in memory, React can apply the minimum number of changes necessary to reconcile the real DOM with the virtual DOM. This also can allow quickly successive changes to be batched for greater efficiency. Taking this approach can lead to great gains in performance that can be noticed by end users.

In addition to solving some of the common problems faced when creating JavaScript applications, React components are modular and emphasize composition over inheritance, which makes code immensely reusable and testable. Additionally, a React component often has rendering logic, markup declaration, and even styles in the same file, which promotes the portability of code and the ability to write shared libraries of components.

Perhaps the most compelling reason to use React and React Native is the astounding amount of community adoption that has taken place in the last two years. People are excited about this technology, and rightly so; it is a novel approach to developing frontend applications that is, by most accounts, accelerating the development time on teams that choose to adopt it. With React Native, the idealistic promise of *learn once, write anywhere* is becoming more and more viable.

Getting started in React

To begin creating an interface in React, the first thing we need to do is break down the interface into conceptual components. We start with a large component, for instance, a news feed. We then say our large component is made up of, or composed of, other smaller components. In the case of our news feed, these smaller components might be individual news items. Each news item, in turn, might be composed of several even smaller components, such as images, a description, and a byline.

This process should continue until the smallest components are bite-sized, reusable visual units that can no longer be easily broken down into smaller pieces. Doing this exercise sets us up well for writing our first code in React. Here is what this process might look like for our hypothetical news reader application.

First, identify and give a name to the largest component we can find, in this case, a NewsFeed:

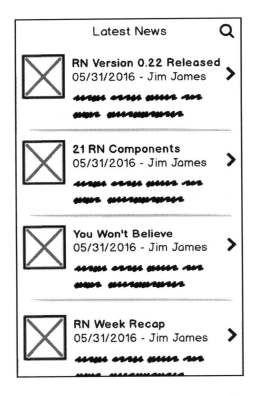

Now, draw boxes around the next largest set of components, the NewsItem components:

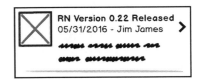

Next, we can zoom in on a single `NewsItem` and identify the components that it is made of. Here, we can see that there is an **Image**, a **Title**, a **Description** and a **Byline**:

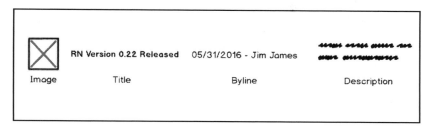

We've now laid the groundwork to start creating a React application. We have identified six components and their relationships: the `NewsFeed`, which is composed of `NewsItem` components, which in turn are composed of `Image`, `Title`, `Description`, and `Byline` components.

Describing components in JSX

In recent years, there have been many developments in JavaScript as a language itself. For instance, the new ECMAScript 2015 (ES2015–sometimes called ES6) specification, which defines the next version of JavaScript, is becoming increasingly solidified. If a developer wishes to write in ES2015–and many do–they need to use a program to convert the newer syntax into one that is compatible with the majority of browsers. Additionally, there are a number of JavaScript-like syntaxes, such as CoffeeScript and TypeScript, that ultimately have to be converted to browser-compatible JavaScript in order to function.

With all of these developments and alternate syntaxes, many developers have become accustomed to transforming code into browser-compatible JavaScript instead of writing it directly. When Facebook created React, they capitalized on this and created a syntax similar to HTML that could be used to describe components. It's called **JavaScript XML (JSX)**, and it is a declarative markup language that is written in tandem with JavaScript to define a component's layout.

Using JSX is not an absolute requirement for writing React, but without it, React becomes verbose and cumbersome. Furthermore, since most developers will be using tools such as Babel already to convert their ES2015 code into JavaScript, writing in JSX does not add much burden because most of those tools come with support for JSX built in.

JSX looks almost exactly like HTML:

```
<h1>
  Hello World!
</h1>
```

It differs from HTML5 only slightly. HTML and JSX have a common ancestor language called **XML (Extensible Markup Language)**. HTML has since diverged in some ways from strict XML that JSX has not. For instance, in the case of a tag such as the image tag (that is, `<img>`) HTML and JSX differ. The `<img>` tag is called **self-closing** in that there is no standalone closing tag like we might see with a `<div>` or a `<p>`. For a self-closing tag in HTML, a forward slash before the end is optional:

```
HTML: <img src="my/image.jpg" >
```

In JSX (and XML, for that matter), this forward slash is required:

```
JSX: <img src="my/image.jpg" />
```

There are other differences between JSX and HTML that arise from JSX being written in the context of JavaScript. The first is that `class` is a keyword in JavaScript, whereas that word is used as an attribute of HTML elements to allow elements to be targeted by CSS for styling. So, when we would use `class` in HTML, we instead have to use `className` in JSX:

```
HTML: <div class="news-item">
JSX: <div className="news-item">
```

A consolation prize for this small inconvenience is we get the benefit of being able to interleave JavaScript into places in our markup where we typically wouldn't in normal HTML. For instance, defining inline styles can use a JavaScript object, rather than cramming all properties into a string.

```
HTML: <div styles="background: green; color: red;">
JSX: <div styles={{background: 'green', color: 'red'}}>
```

Notice here that there are two sets of curly braces on the style attribute's value. The outer set of curly braces is used to show that the code contained is JavaScript. The inner set is a JavaScript object literal containing the CSS style property names and their respective values.

Not only can attribute values be written in JavaScript, but so too can the content contained between JSX tags. This way, we can use dynamic properties to render text content:

```
HTML: <span>Hello World</span>
JSX: <span>{'Hello' + 'World!'}</span>
```

As we'll see in coming section, there are more tags available to us than we would see in normal HTML. In fact, our application-defined components themselves can be added into JSX markup:

```
<NewsItem>
    Hello React!
</NewsItem>
```

Understanding JSX is paramount to starting to create React components; however, JSX makes up only a part of a complete component.

The component

In React, we build applications using composable, modular components. These components represent parts of our visual interface and are rendered as such. In their most simple form, they are simply a description of how to render. We create a component by using ES2015 `class` syntax:

```
import React, { Component } from 'react';

class Title extends Component {

  render() {
    return (
      <h1>
        Hello World!
      </h1>
    );
  }
}
```

Since the only requirement is that a `render()` method is defined, this is now a valid and complete (albeit not especially useful) React component.

In a typical React application project, a component will be self-contained within a file. Files that contain JSX, such as a component file, sometimes have a `.jsx` extension in web projects; however, this practice is less common in React Native projects. This extension helps tools such as Babel know how to transform them into browser-compatible JavaScript. The entire contents of the file that defines and exports the `Title` component, `Title.jsx`, might look like this:

```
import React, { Component } from 'react';
export default class Title extends Component {
```

```
render() {
  return (
    <h1>
      Hello World!
    </h1>
  );
}
}
```

This simple component by itself is not very compelling. So far, everything we've seen in this component could easily be created using only HTML. Rest assured, React provides several ways of making this component more interesting and useful.

Component composition

As was mentioned earlier in this chapter, React favors composition over inheritance. What does this mean? In essence, it means to build complex or derivative components, instead of using something akin to object-oriented inheritance, we use composition to build up complexity from simple building blocks.

Our `Title` component is pretty simple, but we can build up a more complex `NewsItem` component from the `Title` component and other simple components:

```
import React, { Component } from 'react';

class NewsItem extends Component {

  render() {
    return (
      <div className="news-item">
        <Image />
        <Title />
        <Byline />
        <Description />
      </div>
    );
  }

}
```

The JSX returned by the render method of a component is that component's declarative definition. When that JSX includes other components, such as the `<Image />`, `<Title />`, `<Byline />`, and `<Description />` elements we see in the preceding code, it is said to be composed of those components.

Composition has other uses besides making increasingly more complex components from smaller, simpler building blocks. Composition can also be used to make derivative components, a task that in an object-oriented programming world we might use inheritance to achieve. For instance, imagine we want to make a component that is a `WarningTitle`. This component might share many properties with a `Title` component, but also add bright red border around it in order to draw a user's attention:

```
import React, { Component } from 'react';

class WarningTitle extends Component {

  render() {
    return (
      <div style={{ border: '1px solid red' }}>
        <Title />
      </div>
    );
  }

}
```

Using the previous definition, we would then say that `WarningTitle` is composed of `Title` because the latter is returned in the `render()` method of the former.

Props and PropTypes

The components that we've seen so far are completely static in that they take no external input and always render exactly the same. This isn't especially interesting because the same outcome can be achieved by writing plain old HTML. However, React provides a mechanism for making components dynamic by using properties, or **props**.

Accepting props

Props are passed into a component in order to modify their base definition. Let's take another look at our `Title` component:

```
import React, { Component } from 'react';

export default class Title extends Component {

  render() {
    return (
```

[15]

```
      <h1>
        Hello World!
      </h1>
    );
  }


}
```

While the title of a single article might be `Hello World!`, this component needs to be more dynamic if it is to be reused within all of our `NewsItem` components. For this, we'll use a React input property, or prop, called `titleText`. React component methods have a `this` context that gives access to properties that have been passed in:

```
import React, { Component } from 'react';

export default class Title extends Component {

  render() {
    return (
      <h1>
        {this.props.titleText}
      </h1>
    );
  }


}
```

Once again, remember that curly brackets in JSX denotes JavaScript code. Here, we are accessing the component's `titleText` prop in order to render it within the component's markup:

```
<h1>
  {this.props.titleText}
</h1>
```

PropTypes

This by itself is sufficient code to start accepting a `titleText` property. However, as a best practice, we should include in our component's definition a description of what properties it is equipped to accept. While this may seem like over-engineering and unnecessary in small projects maintained by a single developer, as the project and team grows, explicit definition of properties is key in an untyped language such as JavaScript.

Defining `PropTypes` in a component is how we formally tell other developers what properties a component accepts and what value types those properties should be. `PropTypes` are the same across instances of a component and are thus statically attached to the class:

```
import React, { Component, PropTypes } from 'react';

export default class Title extends Component {

  render() {
    return (
      <h1>
        {this.props.titleText}
      </h1>
    );
  }

}

Title.propTypes = {
  titleText: PropTypes.string
};
```

Adding `PropTypes` to a component does not change anything functionally, but it will cause annoying warning messages to be logged to the JavaScript console when they are disobeyed (only when React is in development mode, mind you).

To use `PropTypes`, we'll need to add it to the React import:

```
import React, { Component, PropTypes } from 'react';
```

The `PropTypes` module comes with functions for validating different value types, such as `string`, `number`, and `func`.

Here, what we are communicating is that this component takes one optional property called `titleText`, and that property should be of type `string`:

```
Title.propTypes = {
  titleText: PropTypes.string
};
```

We could also make this a required property:

```
Title.propTypes: {
  titleText: PropTypes.string.isRequired
}
```

In addition to having string type props, we can also have other simple types, such as booleans and numbers:

```
Title.propTypes = {
  titleText: PropTypes.string.isRequired,
  highlighted: PropTypes.bool,
  fontSize: PropTypes.number
};
```

Props can not only be used to define the text content, but can also be used to define attributes of an element, for instance, inline style:

```
import React, { Component, PropTypes } from 'react';

export default class Title extends Component {

  render() {
    return (
      <h1
        style={{
          backgroundColor: this.props.highlighted ? 'yellow' : 'white',
fontSize: `${this.props.fontSize}px`
        }}
      >
      {this.props.titleText}
      </h1>

    );
  }

}

Title.propTypes = {
  titleText: PropTypes.string.isRequired,
  highlighted: PropTypes.bool, fontSize: PropTypes.number
};
```

One thing to note with the preceding example is that CSS properties that have a dash in them when written in traditional CSS use camel case in React inline style. This is because keys in JavaScript objects cannot contain dashes.

React PropType specifications can also be used to validate more complex properties. For instance, we could have a property that is either a string or a number using the oneOfType function, which is as follows:

```
fontSize: PropTypes.oneOfType([
  PropTypes.string,
```

```
    PropTypes.number
])
```

Likewise, we can specify a set of specific values that a property is allowed to take by using the `oneOf` method:

```
size: PropTypes.oneOf([
  'small',
  'medium',
  'large'
])
```

We can of course specify more complex data types, such as arrays and objects, but we can also be more specific and describe the types of values in an array property or the shape that an object property takes:

```
propTypes: {
  //Array that can contain anything
  simpleArray: PropTypes.array,

  //Object that can contain anything
  simpleObject: PropTypes.object,

  //Array that contains only Number values
  arrayOfNumbers: PropTypes.arrayOf(PropTypes.number),

  //Object that takes a specific "shape"
  complexObject: PropTypes.shape({
    id: PropTypes.number,
    name: PropTypes.string
  })
}
```

Now our `Title` component is getting interesting. It has gone from something that can be easily recreated using just HTML to something more like a HTML template–still declaratively defined, but dynamic in that it can take external properties.

Alternatively, `PropTypes` can be added to a React component as a static property using the `static` keyword:

```
import React, { Component, PropTypes } from 'react';

export default class Title extends Component {

  static propTypes = {
    titleText: PropTypes.string.isRequired,
    highlighted: PropTypes.bool,
```

```
      fontSize: PropTypes.number
  }

  render() {
    return (
      <h1
        style={{
          backgroundColor: this.props.highlighted ? 'yellow' : 'white',
fontSize: `${this.props.fontSize}px`
        }}
      >
        {this.props.titleText}
      </h1>

    );
  }

}
```

This syntax is cleaner, but is not officially part of the ECMAScript specification at this point. While most transpiler programs will recognize this syntax, we'll avoid it in this book for that reason.

Passing props

With a component defined that accepts props, the next step is for props to be passed into this component. In the case of our `Title` component, the `NewsItem` component can pass properties into the contained `Title` component. It does this using the attribute syntax of XML:

```
import React, { Component } from 'react';
import Title from './Title';

export default class NewsItem extends Component {

  render() {
    return (
      <div className="news-item">
        <Image />
        <Title
          titleText="Hello World!"
          highlighted={true}
          fontSize={18}
        />
        <Byline />
        <Description />
```

```
      </div>
    );
  }

}
```

Strings are the only value types that can be passed in as a prop directly:

```
titleText="Hello World!"
```

For other JavaScript data types, such as numbers, Booleans, and arrays, we must surround the values in curly braces so that they are interpreted correctly as JavaScript:

```
fontSize={18}
```

For Boolean props, we can shorten their input to where the property name's presence is interpreted as true and its absence is interpreted as false, much like in HTML:

```
<div className="news-item">
  <Image />
  <Title
    titleText="Hello World!"
    highlighted
    fontSize={18}
  />
  <Byline />
  <Description />
</div>
```

Default props

In a previous section, we specified, using `PropTypes`, that the `titleText` property of the `Title` component is required, but the other two properties are optional. This raises an interesting question: what will the value of those properties be if they are not specified? Well, without any intervention from the component developer, those properties will appropriately have the value `undefined` when no value is passed in. This could be problematic in some situations.

For our `fontSize` property, a value of `undefined` could lead to some unpredictable and potentially error-prone code because it is expecting a number. Luckily for us, React has a mechanism for specifying default values for optional properties that have not been passed in explicitly. This mechanism is a method on the component called `defaultProps` and we can use it in `Title`, statically, like this:

```
import React, { Component, PropTypes } from 'react';
```

```
export default class Title extends Component {

  render() {
    return (
      <h1
        style={{
          backgroundColor: this.props.highlighted ? 'yellow' : 'white',
          fontSize: `${this.props.fontSize}px`
        }}
      >
        {this.props.titleText}
      </h1>

    );
  }

}

Title.propTypes = {
  titleText: PropTypes.string.isRequired,
  highlighted: PropTypes.bool,
  fontSize: PropTypes.number
};
Title.defaultProps = {
  highlighted: false,
  fontSize: 18
};
```

defaultProps must be a JavaScript object where keys are property names and the values are the default values to use in the case that no values were passed in for that particular property. We can now define a Title component that isn't highlighted and has the default font size of 18 pixels by simply writing the following:

```
<Title
  titleText="Hello World!"
/>
```

In context, our NewsItem component is now simplified to this:

```
import React, { Component } from 'react';
import Title from './Title';

export default class NewsItem extends Component {

  render() {
    return (
      <div className="news-item">
        <Image />
```

```
        <Title
          titleText="Hello World!"
          highlighted
        />
        <Byline />
        <Description />
      </div>
    );
  }

}
```

Sometimes, a component will receive its props from several levels above. For instance, maybe NewsFeed specifies the title of an individual NewsItem, rather than having NewsItem provide it statically itself, as we have done in the previous examples. Parameterizing this property allows the NewsItem component to be more generic and reusable:

```
import React, { Component, PropTypes } from 'react';
import Title from './Title';

export default class NewsItem extends Component {

  render() {
    return (
      <div className="news-item">
        <Image />
        <Title
          titleText={this.props.titleText}
          highlighted
        />
        <Byline />
        <Description />
      </div>
    );
  }

}

NewsItem.propTypes = {
  titleText: PropTypes.string.isRequired
};
```

Here, we have shown how the NewsItem component can accept a property, and in turn, pass it down to the Title component.

Props.children

Every component has an optional special property that is called **children**. Normal properties, as we have seen, are passed in using something similar to the HTML attribute syntax:

```
<Title
  titleText="Hello World"
/>
```

You can also pass in text or other component elements by placing them in between an opening and closing tag. We can refactor our `Title` component to accept children instead of the `titleText` prop:

```
<Title>
  Hello World
</Title>
```

Now, the `render()` method of our `Title` component becomes this:

```
render() {
  return (
    <h1
      style={{
        backgroundColor: this.props.highlighted ? 'yellow' : 'white',
fontSize: `${this.props.fontSize}px`
      }}
    >
      {this.props.children}
    </h1>
  );
}
```

Note that we could now also pass in other React elements into the `Title` as property by also placing them in between the opening and closing tags:

```
<Title>
  Hello World!
  <img src="icon.png" />
</Title>
```

When validating the `children` prop, we can use a special `PropTypes` called `node`, which means anything that can be rendered by React:

```
Title.propTypes = {
  children: PropTypes.node.isRequired,
  highlighted: PropTypes.bool,
  fontSize: PropTypes.number
};
```

Event handlers

In JavaScript development, we often think of our application as reacting to user events on the page. For instance, we may listen for a submit button on the page to be clicked, and when it is, validate a form. Functions that respond to these user events are sometimes dubbed **event handlers** or **event listeners**.

In a simple JavaScript application, we register these event handlers by querying the DOM for some element and adding an event listener function to run when the event of interest occurs. Here is how we might do this:

```
document.querySelector('form').addEventListener('click', validateForm);

function validateForm() {
  alert('The form is valid!');
}
```

In the early days of JavaScript, we probably would have used HTML event attributes in order to respond to user events on some element. The equivalent code for this inline approach to event handling might look something like this:

```
<form onsubmit="validateForm()">
  ...
</form>
```

In React, the way we do event handling is more like the inline JavaScript of yesteryear. Elements in React can optionally take event handler properties in order to respond to user inputs. A React element is the portion of a component that is returned from the render function. In other words, it is a description of what we want rendered on the screen, generally written in JSX. Our form from the previous example written in JSX would only have a couple of subtle differences:

```
<form onSubmit={validateForm}>
```

To show an example of event handling in context, let's return to our `NewsItem` example. Let's imagine that we want our application to respond to a user clicking on the news item. We can do this by creating an event listener function in the component and adding it to the outer element in JSX:

```
import React, { Component, PropTypes } from 'react';
import Title from './Title';

export default class NewsItem extends Component {

  onClick() {
    alert(`You've clicked on ${this.props.titleText}`);
  }

  render() {
    return (
      <div
        className="news-item"
        onClick={this.onClick.bind(this)}
      >
        <Image />
        <Title
          highlighted
        >
          {this.props.titleText}
        </Title>
        <Byline />
        <Description />
      </div>
    );
  }

}

NewsItem.propTypes = {
  titleText: PropTypes.string.isRequired
};
```

Take note that we are binding the `render` method's `this` context to the `onClick` method when adding it as a click handler:

```
onClick={this.onClick.bind(this)}
```

We need to do this in order to ensure this has the same meaning in the `onClick` method as it does in other component methods. This way, we can still access props and call other component methods. However, the better way to bind the `this` context to the event handler method is to do so within the component's constructor:

```
constructor(props) {
  super(props);
  this.onClick = this.onClick.bind(this);
}
```

Then there is no need to re-bind the event handler in the JSX, which can be simplified:

```
<div
  className="news-item"
  onClick={this.onClick}
>
```

This method is preferred not only because it reduces the amount of typing, but also because React internally optimizes to make it more efficient.

Event listeners in React, much as they do without React, receive an optional argument that is an object representing the user event. We can access this event object in order to suppress default behavior, for instance, in a form submission, by using `event.preventDefault()`. We can also use the event object to, for example, see what document element was targeted by the action or, in the case of a key press event, see which specific key was pressed by the user. To get access to the event, we just need to add it as a parameter to our event listener method:

```
onClick(event) {
  console.log('User event', event);
  alert(`You've clicked on${this.props.titleText}`);
}
```

State

Occasionally, a component will need to keep track of some internal state in addition to the external, read-only, properties that are passed into it. State is necessarily internal to the component and, generally, exclusively tied to some visual display option (for instance, is the component visually expanded or collapsed).

Much in the same way that a component instance can access external properties via `this.props`, a component instance can access its internal state using `this.state`. Using internal state, we could optionally show parts of `NewsItem` only when that item is in an expanded state:

```
render() {
  let body = null;

  if (this.state.expanded) {
    body = (
      <div>
        <Byline />
        <Description />
      </div>
    );
  }

  return (
    <div
      className="news-item"
      onClick={this.onClick}
    >
      <Image />
      <Title
        highlighted
      >
        {this.props.titleText}
      </Title>
      {body}
    </div>
  );
}
```

We can see now that the `body` variable will only be defined if the internal state is expanded. Another thing we can see here is that a `<div>` element has been added around the `description` and `byline`. The reason we do this is because JSX elements must have a single root node in order to return them or store them in a variable. Alternatively, we could have stored each element in its own variable:

```
render() {
  let byline = null;
  let description = null;

  if (this.state.expanded) {
    byline = <Byline />;
    description = <Description />;
  }
```

```
  return (
    <div
      className="news-item"
      onClick={this.onClick}
    >
      <Image />
      <Title
        highlighted
      >
        {this.props.titleText}
      </Title>
      {byline}
      {description}
    </div>
  );
}
```

While this code is completely valid, we can make it even better by splitting out conditional rendering into a separate method:

```
renderBody() {
  if (this.state.expanded) {
    return (
      <div>
        <Byline />
        <Description />
      </div>
    );
  }
  return null;
}
```

Then, we can use this `helper` method within our main `render()` method in order to make things a bit clearer:

```
render() {
  return (
    <div
      className="news-item"
      onClick={this.onClick}
    >
      <Image />
      <Title
        highlighted
      >
        {this.props.titleText}
      </Title>
        {this.renderBody()}
```

```
      </div>
    );
  }
```

We've now seen how to use internal state to render things conditionally, but we have not yet seen how that state is defined or how it is modified. In React, we can specify the initial values of internal state by assigning them in the constructor of the component. The component's initial state, much like its default properties, should be a JavaScript object:

```
constructor(props) {
  super(props);

  this.state = {
    expanded: false
  };

  this.onClick = this.onClick.bind(this);
}
```

This method describes the initial state of a component, but it does not provide us with any means to update that state. In order to update the state of a component, we can use a React component's setState method to assign, or reassign, any internal state value.

Typically, updating state happens as a response to some user input or user event. In the last section, we learned how to define methods that respond to these user events, such as clicks, and how to attach these event listeners to the appropriate React element. Let's modify our onClick event handler to change the expanded state of our component instead of simply alerting:

```
onClick() {
  this.setState({
    expanded: !this.state.expanded
  });
}
```

When we use setState in this way, React will notice that the internal state has changed, and this will trigger a new rendering using the new internal state. For this reason, we should never manipulate the state of a component directly:

```
//Do not do this
this.state.expanded = false;
```

If we change the internal state directly, React's rendering engine will not become aware of it and the component we see on our page will differ from the one in JavaScript. The same goes for props; they are external and should only be changed as a result of new values being passed in through JSX:

```
//Also don't do this
this.props.titleText = 'Hello World!';
```

Now that we've demonstrated how to use internal state to display something conditionally, how to initialize state by setting it in the constructor method, and how to modify internal state in response to some user event using setState, let's look at all of this in context in our NewsItem component:

```
import React, { Component, PropTypes } from 'react';
import Title from './Title';

export default class NewsItem extends Component {

  constructor(props) {
    super(props);

    this.state = {
      expanded: false
    };

    this.onClick = this.onClick.bind(this);
  }

  onClick() {
    this.setState({
      expanded: !this.state.expanded
    });
  }

  renderBody() {
    if (this.state.expanded) {
      return (
        <div>
          <Byline />
          <Description />
        </div>
      );
    }
    return null;
  }

  render() {
```

```
      return (
        <div
          className="news-item"
          onClick={this.onClick}
        >
          <Image />
          <Title
            highlighted
          >
            {this.props.titleText}
          </Title>
          {this.renderBody()}
        </div>
      );
    }

  }

  NewsItem.propTypes = {
    titleText: PropTypes.string.isRequired
  };
```

Now we have a component for our news item that starts out collapsed (not expanded) and not showing the description or byline, but when the user clicks on the news item, it expands to show the two previously hidden elements.

The component lifecycle

Every React component that is rendered into the DOM goes through a series of steps before and after rendering. As React component developers, we can hook into these steps, called the **component lifecycle**, in order to perform tasks or check conditions specific to some stage in that lifecycle:

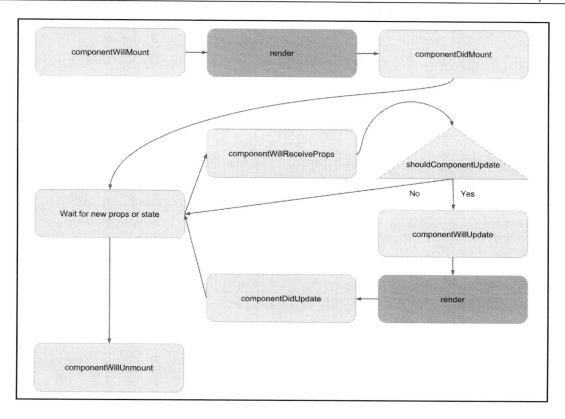

Mounting the component

Before a component is mounted, which means placed into the DOM for the first time, React will look at that component's class to see if it has a method called componentWillMount defined. Should this method exist, React will invoke it. This method is a good place to do things such as set up timers needed by the component or request data the component needs from the server:

```
componentWillMount() {
  //Decrement an internal state counter every second
  setInterval(() => {
    this.setState({
      secondsLeft: this.state.secondsLeft - 1;
    });
  }, 1000);
}
```

The next step in the component's lifecycle is the first render. The `render()` method we've seen before. React calls this method and then, the first time, converts the JSX element output to HTML elements and places them in the DOM. In other words, it mounts the component.

Once mounting is complete, the next step in the lifecycle, an optional method called `componentDidMount`, is called. This is often an integration point for non-React libraries. With that said, a word of warning: it is generally not a good idea to use libraries that manipulate the DOM alongside React. Remember that React works by keeping a virtual representation of the DOM in memory in order to calculate change sets and apply them. When other libraries are modifying the DOM, it can quickly become out of sync with what React expects. This could, and more often than not, will, lead to errors when React tries to reconcile changes:

```
componentDidMount() {
  //Integrate with an external library here
}
```

From here, the component is stable and its lifecycle dormant until one of two things happens. The first thing that could happen is the component's parent could pass it new `props`. The second is some event or interval triggers a change in internal `state`. These two actions, of course, necessitate a re-render. Before a re-render happens, there are a few other lifecycle methods that will be called.

The update cycle

The first method called during a property update cycle is `componentWillReceiveProps`. Here, we not only know that the component is about to receive a new set of properties, but we also can see what those properties are and how they compare to the old ones:

```
componentWillReceiveProps(nextProps) {
  //an object of new props
  console.log(nextProps);

  //The current (old) props
  console.log(this.props);
}
```

This lifecycle method is a good place to update state that is somehow derived from props because it is the only update lifecycle method that is not called for both prop and state changes.

This brings us to the next lifecycle method that is called when either props or state are updated: shouldComponentUpdate. This method is unique among lifecycle methods in that it is the only one that expects a return value. As you may be able to guess, the return value expected is a Boolean. If the method returns true, the lifecycle continues as we expect it. However, if shouldComponentUpdate returns false, the lifecycle is short-circuited here and a re-render does not occur. Within this method, we can see not only the new properties, but also the new state that will be rendered:

```
shouldComponentUpdate(nextProps, nextState) {
  if (this.props.uid !== nextProps.uid) {
    return true;
  }
  return false;
}
```

If a component does not define this method, it is always assumed to be true. React, though, gives you the ability to override this behavior. This can become important in large applications with many components and many layers of component nesting. Using shouldComponentUpdate, we can fine-tune when a component re-renders in order to enhance the performance of our application. This is important because, while React is good at optimizing renders, rendering is still computationally expensive and excessive rendering can slow down an application to the point where a user can feel stuttering.

If shouldComponentUpdate returns true (or is not defined by the component), the next step in the lifecycle is componentWillUpdate, which is the last step before re-rendering. Here, like in shouldComponentUpdate, we have access to both the new properties and the new state:

```
componentWillUpdate(nextProps, nextState) {
  //Prepare for render!
}
```

At this point, React will call render on the component again, getting its new JSX representation. It will compare this new JSX to the old JSX in the virtual DOM and create a change set to apply to the real DOM. Once this process is complete, we arrive at the next step of the lifecycle, which is componentDidUpdate. This method is very similar to componentWillUpdate, except that it receives the previous properties and state as arguments:

```
componentDidUpdate(prevProps, prevState) {
  //Here are the old props
  console.log(prevProps);

  //And here are the current (new) props
```

```
    console.log(this.props);
  }
```

Now, we've completed the update lifecycle. At this point, once again the component remains dormant until another change in properties or state occurs. This process continues over and over again until the component is removed, or unmounted, from the DOM.

Unmounting the component

Just before a component is removed from the DOM, the final stage of the component's lifecycle will be completed. Here, React calls the optional `componentWillUnmount` method, which receives no arguments.

This method is a good place to clean up anything that the component created over the course of its life. For instance, if the component started an interval upon mounting, here would be a good place to stop that interval. In our `componentWillMount` example, we showed starting a countdown interval that fired every second after the component mounted. If we store that interval's ID in state, we can then stop the interval when the component is being unmounted:

```
componentWillMount() {
  //Save the interval in state
  this.setState({
    tickInterval: setInterval(() => {
      this.setState({
        secondsLeft: this.state.secondsLeft - 1;
      });
    }, 1000);
  });
}

componentWillUnmount() {
  //Stop the countdown before unmounting
  clearInterval(this.state.tickInterval);
}
```

While we've gone through and demonstrated how each lifecycle method might be used within a component, it is important to point out that we would very rarely need to use every component lifecycle method in a single component. Remember that each one is optional and need not be defined by the component unless some feature of its functionality necessitates it. In fact, our `NewsItem` component does not need any of these lifecycle methods to do exactly what we want.

Alternate component forms

In React, there are three ways to define a component. The way we've seen so far uses ES2015 classes to define a component and its methods. This is currently the most common method for defining React components and, in fact, the one you'll encounter most often in documentation and in this book.

React.createClass

Before ES2015 and its class syntax became popular and brought into React, the way to define a component was by using the `React.createClass` function. This function takes as an argument a JavaScript object that describes the component and its methods. This conceptually is very similar to the way we have seen so far, but has some syntactic differences. To demonstrate, let's take a look at what our `NewsItem` component looks like using this method:

```
React.createClass({

  propTypes: {
    titleText: PropTypes.string.isRequired
  },

  getInitialState() {
    return {
      expanded: false
    }
  },

  onClick() {
    this.setState({
      expanded: !this.state.expanded
    });
  },

  renderBody() {
    if (this.state.expanded)
      return (
        <div>
          <Byline />
          <Description />
        </div>;
      );
    }
    return null;
```

```
      },

      render() {
        return (
          <div
            className="news-item"
            onClick={this.onClick}
          >
            <Image />
            <Title
              highlighted
            >
              {this.props.titleText}
            </Title>
            {this.renderBody()}
          </div>
        );
      }

    });
```

Other than the obvious syntactic differences, there are a few subtle differences in how we define and use components with `React.createClass` that we should draw our attention to. The first is instead of simply assigning the state in the class constructor, we define a `getInitialState` method in the component, which returns the initial component state as an object:

```
    getInitialState() {
      return {
        expanded: false
      }
    }
```

The next thing we might notice is that, previously, event handler functions were bound to the component's `this` context either in the constructor or within the event attribute assignment. When using the `React.createClass` syntax, we have no longer need to explicitly bind the context:

```
    <div
      className="news-item"
      onClick={this.onClick}
    >
```

We may have also noticed that rather than defining the `propTypes` statically on the class, we instead do it within the component object:

```
propTypes: {
  titleText: PropTypes.string.isRequired
}
```

This component does not need default properties, but if it did, we would also define those inside the component object. We do this by defining a method similar to `getInitialState` called `getDefaultProps` that also returns an object:

```
getDefaultProps() {
  return {
    someProp: 'some value'
  }
};
```

Functional components

For simple components that maintain no internal state, we can define them simply as functions that take props as input and return JSX elements as output. These components are not only succinct, but may in the future be more performant than components defined in other ways. For these reasons, it is recommended that we use functional components wherever possible.

Because of its simplicity and lack of internal state, our `Title` component from an earlier section is a good candidate for being a functional component. Here is what that component would look like with this alternate syntax:

```
const Title = (props) => (
  <h1
    style={{
      backgroundColor: props.highlighted ? 'yellow' : 'white',
      fontSize: `${props.fontSize}px`
    }}
  >
    {props.children}
  </h1>
);
```

Taking advantage of ES2015 arrow function syntax, our large traditionally defined component has been simplified to a single function.

In addition to not having internal state, functional components don't have lifecycle methods. They can, however, have `defaultProps` and `propTypes` that can be specified in the same manner as class components:

```
Title.propTypes = {
  titleText: PropTypes.string.isRequired
};
```

Summary

The React library has created a new way to develop user interfaces for web applications through creating declarative and composable components in the new, but familiar, JSX syntax. Since its introduction, it has grown immensely in popularity. At Facebook's F8 developer conference in 2016, it was estimated that upwards of 250,000 developers were using React in some way. This enthusiasm led the community to look for new places to use their favorite library, and in early 2015, React Native was born.

In this chapter, we covered the fundamentals of React, from conception to implementation. We learned how to take a user interface and structure it as components, the building blocks of React applications. Starting with simple components, such as a static title, we then built up to more complex components by adding props, event handlers, state, and lifecycle methods. Finally, we looked at some alternate ways of representing React components and discussed when each was appropriate.

In the next chapter, we will take this knowledge of React into the realm of native mobile applications by building a `Hello World` application in React Native.

2
Saying HelloWorld in React Native

Now that we've introduced you to the basics of programming in React, it's time to dig into some of the underlying tools and technologies that make React Native work. This will provide valuable context as you progress through the remainder of this book. We'll also touch on some of the more popular mobile development alternatives to React Native. This will help you understand where React Native fits into the broader mobile development ecosystem and better inform your decision-making as to which technology best suites your mobile requirements.

Once we've completed setting context, we'll switch gears and focus on configuring your computer for running and debugging your very first React Native application using the iOS Simulator. Since our immediate goal is to get you up and running quickly, we'll only focus on configuring your environment for iOS. Chapter 9, *Refactoring for Android*, is entirely dedicated to configuring your computer for Android development and refactoring your app to run across both platforms. We will also save much of the React Native API specifics for Chapter 4, *Starting our Project with React Native Components and APIs*.

In this chapter, we'll cover the following topics:

- A review of a few popular mobile development options catered toward JavaScript developers
- A review of the various software and tools we'll use to build React Native applications
- Installing and configuring all the software needed to build our first React Native app
- Walk through basic strategies for debugging in React Native

Understanding the mobile app development ecosystem

When it comes to building mobile applications, the two most popular approaches have been, first, building a native application for each target platform (iOS, Android, and so on), and second, writing a *hybrid application* by using web technologies (HTML, CSS, JavaScript) and wrapping the app inside of a container WebView using a tool such as Adobe PhoneGap. Each option has its pros and cons. Native applications often feel faster and more responsive. They have built-in support for complex touch gestures and they look and feel consistent with their platform. As a post from the Facebook blog states, *the reason we build native apps on these proprietary platforms is that right now, we can create better-feeling experiences that are more consistent with the rest of the platform than we can on the web.* (Source: `https://co de.facebook.com/posts/1014532261909640/react-native-bringing-modern-web-techn iques-to-mobile/`) However, this comes at a cost. For one, the native technology stacks are completely different from one another. Developing a native application for iOS typically involves authoring your code in Objective-C or Swift. Android applications are often written in Java. Additionally, the environment you write your code in is different. Xcode is the de facto choice for iOS development, and Android development is typically done with tools such as Eclipse or Android Studio. Juggling lots of tools and languages shouldn't be anything new to seasoned frontend developers. However, couple these differences with differing best practices, approaches to networking, and a limited number of sharable assets across platforms and you've got quite a bit of work ahead of you just to get a cross-platform app off the ground.

Hybrid applications are a very popular alternative, particularly for those with frontend development experience. Hybrid apps are easier to scale because you only have to author one codebase that can be deployed to multiple platforms. For a large swath of applications, the hybrid approach makes sense, particularly if you or your team's skill set mostly aligns with that of your traditional frontend developer: HTML, CSS, and JavaScript. However, achieving the same level of responsiveness and gesture support as a native app can prove deeply challenging.

In this section, I'll provide an overview of a few mobile development frameworks. This is not intended to be comprehensive list. Other options, such as **Titanium** (`https://www.appc elerator.com/`), **Fuse** (`https://www.fusetools.com`), and others may also be worth exploring.

Adobe PhoneGap

Adobe PhoneGap is a very popular solution to hybrid development. It's built off the open source Apache Cordova library and provides a **Command Line Interface** (**CLI**) for packaging your web application built with HTML, CSS, and JavaScript inside of a native container that can be installed and deployed to native app stores. The native container is a WebView that removes any browser window decoration and runs your web application in full screen. PhoneGap allows you to access different native APIs, such as the device's camera, GPS, and accelerometer. Additionally, Cordova has a rich ecosystem of plugins that provide a bridge to all sorts of phone features that can be interfaced directly within your JavaScript code.

Ionic

Ionic is another hugely popular hybrid application framework. It comprises two major pieces: **Ionic Framework** (`http://ionicframework.com/`) and the **Ionic CLI** (`http://ionicframework.com/docs/cli/`). Ionic Framework is a mobile framework that includes common UI widgets appropriate for mobile interfaces such as action sheets, mobile navigation, infinitely scrolling lists, and popovers. These components are built on top of Google's **Angular JS** (`https://angularjs.org/`) framework using Angular directives. If you're familiar with Angular, working with Ionic should be really straightforward. The **Ionic CLI** is a tool for managing a lot of the tedious parts of mobile app development, such as scaffolding, building, and deploying to phones. Ionic CLI also provides multiple templates for beginning your project based on common UI patterns. Similar to PhoneGap, Ionic is built on top of Cordova. This means you'll be able to leverage the same Cordova plugins in your Ionic applications. Currently, Ionic is built using Angular 1.x. As of this writing, Ionic 2 is available for preview and will pair with the newly released Angular 2 framework.

NativeScript

Telerik's open source NativeScript lets you build native apps for iOS and Android (they also plan to add support for Windows Universal apps soon) with an approach similar to React Native. Unlike the Cordova options, there is no WebView rendering HTML and CSS. NativeScript relies on JavaScript running on the device with JavaScriptCore on iOS and V8 for Android.

Your JavaScript code communicates through NativeScript to the underlying platform rendering real native views. NativeScript uses XML markup for declarative UIs that can even be customized per platform either using separate XML files (that is, `myView.ios.xml` and `myView.android.xml`) or using platform-specific tags within a view.

 As the NativeScript site states, "*NativeScript has a lot of cool features, such as two-way data binding between JavaScript objects and native UI components, and a CSS implementation for native apps.*" (Source: `http://developer.telerik.com/featured/nativescript-works/`).

One important differentiator between NativeScript and alternative offerings is its ability to directly access all native platform APIs through JavaScript. The Telerik site provides several good examples of what this might look like in an application:

```
var alert = new UIAlertView();
alert.message = "Hello world!";
alert.addButtonWithTitle("OK");
alert.show();
```

(Source: `http://developer.telerik.com/featured/nativescript-works/`)

In the preceding sample, `UIAlertView` is a native class in Objective-C. NativeScript allows you to access these native APIs without needing to touch Objective-C or Java. The NativeScript runtime injects into the global namespace of the platform's JavaScript virtual machine all the meta information of the iOS or Android API. This allows you to successfully execute something like the following in an Android environment:

```
var time = new android.text.format.Time();
```

(Source: `http://developer.telerik.com/featured/nativescript-works/`)

NativeScript allows you to style your application using a subset of the CSS language. You can place your CSS inline, in page-specific CSS files, or in application-wide CSS files. You can also layout your views using the predefined layouts–`AbsoluteLayout`, `DockLayout`, `GridLayout`, `StackLayout`, and `WrapLayout`. These web-like paradigms make NativeScript a very enticing option for frontend developers looking to develop native applications.

React Native

React Native is an open source project released by Facebook in March 2015. The goal of React Native is to allow developers to write high-quality native applications for iOS and Android using familiar web technologies. It uses the same declarative approach to constructing user interfaces as React for the web. React Native also aims to reduce many native development inefficiencies. Rather than deal with the slow process of write > compile > deploy > debug, which can cripple development on larger native apps, React Native allows you to simply *refresh* the app after making a change without the slow compile and deploy steps, just like on the Web! This makes for a much improved developer experience. And, unlike normal native development, React Native allows you to share far more code across platforms. However, Facebook points out that React Native is not intended to be a *write once, run anywhere* solution. They acknowledge that each platform has its own look, feel, and capabilities. Instead, React Native allows you to leverage common technologies to build across multiple platforms. They call this *learn once, write anywhere*.

React Native apps are authored very similarly to React for the Web. You write your business logic in JavaScript and compose your views using JSX. Similar to NativeScript, React Native does not rely on WebViews. React Native runs an embedded instance of JavaScriptCore that communicates through the React Native bridge to platform-specific native components that look and feel as they should on the platform. React Native also exposes underlying platform APIs, allowing you to access the device's camera, GPS, and the like all in JavaScript. However, unlike NativeScript, React Native has you compose your application just like React–by creating a nested component tree structure.

React Native maintains its high performance by executing layout calculations and JavaScript on separate threads, leaving the main thread focused on rendering native views, handling gestures responses, and smooth animations. React components are themselves pure, side-effect-free representations of the application state. UI updates are prompted by changes to a component's props or state. React then goes through its usual update lifecycle and asynchronously batches up the minimal updates necessary to send over the React Native bridge. The bridge is how JavaScript then communicates to the native side and how the native side messages back to JavaScript. However, you can think of the bridge as an implementation detail that can be largely ignored in your day-to-day development. For the most part, you can focus on writing your code in JavaScript using the React Native APIs and let React Native take care of the ugly parts.

React Native comes bundled with support for many APIs you're used to seeing on the Web. This include, among others, networking APIs for fetch, XMLHttpRequest, and WebSockets along with geolocation and requestAnimationFrame. React Native has built-in support for ECMAScript 2015 and parts of ECMAScript 2016. The **React Native Packager** (more on this later) runs **Babel**, a tool for transpiling ES2015 and ES2016 into ECMAScript 5. This is necessary as many older JavaScript runtimes only support parts of ES2015 at this point. But thanks to Babel, this means you can leverage many of the new JavaScript language features in your React Native apps.

 If you're unfamiliar with Babel, you can experiment with it in the Babel REPL available on their website at https://babeljs.io/repl/.

Extending React Native

Being a JavaScript framework, you're automatically able to leverage a vast number of JavaScript libraries such as Moment.js and Lodash. But every now and then you'll need to do something that requires native code that isn't available in the React Native API. Through React Native's Native Modules, you can extend the capabilities of React Native allowing you to access platform APIs, reuse existing native code, or perhaps offload an expensive task to the native side. A rich ecosystem of React Native plugins already exists, adding support for things like Google's Material Design, barcode scanners, and an assortment of user interface components. As a testament to how far React Native can be extended, during Facebook's 2016 F8 conference, a React Native plugin for the Microsoft Windows Universal Platform was announced. This opens up React Native development to both Windows and Xbox. We'll touch more on this in Chapter 12, *React Native Tools and Resources*. We'll also review how you can build your own Native Module in Chapter 10, *Using and Writing Native Modules*.

Introducing style and layout in React Native

Before we wrap up our introduction to React Native, we must discuss style. Similar to NativeScript, React Native borrows many ideas of styling for the Web. However, unlike NativeScript, you don't author CSS selectors in a CSS file. Instead, you write JavaScript objects that align with many familiar CSS properties. For example, in CSS, you might write the following:

```
.container {
    width: 400px;
    height: 400px;
```

```
    background-color: #222222;
}

.box {
    border-width: 2px;
    border-color: #cc0000;
}
```

However, in React Native, you would write the following in JavaScript:

```
const styles = StyleSheet.create({
    container: {
        width: 400,
        height: 400,
        backgroundColor: '#222222'
    },
    box: {
        borderWidth: 2,
        borderColor: '#cc0000'
    }
});
```

Note that instead of writing properties such as `border-color`, you instead write the camel cased `borderColor`. This approach actually follows the same conventions used when updating DOM `style` properties for the Web. Because these are JavaScript objects, you'll need to add quotes around strings. Also, you must omit units such as `px` for numeric values.

There are several reasons why the React Native team chose not to implement CSS as it exists on the Web. CSS at scale is hard. It's not impossible. But it is hard. There are many approaches for scaling large CSS libraries for the Web, such as OOCSS, BEM, and SMACSS. Each has its own take but none can escape one of CSS's biggest hurdles: everything is entirely global. CSS was never intended to be isolated from the global namespace. For many developers, this seems counterintuitive since global variables are usually a bad practice. Even tools such as Bootstrap and Zurb's Foundation rely heavily global SCSS variables. Writing CSS in JavaScript allows you to isolate styles from the global name space.

There's one other major piece to React Native's approach to layout. React Native uses flexbox as the default layout system. If you're familiar with flexbox for the web, it operates very similarly. We'll go much deeper on style and layout in `Chapter 3`, *Styling and Layout in React Native*. For now, let's get our environments configured to build our first React Native application.

Understanding all the React Native tools

Like most modern development, there are a few tools required to build a React Native application. Luckily, React Native is pretty easy to configure relative to many frameworks out there. We'll get into installing all these tools shortly. First, let's review what all the tools are how they fit into the bigger picture of developing a React Native app.

Xcode

In order to build an iOS application, you'll need Apple's Xcode IDE. React Native runs on iOS 7 and above. This means that you'll need Xcode version 7.0 or higher. (We'll be using Xcode 8 in this book.) Whether you love, hate, or are altogether indifferent about Xcode, we won't actually be spending much time in it.

Initially, we'll just use Xcode to launch our app in the iOS Simulator. Also, because we'll mostly be testing our app in the iOS Simulator, you don't need to worry about enrolling in the Apple iOS Developer Program. However, if and when you wish to ship an app to the App Store, you will need to register. Gustavo Ambrozio has a wonderful series on how to configure everything required for submitting to the Apple App Store; for more information, refer to `https://www.raywenderlich.com/8003/how-to-submit-your-app-to-apple-fro m-no-account-to-app-store-part-1`.

Google Chrome

Wait, Chrome? I thought we were making native mobile apps? Don't worry. We are. If you've been developing web apps for some time, chances are you've had some time to play with Chrome's amazing **DevTools**. Thankfully, the Facebook team feels the same way. You can actually debug your React Native apps running on the iOS Simulator or your native device in Google Chrome. It's pretty amazing and is from my experience one the biggest selling points when showing off React Native to other developers.

Homebrew (also known as brew)

Homebrew is a package manager for **macOS** (formerly known as **Mac OS X**). We won't be interfacing with this tool much at all in this book. It'll simply be used for installing some of the other tools we'll need to get our environments up and running. Once everything is configured, you can almost forget it exists. If you're curious, though, you can find out more about Homebrew on its website, `http://brew.sh/`.

Node.js and npm

Node.js is a server-side JavaScript runtime environment. React Native ships with some tools that are written for Node.js. Additionally, we will use Node's package manager, **npm**, to install the React Native command-line tool along with other libraries in later chapters.

It's very likely you've encountered Node and npm in the past. Almost all modern frontend tooling, such as Gulp, Babel, or Webpack, run on top of Node.

Watchman

Watchman is an open source tool created by Facebook (`https://facebook.github.io/wat chman/`). React Native's packager uses Watchman to recursively watch for changes to our source code files across one or more directory trees. Once it detects a change, it automatically rebuilds the JavaScript bundle. This allows us to sidestep one of the slowest and most painful parts of native development.

Much like several of our other tools, once Watchman is installed, you won't have to worry about it. The React Native Package Manager handles running Watchman for us.

Flow

Unlike the other tools mentioned, **Flow** is entirely optional. Flow is yet another open source tool created by the Facebook team (`http://flowtype.org/`). It's used to add type annotations to our JavaScript code. JavaScript, as you likely already know, is a dynamically typed language. This means you never need to declare a variable as an `int` or a `string`. You just declare a variable and set a value. The type is implicitly set based on the value you assigned. This makes JavaScript an incredibly powerful and dynamic language. But as the saying goes, with great power comes great responsibility.

That said, many JavaScript developers are embracing type annotation tools such as Flow as a way to guard against potential errors in their code. Once you've annotated your code with types, you can run `flow` from the terminal to verify everything is as expected.

Following is a simple example from the Flow website:

```
// @flow
function foo(x) {
    return x * 10;
}
foo('Hello, world!');
```

The previously code will execute without error but it isn't likely going to return a result that's particularly useful. Passing a string to foo will result in **NaN** (**Not a Number**). So here's how we might try to guard against this using Flow:

```
// @flow
function foo(x: number): number {
    return x * 10;
}
foo('Hello world');
```

Note the number type annotations that were added to both the function's parameters and the function's return value. Now, running flow will produce an error alerting you that the argument `'Hello world'` is incompatible with the expected type.

Flow can be configured for a project by creating a `.flowconfig` file in the root directory of your project. The React Native CLI actually provides you an initial configuration when it creates your project.

React Native command-line interface (CLI)

The React Native CLI is a small Node app that offers a simple `init` command used to create new React Native applications. There really isn't much to it. As we'll see shortly, once you run the CLI, it will create a standard React Native app with all the necessary files and dependencies needed to build an app for iOS and Android.

Installing our tools

At this point, we have covered what each of the tools in our tool chain is responsible for doing. So with that out of the way, let's begin installing each of them.

Installing Xcode

The first thing you'll need to do is ensure you have version 7 or later of **Xcode** installed. However, I recommend you install Xcode 8 as that's what we'll be using throughout this book. If you already have Xcode installed, verify the version by launching the program and then clicking on **Xcode | About Xcode**. You should see an image similar to the following screenshot:

If you don't have Xcode installed, you'll need to download it from the Apple App Store. To do this, launch the App Store application and search for Xcode using the search bar in the top right corner of the window. Once you find it, click on the **Get** button and then **Install App**. You may need to enter your Apple credentials before downloading. The Xcode installer is pretty large, so while we wait on that, you can start downloading the next set of tools.

Installing Homebrew

The next series of tools must be installed through the terminal. You can use the macOS Terminal app or another terminal of your choosing. You can search for Terminal (or any other application) by using *Command + Space* on your keyboard. Then type `Terminal` and launch it.

Once the terminal is open, visit `http://brew.sh` in your web browser. Copy and paste the `Install Homebrew` command into your terminal and press Enter. You'll need to have administrator privileges in order to install Homebrew and most other tools. You may have to press *Return* a second time for the terminal to ask for your password. Type in your account password, press *Return,* and wait for Homebrew to finish installing:

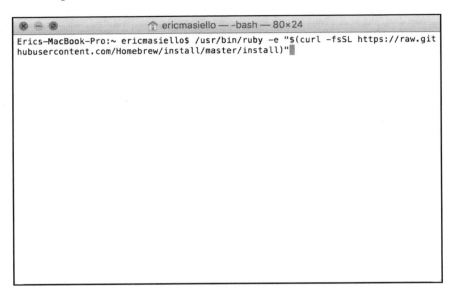

Once it's done installing, your terminal window should look like the following:

```
remote: Total 1037 (delta 93), reused 631 (delta 67), pack-reused 0
Receiving objects: 100% (1037/1037), 1.04 MiB | 1.65 MiB/s, done.
Resolving deltas: 100% (93/93), done.
From https://github.com/Homebrew/brew
 * [new branch]      master     -> origin/master
HEAD is now at 2b45ae4 Merge pull request #926 from MikeMcQuaid/os-rubocop
==> Tapping homebrew/core
Cloning into '/usr/local/Homebrew/Library/Taps/homebrew/homebrew-core'...
remote: Counting objects: 3727, done.
remote: Compressing objects: 100% (3615/3615), done.
remote: Total 3727 (delta 15), reused 1624 (delta 4), pack-reused 0
Receiving objects: 100% (3727/3727), 2.90 MiB | 3.59 MiB/s, done.
Resolving deltas: 100% (15/15), done.
Checking connectivity... done.
Tapped 3606 formulae (3,754 files, 9M)
Already up-to-date.
==> Installation successful!
==> Next steps
Run `brew help` to get started
Further documentation: https://git.io/brew-docs
==> Homebrew has enabled anonymous aggregate user behaviour analytics
Read the analytics documentation (and how to opt-out) here:
  https://git.io/brew-analytics
Erics-MacBook-Pro:~ ericmasiello$
```

Installing Node and npm

Next on our list are Node and npm. As the React Native docs recommend, you can install this through brew:

```
brew install node
```

Node comes with npm, so you don't have to worry about installing that separately. I recommend installing the latest version of Node and npm, version 6 and 3, respectively, at the time of writing.

Once you've installed Node, you can run npm -v and node -v from the terminal. If you see version numbers, you're good to go:

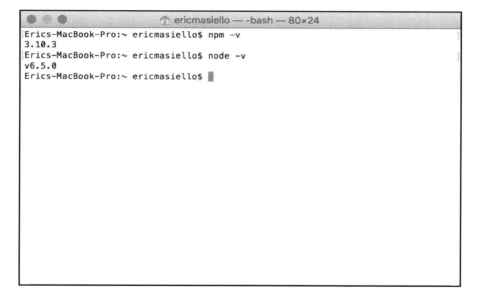

Installing Watchman and Flow

Next up are Watchman and Flow. Again, Flow is entirely optional. If you wish to experiment with it, you're welcomed to install it. It won't hurt anything. If you'd rather skip it for now, that's totally fine as well.

From the terminal, run `brew install watchman`:

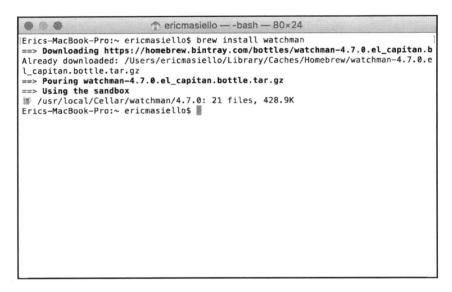

And if you wish, run `brew install flow`.

Installing the React Native CLI

Okay! We're almost done with installing everything. There's just one more it we need: the React Native CLI. Again, from the terminal, run `npm install -g react-native-cli`. Using npm, this will globally (`-g`) install the React Native CLI that you'll use to scaffold your React Native applications. However, don't be surprised if you see an error that looks like the following:

```
● ● ●                     ⌂ eric — bash — 80×24
npm ERR! Darwin 14.5.0
npm ERR! argv "/usr/local/bin/node" "/usr/local/bin/npm" "install" "-g" "react-n
ative-cli"
npm ERR! node v5.7.0
npm ERR! npm  v3.6.0
npm ERR! path /usr/local/lib/node_modules
npm ERR! code EACCES
npm ERR! errno -13
npm ERR! syscall access

npm ERR! Error: EACCES: permission denied, access '/usr/local/lib/node_modules'
npm ERR!     at Error (native)
npm ERR!  { [Error: EACCES: permission denied, access '/usr/local/lib/node_modul
es']
npm ERR!   errno: -13,
npm ERR!   code: 'EACCES',
npm ERR!   syscall: 'access',
npm ERR!   path: '/usr/local/lib/node_modules' }
npm ERR!
npm ERR! Please try running this command again as root/Administrator.

npm ERR! Please include the following file with any support request:
npm ERR!     /Users/eric/npm-debug.log
hmasiello:~ eric$ ▮
```

This is pretty common permission error. One way to get around this is by prefacing the command with `sudo`, which will required you type your password. However, we can fix our permissions pretty easily so that `sudo` is unnecessary. Here are the steps:

1. Type in `npm config get prefix`.
2. If you see `/usr/local`, then simply run `sudo chown -R $(whoami) $(npm config get prefix)/{lib/node_modules,bin,share}`.
3. You'll be prompted for your user password. Enter it and press Return, and your permissions should be set.
4. If after running `npm config get prefix` you get a different response, check out `https://docs.npmjs.com/getting-started/fixing-npm-permissions`. There are more detailed instructions and different options for how to fix npm permissions.

Once you have your permissions buttoned up, rerun `npm install -g react-native-cli`. Once it's done, you should see something like the following:

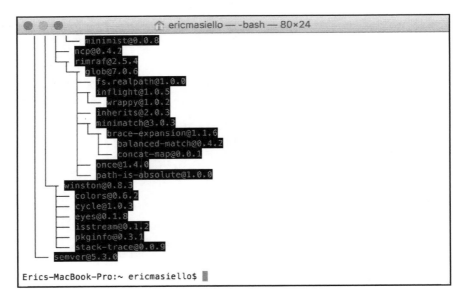

Finally, you're all set. Now let's create an app!

Creating our first React Native app

If you're fairly well versed in navigating the terminal, go ahead and `cd` into whichever directory you plan to place your code. We'll be putting this project on our desktop. You can always move it later if wish.Enter the following into the terminal:

```
cd ~/Desktop
```

Then type the following:

```
react-native init HelloWorld.
```

This uses the React Native CLI we installed earlier to create a directory called `HelloWorld`. It then downloads all the necessary dependencies needed to create our first React Native app. Downloading these assets should only take a few minutes if you're on a reasonably fast Internet connection. Once it's done installing, you should see something like the following in your terminal:

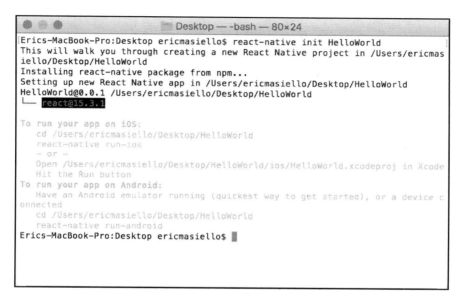

Now back in your terminal, run the following:

```
cd HelloWord
```

Then type the following:

```
open .
```

This will open up a new Finder window in your HelloWorld directory, as shown in the following screenshot:

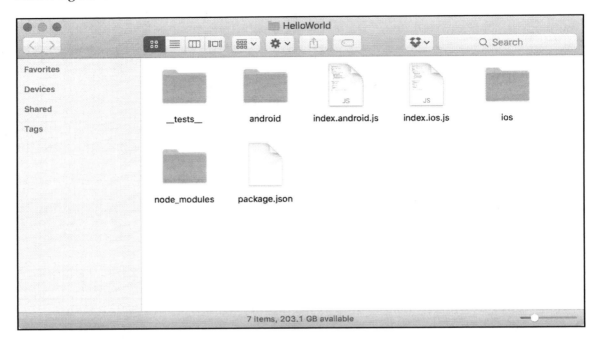

Open the `ios` folder and then open `HelloWorld.xcodeproject` in Xcode, as shown in the following screenshot:

Once Xcode has completed indexing your project, you should see the message HelloWorld: Ready at the top center of the window. Click the build and run play button in the top left. This will launch your HelloWorld application in the selected simulator. In the preceding screenshot, the default simulator is the iPhone 7 Plus. If you'd like to change it to a different device, select a different simulator from the dropdown. Then click build and run.

You may be prompted with a message asking if you wish to **Enable Developer Mode** on this Mac. Click on **Enable** and the app will continue building.

It's possible that the simulator device may look humongous on your screen, particularly if you picked one of the recent iPhones. To adjust this to something more reasonable, make sure the iOS Simulator is in the foreground. From the menu, select **Window** | **Scale** | 33%. Feel free to pick a different scale option that best suits your computer screen. Refer to the following screenshot:

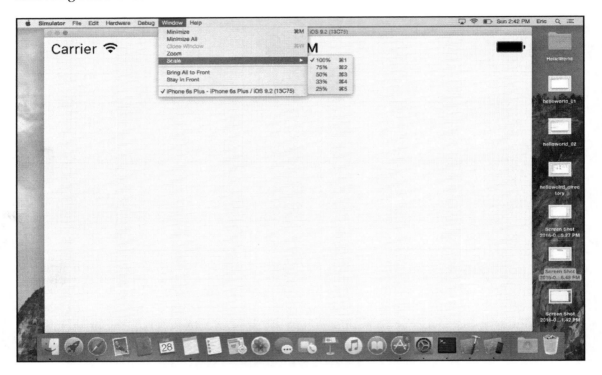

Assuming everything ran successfully, you should see the default React Native app, as shown in the following screenshot:

Going forward, you actually don't even need to open Xcode to run React Native apps. Instead, run the following command from the root directory of your project:

```
react-native run-ios
```

This will launch the app directly in iOS simulator without needing to open Xcode.

React Native Packager

You may have noticed a separate terminal window spawn when running your HelloWorld app. This is the React Native Packager. It's a program similar to **Browserify** and **Webpack**, which are responsible for resolving dependencies, transpiling, and bundling the JavaScript, JSX, and other assets to be run on the device or simulator.

Understanding our HelloWorld app

This is great. We've got the app running in our simulator. Sure, it required a little bit of work to install the necessary tools, but the good news is that the only thing we'll need to do from this point forward is run the `react-native init AppName` command whenever we wish to create a new app. All our tools are installed and we're ready to start developing. But before we get into the meat and potatoes of React Native, let's quickly take a look at what exactly the React Native CLI provided us. Open up `package.json` in your text editor of choice. I'm using **Atom** (`https://atom.io/`) as shown in the following screenshot:

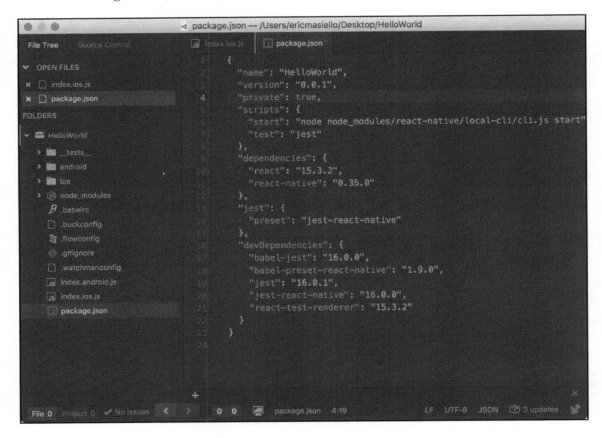

I want to call your attention to dependencies section. Here, you should only see two items listed: react and react-native. At the time of writing, React Native is at stable version 0.35.0. Given the pace of updates to React Native, yours is likely newer. That's fine. Just keep your version in mind when seeking out help with React Native questions. The last file I want to call your attention to is `index.ios.j` from the following screenshot:

```
                    index.ios.js — /Users/ericmasiello/Desktop/HelloWorld
   index.ios.js      package.json

    /**
     * Sample React Native App
     * https://github.com/facebook/react-native
     * @flow
     */

    import React, { Component } from 'react';
    import {
      AppRegistry,
      StyleSheet,
      Text,
      View
    } from 'react-native';

    export default class HelloWorld extends Component {
      render() {
        return (
          <View style={styles.container}>
            <Text style={styles.welcome}>
              Welcome to React Native!
            </Text>
            <Text style={styles.instructions}>
              To get started, edit index.ios.js
            </Text>
            <Text style={styles.instructions}>
              Press Cmd+R to reload,{'\n'}
              Cmd+D or shake for dev menu
            </Text>
          </View>
        );
      }
    }
33
    const styles = StyleSheet.create({
      container: {

File 0   Project 0   ✔ No Issues   <   >        LF   UTF-8   JavaScript (JSX)   3 updates
```

There are four major parts to this file. Let's walk through them one by one.

Importing dependencies using ECMAScript 2015

It's worth calling this out since we'll be doing this a lot. At the top of this file, you'll see two ES2015 `import` statement. The syntax follows the pattern `import something from 'somewhere';`. Using the first import as an example, we are telling the React Native Packager that we require the `React` object from the React package found in the `node_modules` directory. When our application runs, the React Native Packager will resolve this dependency automatically, making the React object available in this file. You'll need to do this in every file you create that creates a React component.

Additionally, you'll see other variable(s) inside curly braces beside the `import React` statement:

```
import React, { Component } from 'react';
```

If you're new to ES2015, this syntax probably looks a bit foreign to you. Somewhat confusingly, it also looks similar to ES2015 destructuring. However, it's not the same. In this example, `React` and `Component` are both exported values from the `React` package. React is what's known as the default export. This is why it appears outside the curly braces. Anything inside the curly braces is named exports (to which you can have many). If you still find this a bit confusing, the Mozilla Developer Network has a great write-up on this topic. For more information, refer to `https://developer.mozilla.org/en-US/docs/Web/J avaScript/Reference/Statements/import`.The second `import` statement is where we bring in everything that's React Native-specific. Take a look at the following code:

```
import {
  AppRegistry,
  StyleSheet,
  Text,
  View
} from 'react-native';
```

This includes a handful of React Native Components and APIs we'll be using extensively throughout this book. However, I'll save the deeper exploration of these topics for the coming chapters.

Our HelloWorld component

The next part of our code is the component itself:

```
class HelloWorld extends Component {
  render() {
    return (
      <View style={styles.container}>
        <Text style={styles.welcome}>
          Welcome to React Native!
        </Text>
        <Text style={styles.instructions}>
          To get started, edit index.ios.js
        </Text>
        <Text style={styles.instructions}>
          Press Cmd+R to reload,{'\n'}
          Cmd+D or shake for dev menu
        </Text>
      </View>
```

```
    );
  }
}
```

This component is what will actually be rendered in our application. Don't worry just yet about what a `View` or a `Text` component is. We'll cover all that in `Chapter 4`, *Starting our Project with React Native Components and APIs*. But for now, let's change the code to see how quickly we can test our application in the simulator. Take a look at the following steps:

1. Change `Welcome to React Native!` to `Welcome to my first React Native application!` and save the file.
2. Switch back to your simulator and press *Command + R*.

Your app will quickly refresh and you'll see your changes immediately. Pretty amazing! The following screenshot will give you a clear idea about the new interface:

HelloWorld style code

The following block of code represents the style and layout code:

```
const styles = StyleSheet.create({
  container: {
    flex: 1,
    justifyContent: 'center',
    alignItems: 'center',
    backgroundColor: '#F5FCFF',
  },
  welcome: {
    fontSize: 20,
    textAlign: 'center',
    margin: 10,
  },
  instructions: {
    textAlign: 'center',
    color: '#333333',
    marginBottom: 5,
  },
});
```

Feel free to experiment with these properties and values. As we mentioned earlier, this should all feel similar to CSS. If you're unfamiliar with flexbox, don't fret as we'll be covering it in much greater depth in the next chapter.

Registering the root component

The last piece of code of note is as follows:

```
AppRegistry.registerComponent('HelloWorld', () => HelloWorld);
```

The preceding code tells React Native that for our application called `'HelloWorld'`, set the root component to be `HelloWorld`. You only need to call `AppRegistry.registerComponent` once per app. Every other component will be a child component contained within `HelloWorld`.

Why import React?

You may have noticed that we never directly reference the `React` object we imported at the top of our file. So why do we need it? Can we just delete it? Try changing the first import statement to the following:

```
import { Component } from 'react';
```

Now press *Command + R* in the Simulator to see what happens:

Right at the top, you'll see the message **Can't find variable: React**. This seems odd seeing that we're not actually using the React variable anywhere, no? Well, here's what is happening. Remember how we said that the React Native Packager transpiles our ES2015 and ES2106 code into ES5? This is also true of JSX code. As you probably already know, `<Text>Hi there<Text>` is not a valid JavaScript expression. The React Native Packager, using Babel, transpiles the JSX code into something similar to the following:

```
return React.createElement(Text, null, 'Hi there');
```

Note that Babel automatically converts our JSX code into `React.createElement` statements. This is why you must always make the `React` object available to your source code whenever you write JSX.

Debugging a React Native app

While being able to write in a familiar language makes writing React Native apps relatively easy for JavaScript veterans, there's another equally important part of the development experience that we haven't touched upon–debugging. Earlier, we mentioned how Google Chrome contains amazing JavaScript debugging tools. They are among the best out there and are often why many frontend developers choose Chrome as their primary browser for testing and development. Thankfully, the Facebook team has crafted React Native such that we can debug our React Native JavaScript code in these familiar tools. When you debug your React Native application, it runs in a *proxy mode*, whereby your application's JavaScript is actually run inside of Chrome's V8 JavaScript engine instead of on the device or simulator's JavaScriptCore engine. The React Native Packager will then broker communication between the app and Chrome using web sockets.

Enabling the Chrome Debugger

As you may have noticed, our HelloWorld app actually provides some useful instructions for us. For one, you can press *Command + R* to quickly reload your application after making changes to your source code. Additionally, you can press *Command + D* to trigger the `dev` menu. Let's try this out by following these steps:

1. Select your iOS Simulator and press *Command + D*.
2. An action sheet will appear providing you with a few options.
3. Click on **Debug JS Remotely**. This will launch a new tab in Chrome.

Take a look at the following screenshots:

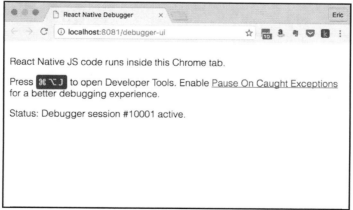

If your app doesn't not respond to your keyboard presses, such as Command + R, ensure the simulator is configured correctly. From the simulator, select **Hardware | Keyboard** and make sure **Connect Hardware Keyboard** is selected.

From Chrome, press *Command + Option + J* on your keyboard to open up the Chrome DevTools console. With the developer tools open, let's experiment with some simple debugging options in our HelloWorld app. Inside index.ios.js, add a console.log statement. Take a look at the following code:

```
class HelloWorld extends Component {
  render() {
    console.log('Debugging from React Native');
    return (
      <View style={styles.container}>
        <Text style={styles.welcome}>
          Welcome to React Native!
        </Text>
        <Text style={styles.instructions}>
          To get started, edit index.ios.js
        </Text>
        <Text style={styles.instructions}>
          Press Cmd+R to reload,{'\n'}
          Cmd+D or shake for dev menu
        </Text>
      </View>
    );
  }
}
```

Now, select your iOS Simulator and press Command + R on your keyboard. This will refresh the app in the simulator. Now, if you look in Chrome's console, you should see the message Debugging from React Native. Take a look at the following screenshot:

Breakpoints

Strategically placing console log calls can be useful for monitoring the state of your application. But what's often far more useful is setting breakpoints within Chrome's DevTools. This will let you step line by line through your code to understand what exactly is going on. To do this, follow these steps:Select the **Sources** tab in the Chrome DevTools:

1. Then press *Command + P* on your keyboard.
2. Search for the `index.ios.js` file. There may be two results that show up as options. Try opening each of them until you find the one that matches our source code.
3. Scroll down until you find your `console.log` statement you added. Then click on the line number that appears to the left your code in the gray margin. This will put a blue marker signifying a breakpoint has been set.

Now that we've set the breakpoint, let's test it to make sure our code actually hits it. To do this, don't refresh the Chrome tab we're in. Instead, refresh the app inside the iOS Simulator. Execution will now pause at our breakpoint and the app will appear as a blank white screen, as shown in the following screenshot:

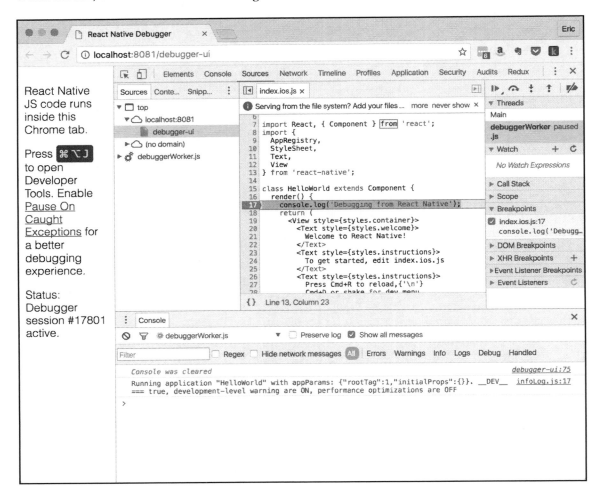

Here, we obviously don't have much of interest to step through. You can click on the Resume (Play) button in Chrome's DevTools or press *Command* + \ on your keyboard and the app will render as normal. You can remove your breakpoint by clicking on that same blue marker we added earlier. Setting breakpoints throughout our app will become increasingly useful as we begin to build more and more complex applications.

Summary

In this chapter, we covered a lot of ground. We talked about some of the different approaches to building mobile applications and the inherit tradeoffs. We introduced what it means to develop in React Native and how it ties together with the underlying tools and technologies. And, far more importantly, we configured our computers for building and debugging our very first React Native app. Now that we've covered the basics of React, React Native, and debugging, in the next chapter, we'll dive deeper into how you can style and lay out your application using flexbox.

3
Styling and Layout in React Native

So far, we've covered the basics of React development. We understand how to work with props and state and how to compose smaller, reusable components to form more complex views. We've installed the necessary tools to get a React Native app off the ground and now have a working Hello World app running in the iOS Simulator. The React Native API comes with a large library of built-in components, which we'll explore in the next chapter. But before we dive into the various component APIs, it's important we understand how to style and layout these components, much like we would with CSS in the web world.

React Native's approach to style and layout is heavily inspired by the Web. Many of the properties used to decorate your app will feel very familiar to CSS. For layout, rather than relying on floats, the Facebook team has ported the powerful **flexbox** layout system to React Native enabling us to make declarative, flexible layouts for our mobile apps. With all the similarities to the Web, seasoned web developers might think they can skip past this chapter. However, there are several notable differences between React Native and CSS that are worth understanding before venturing on. We'll uncover these differences as we explore the following topics:

- How to construct and apply styles
- Styling without inheritance
- Flexbox and the box model
- Styling text
- Styling images
- Debugging styles
- Adding media-query-like behavior to your apps

Constructing and applying styles

Let's begin our exploration of component styling by first answering two key questions: what should my style code look like and where does it go inside of my project?

Inline styles

Similar to HTML, styles in React Native can be applied inline by setting the value of the style property, as shown in the following code:

```
<View style={{ backgroundColor: 'blue', flex: 1, justifyContent: 'center',
alignItems: 'center' }}>
    <Text style={{ color: '#fff', fontSize: 22 }}>Hello World</Text>
</View>
```

The output of the code will be as shown in the following screenshot:

You can think of a `View` much like a `div` and `Text` similar to a `span` or `label`. Those differences aside, the style properties and values should feel pretty familiar. The `color` property sets the text color just like in CSS. `fontSize`, `backgroundColor`, `justifyContent`, and `alignItems` are by and large the camel case version of their CSS equivalents.

Styles as objects in your React Native components

As you may have noticed, `style` values are defined as JavaScript objects. You can define them inline as we did in the previous section or you can define them outside of your component and simply reference them, as shown in the following code:

```
const DemoComponent = () => (
  <View style={viewStyles}>
    <Text style={textStyles}>Hello World</Text>
  </View>
);

const viewStyles = {
  backgroundColor: 'blue',
  flex: 1,
  justifyContent: 'center',
  alignItems: 'center'
};

const textStyles = {
  color: '#fff',
  fontSize: 22
};
```

This will produce an app that looks identical to the inline style example. However, now that we've moved our style declarations outside of the component, our code is far more readable.

In CSS, you can apply multiple CSS classes to an individual element:

```
<button class="btn btn-primary">Submit</button>
```

For those new to CSS, you might think that because you added `btn-primary` after `btn`, the `btn-primary` rules would trump any conflicts with `btn`. In reality, conflict resolution in CSS is controlled by *specificity*. In React Native, specificity rules operate differently and arguably more predictably. In the following example, we'll use the built-in `TouchableHighlight` component. Think of these as just buttons for React Native. Take a look at the following code:

```
const DemoComponent = () => (
  <View style={viewStyles}>
    <TouchableHighlight style={[btn, btnPrimary]}>
      <Text>Submit</Text>
    </TouchableHighlight>
  </View>
);

const viewStyles = {
  flex: 1,
  justifyContent: 'center',
  alignItems: 'center'
};

const btn = {
  borderStyle: 'solid',
  borderColor: '#d5d5d5',
  borderWidth: 1,
  backgroundColor: '#eee',
  borderRadius: 3,
  padding: 3,
  paddingLeft: 5,
  paddingRight: 5
};

const btnPrimary = {
  backgroundColor: '#60b044',
  borderColor: '#5ca941'
};
```

Firstly, note that you combine multiple style definitions by wrapping the objects in an array. The net result of this in React Native is effectively the same, as follows:

```
style={Object.assign(btn, btnPrimary)}
```

`Object.assign` will merge the two objects together, favoring later arguments. In our case, the `btn` and `btnPrimary` objects will merge. If properties on `btnPrimary` exist that do not exist on `btn`, they will be added. If properties exist on both, `btnPrimary` properties will trump `btn`. In our example, this results in the following:

```
{
    borderStyle: 'solid',
    borderColor: '#5ca941',
    borderWidth: 1,
    backgroundColor: '#60b044',
    borderRadius: 3,
    padding: 3,
    paddingLeft: 5,
    paddingRight: 5
}
```

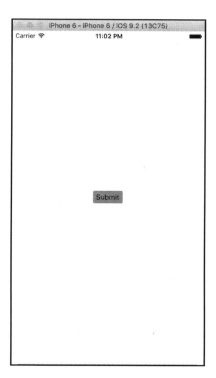

Stylesheet

You may have noticed in the previous chapter that the style code produced for us through the React Native CLI looked a little bit different than what we've demoed thus far. In our HelloWorld application, the style code looks like the following:

```
const styles = StyleSheet.create({
  container: {
    flex: 1,
    justifyContent: 'center',
    alignItems: 'center',
    backgroundColor: '#F5FCFF',
  },
  welcome: {
    fontSize: 20,
    textAlign: 'center',
    margin: 10,
  },
  instructions: {
    textAlign: 'center',
    color: '#333333',
    marginBottom: 5,
  },
});
```

For starters, everything is wrapped in a container object. This means we'll apply individual style rules like so—styles.container, styles.welcome, and styles.instructions. But more importantly, we've made our container an argument to StyleSheet.create().

The StyleSheet component comes from the top of our index.io.js file in the import statement. The create() method does a few things for us. For one, it will validate all the style properties passed to it. Therefore, see what happens if you run the following code:

```
const stylesWithError = StyleSheet.create({
  container: {
    flex: 1,
    madeUpStyleRule: 'thisWillFail'
  }
});
```

React Native would throw a big red error on screen letting you know you made a mistake. Knowing this upfront can definitely come in handy when trying to debug style and layout. Take a look at the following screenshot:

If you were to apply a similarly invented style without wrapping it in `StyleSheet.create()`, you would probably only see a warning. Ultimately, `StyleSheet.create()` will return an object allowing you to reference each individual property name by an ID. This might not be immediately useful to us as developers, but it potentially allows Facebook to optimize React Native's messaging of these style definitions and updates across the bridge. The style object would only have to be sent once. Any subsequent usage of that object can just send the ID over the bridge. As the Facebook documentation notes, this isn't yet implemented but something they could optimize for in the future.

Using Stylesheet.hairlineWidth

There's one other property of the `StyleSheet` object worth mentioning. While you'll usually define widths using numeric values, the `StyleSheet` object also exposes a `hairlineWidth` property. To demonstrate, let's use what we've learned thus far to create four buttons. Two will be default buttons and two will be primary buttons. However, we'll assign one gray button and one primary button to have a `hairlineWidth` border, as shown in the following code snippet:

```
const buttonStyles = StyleSheet.create({
  core: {
    borderStyle: 'solid',
    borderColor: '#d5d5d5',
    borderWidth: 1,
    backgroundColor: '#eee',
    borderRadius: 3,
    padding: 3,
    paddingLeft: 5,
    paddingRight: 5
  },
  primary: {
    backgroundColor: '#60b044',
    borderColor: '#355f27'
  },
  hairlineBorder: {
    borderWidth: StyleSheet.hairlineWidth
  },
  spacer: {
    marginBottom: 10
  }
});
```

Now, we'll update the component with our four sample buttons:

```
<View style={viewStyles}>
  <TouchableHighlight
    style={[buttonStyles.core, buttonStyles.spacer]}
  >
    <Text>Default Normal</Text>
  </TouchableHighlight>
  <TouchableHighlight
    style={[buttonStyles.core, buttonStyles.hairlineBorder,
buttonStyles.spacer]}
  >
    <Text>Default Hairline</Text>
  </TouchableHighlight>
  <TouchableHighlight
```

```
    style={[buttonStyles.core, buttonStyles.primary, buttonStyles.spacer]}
  >
    <Text>Primary Normal</Text>
  </TouchableHighlight>
  <TouchableHighlight
    style={[buttonStyles.core, buttonStyles.primary,
buttonStyles.hairlineBorder]}
  >
    <Text>Primary Hairline</Text>
  </TouchableHighlight>
</View>
```

In order to create some whitespace between the buttons, I also added the `buttonStyles.spacer` to the first three buttons. This adds a margin below these buttons much like it would in CSS, as shown in the following screenshot:

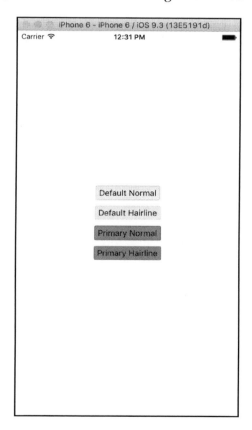

You may need to look closely, but the second default and second primary buttons each have a slightly thinner border width. If you were to use `console.log(StyleSheet.hairlineWidth)`, you would actually see a numeric value. On this particular iOS simulated device, the value is 0.5. You could just as easily have set the `borderWidth` to 0.5 in your style definition and get the same effect on that particular device. However, React Native actually computes a relative `hairlineWidth` based on the device's pixel ratio. This should produce more consistent results across devices of varying pixel densities.

Applying component-specific style properties

Finally, some React Native components possess style properties that are specific to that component. The way you apply them is not through the typical `style` property. Instead, you'll need to set the property on the component itself as defined by the component's specification. It's not feasible to review every single component's specific style properties here. Instead, we'll just cover a few examples so that you can identify them as you develop future React Native apps.

`TouchableHighlight` is a commonly used React Native component. We used it in our earlier example as a stand-in for a button. `TouchableHighlight` has two additional style properties—`activeOpacity` and `underlayColor`. `activeOpacity` sets the opacity level of any child components with any numeric value between 0 and 1; 0 means transparent and 1 means fully opaque. `underlayColor` accepts a color value just like `backgroundColor`. Both are used whenever the button is in an active state (meaning it's being pressed down). However, in order to actually demonstrate this, we need to set an `onPress` handler. For now, our `onPress` handler will point to an empty function. Take a look at the following code snippet:

```
<TouchableHighlight;
  style={[buttonStyles.core, buttonStyles.hairlineBorder,
buttonStyles.spacer]}
  underlayColor="#efefef"
  activeOpacity={0.8}
  onPress={() => {}}
>
  <Text>Default Hairline</Text>
</TouchableHighlight>
```

Pressing the button, you'll can now see the active state. Let's do the same for our primary button, but let's try out a different way of writing a hexadecimal (hex) color value. React Native supports your standard hex color values in the standard six-digit style (for example, `#00ff00`) and the shorthand three-digit style (for example, `#0f0`). Additionally, it supports a new eight-digit and shorthand four-digit format. In the eight-digit format, the additional two digits are used to represent opacity. `00` means transparent and `off` means fully opaque. Any value between these represents some level of transparency. The four-digit style is just like the three-digit version, except with the additional single digit representing the opacity level.

React Native also supports many other color values common to web development, including the `rgb`, `rgba`, `hsl`, and `hsla`, color keywords, and the value `'transparent'`.
Following are some examples:
```
'rgb(50, 255, 100)'
'rgba(0, 0, 0, 0.75)'
'hsl(360, 100%, 100%)'
'hsla(360, 100%, 100%, 0.9)'
aqua
```

Following is an example of the eight-digit hex color applied to our primary button:
```
<TouchableHighlight
  style={[buttonStyles.core, buttonStyles.primary,
            buttonStyles.hairlineBorder]}
  underlayColor="#60b044cc"
  activeOpacity={0.9}
  onPress={() => {}}
>
  <Text>Primary Hairline</Text>
</TouchableHighlight>
```
In the preceding example, we used the same hex color value as our background, `#60b044`, but added `cc` at the end to reduce the opacity.

Once you've established styles for components, it would be tedious to copy and paste the same style code into each instance. Thankfully, React allows us to create our own reusable components that encapsulate styles.

Styling without inheritance

Much of how we think about using CSS on the Web is predicated upon the concept of inheritance. We as web developers have built up many best practices that assume inheritance from the `html` container all the way down the DOM tree. As an example in CSS, we'll often define several styles on the `html` or `body` elements such as `color`, `font-family`, or `font-size`. By default, these definitions will be inherited by the entire subtree, making it easy to establish a baseline. With this basic example, this approach feels clean and relatively straightforward. However, as your CSS grows, all these inherited styles and conflicting rules can make styling larger applications unpredictable and difficult to scale.

React Native takes a different approach to styling. Rather than applying the same inheritance model as CSS, React Native styles are almost entirely scoped to the elements where they are applied. This encourages a different approach to styling your application. Rather than relying on global styles, you're encouraged to create reusable components that encapsulate styles. Using our previous example of the styled `TouchableHighlight`, we can create a reusable `Button` component that wraps `TouchableHighlight` along with our styles, as shown in the following code snippet:

```
<Button>
  <Text>Custom styled button</Text>
</Button>
```

Or, we can add additional properties to customize each instance, as shown in the following code snippet:

```
<Button onPress={() => {}} style={buttonStyles.spacer}>
  <Text>Custom button with props</Text>
</Button>
```

The implementation of our `Button` component might look like the following:

```
const Button = ({ style, children, ...otherProps }) => (
  <TouchableHighlight
    style={[buttonStyles.core, buttonStyles.hairlineBorder, style]}
    {...otherProps}
    underlayColor="#efefef"
    activeOpacity={0.8}
  >
    {children}
  </TouchableHighlight>
);

Button.propTypes = {
  style: TouchableHighlight.propTypes.style,
```

```
    children: React.PropTypes.node
};
```

Here, we've created a functional component that accepts props. Those props are destructured inside the function definition as style and children with any remaining props placed inside `otherProps`. The style variable is then placed at the end of the array of styles, allowing it to override them. Children are sandwiched inside the `TouchableHighlight` allowing you to put any content inside the button. And `otherProps` is spread across the `TouchableHighlight` to cover everything else you may want to add to it. We've also added `propType` validation to ensure the style and children passed to `Button` match the types we expect.

Adding `propTypes` is considered a best practice when authoring React or React Native components. You can learn more about general prop validation on the React docs at https://facebook.github.io/react/doc s/reusable-components.html#prop-validation.
Additionally, because style is somewhat unique to React Native, you can enforce that a prop adheres to the style rules of a particular component (for example, `TouchableHighlight.propTypes.style`, `View.propTypes.style`, or `Text.propTypes.style`)

Understanding React Native's take on the box model and flexbox

While React Native supports web layout techniques such as relative and absolute positioning, you probably don't want to design an entire app with these. For far too long, the web has used hacky CSS float techniques to create columned layouts. Floats do the job, but they were never intended for complex layouts. Nowadays, we have something far better in the form of the flexbox layout module. And what's even better is that React Native implements a form of flexbox that closely mirrors the API found in CSS. There are, however, a few differences worth noting. We'll cover these along with the related *box model-like* properties in this section.

Box model

Let's briefly start with the box model. Nowhere in the React Native documentation will you see the term box model referenced. I only mention it as it is a relatable web paradigm with numerous similarities to React Native. For starters, React Native allows you to style all the properties that affect the box model on the Web–padding, width, height, border, and margin. React Native's implementation of the box model is closest to CSS's box-sizing: border-box.

The following represents the CSS equivalent baseline implementation of components inside of React Native:

```
div, span {
  box-sizing: border-box;
  position: relative;
  display: flex;
  flex-direction: column;
  align-items: stretch;
  flex-shrink: 0;
  align-content: flex-start;
  border: 0 solid black;
  margin: 0;
  padding: 0;
  min-width: 0;
}
```

Source: https://github.com/facebook/css-layout.

We can demonstrate how the box model works with some sample code. We'll do so inside the iPhone 6 simulator, which has screen dimensions of 375 by 667 points.

Note that units in React Native are represented as points, not pixels. Points are an abstract unit of measure. For more information on points versus pixels, refer to
http://www.paintcodeapp.com/news/iphone-6-screens-demystified.

Take a look at the following code snippet:

```
const BoxModelDemo = () => (
  <View style={styles.main}>
    <Text style={styles.content}>Column 1</Text>
    <Text style={styles.content}>Column 2</Text>
    <Text style={styles.content}>Column 3</Text>
  </View>
);

const styles = StyleSheet.create({
  main: {
    flex: 1,
    paddingVertical: 20,
    flexDirection: 'row',
    flexWrap: 'wrap'
  },
  content: {
    padding: 20,
    margin: 0,
    backgroundColor: '#ef4c',
    width: 125,
    height: 125,
    borderWidth: 1,
    borderColor: 'red',
    textAlign: 'center'
  }
});
```

For the time being, ignore the flex properties. Our main container is set up to display its children in a row. The three child content elements all share the same styling. Each of them has a background, a border, padding, and zero margin. (Margins are by default set to zero. I only explicitly set them to zero for demonstration purposes.) Additionally, each one has a width of 125 points ($125 \times 3 = 375$, which is the total width of the simulated device). Also notice that even though we have a left and right border width of 1 point and left and right padding of 20, each column still fits nicely on screen, occupying one-third of the total width.

However, similar to the Web, adding left or right margins to these elements will cause them to break to a new line. To demonstrate this, we'll replace `margin: 0` with `marginHorizontal: 10`, as shown in the following screenshots:

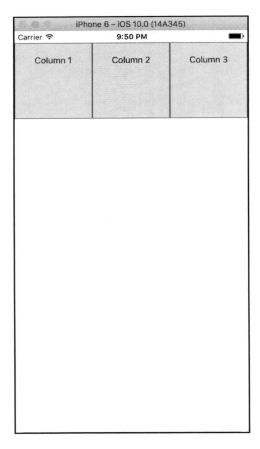

Without margin

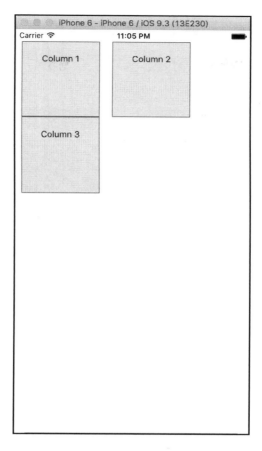

With margin

As you can see, the single row has now broken into two due to the added margin.

 React Native only allows you to set a single numeric value for `margin`, `padding`, and `borderWidth`. Therefore, it is not possible to set varying vertical and horizontal values with a single assignment like you can with CSS. You can, of course, leverage properties such as `marginTop`, `paddingLeft`, or `borderRightWidth` to set an individual dimension. React Native also exposes vertical and horizontal shorthands for padding and margin: `paddingHorizontal`, `paddingVertical`, `marginHorizontal`, and `marginVertical`. No such horizontal or vertical shorthand exists at the moment for `borderWidth`.

Understanding Flexbox

All components in React Native are flex containers and are positioned relatively. In CSS, you would express the default stylesheet, as shown in the following code snippet:

```
* {
  display: flex;
  position: relative;
}
```

In React Native, there are no alternative `display` values. In fact, `display` isn't even a valid style property. And, because everything is set as a relative position container, you can assume that any element positioned as `absolute` will always be relative to its immediate parent.

Flexbox can be thought of as relationship between the container and its immediate children. The container can align items either horizontally or vertically. In CSS, the default `flex-direction` is set to `'row'`. You can change that value to `'column'` and `flex` items will be stacked vertically. In React Native, you express this with the style property `flexDirection`. However, unlike the Web, the default direction is set to `'column'` and can be changed to `'row'`. The `flex` container will then expand or contract the size of its children to fit within it.

There are two properties that influence the alignment of `flex` items within the container across the *x* and *y* axis. In the flexbox world, we refer to these as the *main axis* and *cross axis*. The main axis is set by the `flexDirection`. That said, when the `flexDirection` is set to `'column'` (or not set at all as this is the default value), the main axis corresponds to the *y* axis. When `flexDirection` is set to `'row'`, the main axis is now the *x* axis. You align items along the main axis through the `justifyContent` property. Whichever axis is *not* the main axis is referred to as the cross axis. Items along the cross axis are aligned through `alignItems`.

This graphic from the W3C's website helps illustrate these concepts visually for a flex `'row'` container:

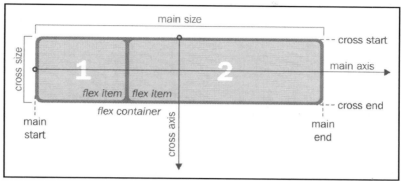

Source: `https://drafts.csswg.org/css-flexbox-1/#main-size-property`.

Flexbox can be difficult to understand without some visual examples. Let's explore some basic flexbox layouts to see how all these pieces fit together:

```
const FlexBoxLayout = () => (
  <View style={styles.container}>
    <View style={styles.item} />
    <View style={styles.item} />
    <View style={styles.item} />
  </View>
);

const styles = StyleSheet.create({
  container: {
    flex: 1,
    flexDirection: 'column',
    justifyContent: 'flex-start',
    alignItems: 'flex-start'
  },
  item: {
    backgroundColor: 'lightgoldenrodyellow',
    borderWidth: 1,
    borderColor: 'goldenrod',
    height: 150,
    width: 150
  }
});
```

The preceding example represents a very basic `flex` layout. Each item represents a `flex` item and the container is our flex container. I have explicitly set the `flexDirection`, `justifyContent`, and `alignItems` to their default values for illustrative purposes. I've also explicitly set a `width` and `height` for each `flex` item otherwise they would not be visible on screen since they contain no inner content. Take a look at the following screenshot:

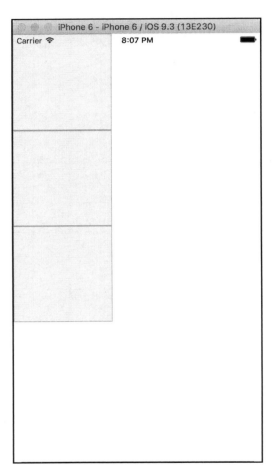

We can start by modifying the justifyContent property to some of its alternative values. Setting the value to 'flex-end' will move the items to the end of the main axis (*y* axis). And as you'd expect, setting it to 'center' will place the items right in the middle, as shown in the following screenshots:

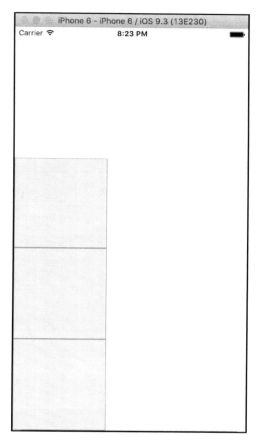

justifyContent: 'flex-end'

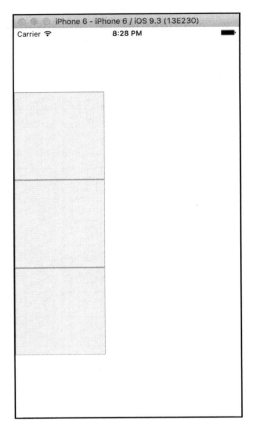

justifyContent: 'center'

The remaining two values, `'space-between'` and `'space-around'`, require a bit more explanation. First, let's examine the following two layouts in action:

justifyContent: 'space-between'

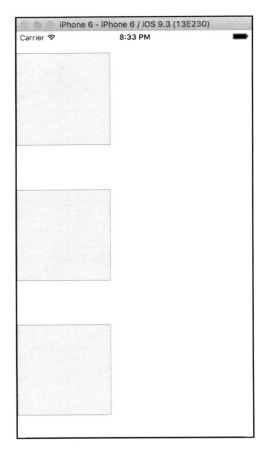

justifyContent: 'space-around'

'space-between' will take the first and last items inside the container and effectively *stick* them to either end. Any space left over will be evenly distributed between each of the flex items. 'space-around' calculates the available unused space (in our example that's the vertical white space). It then even distributes the white space between items. Additionally, it takes half the white space available and uses it to pad the first and last items from the start and end. Looking at our 'space-around' in the preceding screenshot, this means that the vertical white space that separates the top and bottom of the device from its nearest flex item is exactly half the space separating each flex item.

Covering the other axis

To this point, we've only addressed how to align the position of our `flex` items across the main axis. Again, because we set `flexDirection: 'column'`, our main axis is the *y* axis. Keeping that in mind, let's explore what options we have available to control items along the cross axis.

Much like with main axis, the cross axis can be controlled by setting `alignItems` to `'flex-start'`, `'center'`, `'flex-end'`, or `'stretch'` on the container. Alternatively, the individual `flex` items can override their cross axis position by setting the `alignSelf` property. To demonstrate, we'll set each of the three flex items to different `alignSelf` values, as shown in the following code snippet:

```
const FlexBoxLayout = () => (
  <View style={styles.container}>
    <View style={[styles.item, { alignSelf: 'flex-start' }]} />
    <View style={[styles.item, { alignSelf: 'center' }]} />
    <View style={[styles.item, { alignSelf: 'flex-end' }]} />
  </View>
);
```

In the case of `flexDirection: 'column'`, if you omit the width property, or in the case of `flexDirection: 'row'`, if you omit the `height` property, you can make your flex item span the entire cross axis by setting the value to `'stretch'`. Take a look at the following code snippet:

```
const FlexBoxLayout = () => (
  <View style={styles.container}>
    <View style={[styles.item, { alignSelf: 'flex-start' }]} />
    <View style={[styles.item, { alignSelf: 'stretch', width: undefined }]}
/>
    <View style={[styles.item, { alignSelf: 'flex-end' }]} />
  </View>
);
```

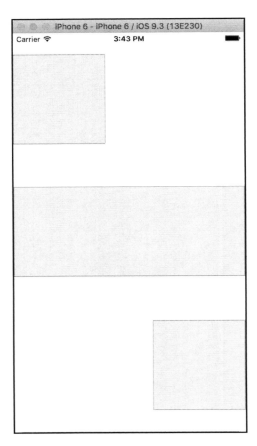

Flex shrinking and growing

Sizing elements with purely flexbox properties can be a bit confusing. I've seen many developers fall into the trap of thinking `flexGrow` is the same as setting a percentage width. Take a look at the following code:

```
[flex grow: .25] + [flex grow: .75] != [width: 25%] + [width: 75%]
```

This is simply untrue. Additionally, I've also seen developers blindly throw `flex: 1` on just about everything in the hope that it fixes whatever layout problem they are encountering. As you've probably already concluded, flexbox isn't the most straightforward topic, and sadly there are three other important `flexbox` properties we haven't even touched on—`flexGrow`, `flexShrink`, and `flexBasis`. (Technically, there's even a fourth called `flex`, but that's really just a shorthand property.)

Setting flexBasis

This property is simultaneously the most confusing and the simplest. `flexBasis` works just like `width` and `height`. The key point is that it will set the size of the element that corresponds with the main axis (`flexDirection`). If it's set to `'column'`, then `flexBasis` sizes the `height`. If it's set to `'row'`, then it sets the `width`. But that's pretty much it. In the CSS world, there are a few other considerations, but thankfully they aren't applicable in the React Native world.

Growing and shrinking flex items

Let me paint a scenario. Imagine you have a column with three items in it. The column is 667 points tall. The three items within the column are each 50 points tall. This means that there are 517 points of remaining space available with me so far?

So here's how `flexGrow` works. I'm going to leave one of the items alone so that it remains 50 points tall. The next one I'll set to `flexGrow: 1` and the other to `flexGrow: 2`. The way this calculation works is as follows: of the available free space (517 points), I will give twice the amount of free space to the `flexGrow: 2` item as the `flexGrow: 1` item. The equation looks something like the following:

*total size = initial size + (remaining space * (flex grow factor/total number of flex grow factors))*

In the case of the `flexGrow: 2`, the numerator is 2 and the denominator is 3 (2 + 1). So plugging in our values, we end up with the following:

*total height = 50 + (517 * (2/3))*

This comes out to roughly 394.66. This then means that our item with `flexGrow: 1` would come out to roughly 222.33. Take a look at the following screenshot:

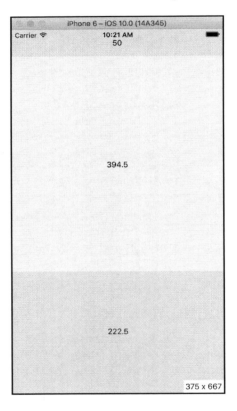

`flexShrink` works similarly to `flexGrow`. Again, it manages items along the main axis but it instead handles how to size items when there is too little room. You can think of it as this– *how much space should I remove relative to my flex item siblings?* `flexShrink: 2` will take away twice as much size from a sibling with a `flexShrink: 1`. An item set to `flexShrink: 0` will simply never shrink.

 As mentioned earlier, `flex` is simply a shorthand for setting `flexGrow`, `flexShrink`, and `flexBasis`. If flex is set to a positive number, it sets `flexGrow` to that same value and sets `flexShrink` and `flexBasis` to 0. If flex is a negative value, it sets `flexShrink` to the inverse of that value and `flexGrow` to 0, and leaves `flexBasis` unset.

Before we totally switch topics, I want to call out the most commonly used `flexbox` setting, `flex: 1`. Let's go back to the earlier example where we had three items each set to 50 points tall. If we only defined a `flexGrow` (or `flex`) value for one of those three items, then that one item will take up all the available space. That's why it's rather common to see `flexGrow: 1` or `flex: 1` set on an item that you want to consume a large portion of the screen. We'll be using `flexbox` a lot throughout this book, so it's important to have a baseline understanding. If you still find yourself a bit perplexed, check out the online game **Flexbox Froggy**. It's a fun interactive game that teaches you how to use flexbox; for more information, refer to `http://flexboxfroggy.com/`.

Styling text with React Native

While most of the rules around React Native styling are equally applicable to text, there is one notable exception: nested `Text` elements actually inherit type styles from one another. As an example, imagine in the HTML/CSS world you have a `span` element that contains several words, one of which you'd like to appear bold. You could simply wrap that single word with a `strong` element and achieve your goal. The inner `strong` element would inherit the typographic styles of the parent span but make its own text bold. This same concept applies in React Native. Take a look at the following code snippet:

```
const BasicType = () => (
  <Text style={styles.headline}>
    Welcome to <Text style={styles.bold}>React</Text> Native {'\n'}
    <Text style={styles.subheader}>This is <Text style={styles.bold}>so
cool!</Text></Text>
  </Text>
);

const styles = StyleSheet.create({
```

```
  headline: {
    fontFamily: 'Georgia',
    fontSize: 20
  },
  subheader: {
    color: 'blue'
  },
  bold: {
    fontWeight: 'bold'
  }
});
```

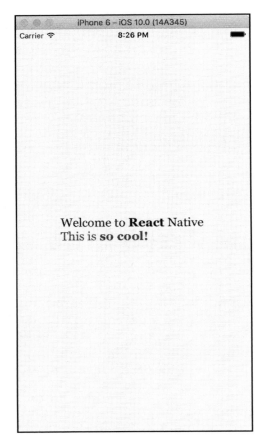

In this example, we've set some baseline styles that apply a `fontFamily` and `fontSize` to an outer `Text` element. Within that, we have several nested `Text` elements that inherit those styles but also possess their own additional styles. On iOS, React Native is actually flattening all of these nested `Text` elements into a single `NSAttributedString`. This yields a single rendered *box* rather than multiple nested boxes. This also means you'll only be able to apply box styles such as padding and margin to the outer `Text` element. Child `Text` elements will ignore these properties.

 For performance reasons, the React Native team has applied an unusual behavior to the `Text` component. In HTML, elements default to a transparent background. As a result, nested HTML elements challenge the compositing engine as each nested element may require blending with other child elements. This can create performance issues with complex or deeply nested trees, particularly on phones that typically do not possess the same performance characteristics of a modern laptop or desktop computer. For this reason, rather than defaulting to a transparent background, `Text` components inherit the background color of their container. Typically, this produces the exact same effect as having a transparent background but without the performance hit. However, there may be times where you'll need to explicitly set the `backgroundColor` of a Text element to be 'transparent'. Source: https://github.com/facebook/react-native/releases/tag/v0.6.0-rc.

Text style properties

React Native only allows you to set certain style properties on particular components. As an example, you cannot set `fontSize` on a `View` component, only a `Text` component. `Text` components also support many CSS-like text and font properties including `color`, `fontSize`, `fontFamily`, `fontStyle`, `fontWeight`, `lineHeight`, and `textAlign`. Rather than review every one of these, let's demonstrate how they behave with some simple examples.

Here we have several nested `Text` elements with different styles applied. Take a look at the following code:

```
const AdvancedType = () => (
  <View>
    <Text style={styles.text}>
      Fun styling <Text style={styles.bold}>text</Text> inside of <Text
style={styles.italic}>React Native.</Text>
    </Text>
```

```
        <Text style={[styles.text, styles.moreLineHeight, styles.right]}>
          I am right aligned and have more <Text
style={styles.code}>lineHeight</Text> than the text above.
        </Text>
        <Text style={[styles.text, styles.center, styles.thin]}>
          I am centered and very thin!
        </Text>
      </View>
  );

const styles = StyleSheet.create({
  text: {
    fontSize: 22,
    marginBottom: 20
  },
  bold: {
    fontWeight: 'bold'
  },
  thin: {
    fontWeight: '200'
  },
  italic: {
    fontStyle: 'italic'
  },
  moreLineHeight: {
    lineHeight: 40
  },
  right: {
    textAlign: 'right'
  },
  center: {
    textAlign: 'center'
  },
  code: {
    fontFamily: 'Courier'
  }
});
```

Encapsulating text styles in reusable components

The past few code samples haverequired that we repeat several style definitions. Similar to what we did with our `Button` component earlier, we can encapsulate common text styles in custom, reusable components. As an example, let's create three components—one for our headline copy, one for normal copy, and one for bold copy. When we're done, we'll have something like the following:

```
<View>
  <Headline>This is a header</Headline>
  <BodyCopy>This is my regular or <Bold>bold</Bold> text.</BodyCopy>
</View>
```

To get there, we need to create three custom components: `Headline`, `BodyCopy`, and `Bold`. Each of these follow the same pattern–a functional component that pairs with a `StyleSheet`. A rudimentary implementation may look like the following:

```
const Bold = ({ children }) => <Text
style={boldTextStyles.text}>{children}</Text>;

Bold.propTypes = {
  children: React.PropTypes.node.isRequired
};
const boldTextStyles = StyleSheet.create({
  text: {
    fontWeight: '600'
  }
});

const BodyCopy = ({ children }) => <Text
style={bodyCopyStyles.text}>{children}</Text>;

BodyCopy.propTypes = {
  children: React.PropTypes.node.isRequired
};
const bodyCopyStyles = StyleSheet.create({
  text: {
    fontFamily: 'Helvetica',
    fontSize: 18,
    color: '#333'
  }
});

const Headline = ({ children }) => <Bold><Text
style={headlineStyles.text}>{children}</Text></Bold>;

Headline.propTypes = {
  children: React.PropTypes.node.isRequired
};
const headlineStyles = StyleSheet.create({
  text: {
    fontFamily: 'Optima',
    fontSize: 30,
    color: '#333'
  }
});
```

Here, our `Bold`, `BodyCopy`, and `Headline` are really just styled versions of a `Text` component. However, this basic implementation lacks the ability to pass additional styles or other props aside from children. We can remedy this just like we did with `Button`. We'll extract style and children and then use the ES2015 rest operator to extract any remaining props. Here is how this looks when applied to our `Bold` component:

```
const Bold = ({ children, style, ...otherProps }) => <Text
style={[boldTextStyles.text, style]} {...otherProps}>{children}</Text>;

Bold.propTypes = {
  children: React.PropTypes.node.isRequired,
  style: Text.propTypes.style
};
```

Again, note how we *spread* `otherProps` across the `Text` element. This way, the consumer of our `Bold` component can still control other `Text` properties such as `onPress` or `numberOfLines`, as shown in the following code:

```
const Demo = () => (
  <View>
    <Bold
      onPress={() => console.log('Pressed!')}
      numberOfLines={2}
      style={styles.green}
    >Lorem ipsum dolor sit amet, consectetur adipiscing elit. Donec magna
ipsum, lobortis quis rhoncus ac, suscipit sed dolor.
    </Bold>
  </View>
);

const styles = StyleSheet.create({
  green: {
    color: 'green'
  }
});
```

Styling images

Images in React Native are somewhat unusual. The `Image` component has qualities of both the inline HTML `img` element and background properties of CSS. We'll explore these behaviors in this section to better your understanding of how to use images as both content and as design accents within your applications.

Within your React Native project, you can reference either a local image resource or a remote one. To reference an image contained within your project, use the following syntax:

```
<Image source={require('./images/pizza.jpg')} />
```

If you wish to reference an image located remotely on a server, you'll follow a similar but slightly different pattern:

```
<Image
    source={{ uri:
'https://pixabay.com/static/uploads/photo/2014/11/08/17/05/pizza-522485_960
_720.jpg' }}
    style={{ width: 150, height: 300 }}
  />
```

There are two key differences when referencing a local image versus a remote one. For starters, a local image is loaded through require. However, with a remote image, you must pass the source property an object with an `uri` pointing to the remote resource. Additionally, remote images require you specify both `width` and `height`. If you don't, the image will render as 0 × 0 points. In contrast, an HTML `img` element with no `width` or `height` specified will initially render as 0 × 0 pixels. Once the image has been downloaded, the element will automatically resize to the same dimensions as the source image. While this is convenient, it will cause your UI to jump around as it pushes content to accommodate space for the image. The Facebook team has intentionally not implemented this as they feel it leads to an overall improved user experience.

As stated earlier, the `Image` component shares some traits of CSS backgrounds. For starters, you can set the `resizeMode` to `'stretch'`, `'contain'`, `'cover'`, `'repeat'`, or `'center'`. Given the same source image, this is how each of these properties affects the output:

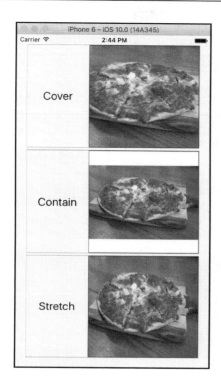 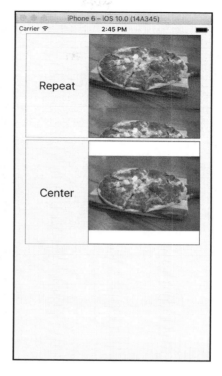

Background images

Unlike an HTML `img`, the React Native `Image` component allows for nested content. When used in this way, `Image` acts as a background to its child elements. Using our pizza photograph in this way, we can make something that feels like a mobile restaurant menu for a pizza shop. Here is an excerpt of what this code could look like:

```
<Image source={pizzaImage} style={styles.image}>
  <View style={styles.content}>
    {/* content goes here */}
  </View>
</Image>
```

Inspecting and debugging styles

Up to this point, we have reviewed much of what React Native offers to style and layout your applications. One thing we've glossed over is how to debug your style rules in React Native. In the Web world, we often refer to this as **inspecting styles** (a reference to Chrome's DevTools that allow you to inspect any CSS properties applied to an element). Unfortunately, this is one area where React Native currently falls a bit short. You cannot use Chrome's inspector to edit or view each element's style properties. However, React Native does offer a built-in inspector. It's very basic when compared to Chrome's inspector, but for the moment it's one of the few tools available to developers.

Using the React Native Inspector

To give the React Native Inspector a run through, we'll need something to inspect. Fire up any React Native app in the iOS Simulator and then press Command + D on your keyboard just like you would to launch **Debug JS Remotely**, except this time click on **Show Inspector**. You'll see a gray overlay across the bottom of the screen with the message **Tap something to inspect it**. If you begin clicking around different parts of the app, you should see three pieces of content update. Across the top, you'll see hierarchy of components listed as a breadcrumb navigation. You can click on each item in the breadcrumb to inspect the styles. In the following screenshot, you'll see any style properties set on the element such as `padding`, `border`, and `flex` properties, and so forth. Additionally, you'll see what amounts to our box model outlining the `width`, `height`, `padding`, and `margin` values. While this is a read-only view, it can be helpful when trying to understand what styles are or are not being applied to an element:

In Chapter 12, *React Native Tools and Resources*, we'll review a few software packages that are designed for React Native development. Nuclide is a custom package built for the Atom editor that includes a tool called **Nuclide React Native Inspector**. While it too is read-only, it does provide a much richer, more Chrome DevTools-like experience for debugging React Native element styles.

Adding media query behavior to React Native

In the current web world, we are accustomed to building sites that adjust their presentation to best fit the screen space available. Most often, that's done by detecting the width or height of the viewport and adjusting CSS rules accordingly. Doing this type of screen detection has actually been possible for a long time through JavaScript. But the grand idea of **responsive design** didn't become popular until browsers added support for media queries through @media in CSS. Currently, React Native styles don't have an equivalent of @media. However, there are a few useful hooks built into React Native for determining the width and height of the device or individual components that can help us achieve similar, if not cooler results.

Using Dimensions

React Native has its own version of window.innerHeight and window.innerWidth that provides static values for width, height, and scale. These properties are made available through the Dimensions object inside in the React Native library, as shown in the following code snippet:

```
import {
  Dimensions
} from 'react-native';

const getDimensions = () => {
  const { width, height, scale } = Dimensions.get('window');
  console.log(`width: ${width}, height: ${height}, scale: ${scale}`);
};
```

In the preceding example, we've imported Dimensions from React Native and created a function that can be called within our application. Calling Dimensions.get('window') returns an object with three properties–width, height, and scale. If you were to call this method from an iPhone 6 simulator, you'd see the following outputted to the console:

```
width: 375, height: 667, scale: 2
```

When running this same code with the iPhone 4s simulator, you'll see the following:

```
width: 320, height: 480, scale: 2
```

Knowing this, you can imagine a scenario where having these dimensions could inform how you layout your views or size various components within your app. Unfortunately, Dimensions does not update after the app is launched. That is to say, if you change the orientation of your device from portrait to landscape and then query Dimensions.get('window') again, you will see the exact same width and height values as before. Therefore, Dimensions should not be used to detect orientation changes within your app.

Using onLayout per View

If you're interested in detecting whenever the device has rotated from portrait to landscape (or vice versa), there is another useful tool at your disposal. The View component implements an onLayout event handler that is called whenever layout is calculated, either on mount or on change. You can leverage this for detecting device rotation and then make any modifications you'd like to your application's presentation.

The onLayout handler is passed an event object that holds lots of information. However, for the purposes of achieving a responsive design, we'll only inspect the event.nativeEvent.layout object. It contains four pieces of data–x, y, width, and height. Keep in mind that these properties don't necessarily represent the state of your entire viewport but just a single component within it. For example, you might have a View stuffed at the bottom of your app acting as a footer. These four properties will reflect the values of that particular View when its onLayout handler is executed. This may still be useful in particular contexts. However, what we're probably more interested in is the width and height of the entire viewport. So let's see how we can achieve this with a very simple demo application:

```
class DemoOnLayout extends Component {
  constructor(props) {
    super(props);
```

```
    this.state = {
      width: 0,
      height: 0
    };

    this.onLayoutChange = this.onLayoutChange.bind(this);
  }

  onLayoutChange(event) {
    const { width, height } = event.nativeEvent.layout;
    this.setState({ width, height });
  }

  render() {
    return (
      <View onLayout={this.onLayoutChange} style={styles.container}>
        <Text style={styles.text}>Width: {this.state.width}, Height:
{this.state.height}</Text>
      </View>
    );
  }
}

const styles = StyleSheet.create({
  container: {
    flex: 1,
    alignItems: 'center',
    justifyContent: 'center'
  },
  text: {
    fontSize: 18
  }
});
```

Here we have a very simple app that only does one thing–display the width and height of the View element. You'll note that because we're using state, we need to call constructor and thus we need to define this component using component class syntax. But more to the point, we've attached an onLayout handler to a method within our class called onLayoutChange. Additionally, we've ensured that the View element with the onLayout handler fills the entirety of the device by setting the style property flex: 1. By doing so, we can approximate the same effect as @media for a viewport.

When DemoOnLayout first mounts, it triggers the onLayout handler and thus executes onLayoutChange. Within onLayoutChange, we destructure the width and height properties from event.nativeEvent.layout. Then, using ES2015 shorthand, we update this.state with those values. This, in turn, triggers the render method to re-execute, and the values displayed on screen are updated. Then, whenever you rotate the device, `onLayout` will again call `onLayoutChange` and thus update the view all over again. Take a look at the following screenshot:

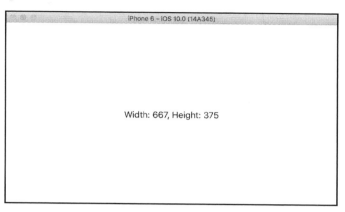

 Within the iOS Simulator, you can make it change orientation by going to **Hardware** | **Rotate Left** or **Hardware** | **Rotate Right**. Alternatively, you can use the keyboard commands *Command* + Left Arrow Key or *Command* + Right Arrow Key.

Summary

Styling is a big topic, and we've covered a lot of ground. We introduced how styling works in React Native and how in many ways it's similar to CSS. We also discussed where React Native and CSS differ, particularly with their approach to inheritance. To address this, we demonstrated how to create reusable components that encapsulate styles. Then we discussed all the different ways you can apply style properties, be it for Text or non-Text components. Because flexbox is critical to layout in React Native, we did a deep dive on the many facets of flexbox. And while debugging React Native styles is not as great a developer experience as debugging business logic, we reviewed how you can diagnose some of those pesky layout questions you're bound to encounter.

Although we did not touch on every single style or layout property found in React Native, we've covered more than enough to put you on a solid footing. With this much deeper understanding of layout and style, we'll next explore many of React Native's out-of-the-box components for building rich mobile applications.

4
Starting our Project with React Native Components

In much the same way in which React for the Web comes with a multitude of JSX elements that represent native HTML elements (`div` and `span`), React Native comes with many components representing native iOS and Android components built in. These components are the building blocks of React Native applications and give you access to real, native interfaces that look and feel appropriate to the platform on which they are running.

In addition to these React Native components, the React Native library gives access to many native APIs, which allow us to perform other native tasks that don't comfortably fit into a component. It is important to note that React Native does not expose every native interface component and API. On occasion, we will have to create our own native modules. We'll learn more about writing and using custom native modules in Chapter 10, *Using and Writing Native Modules*.

In this chapter, we'll cover the following topics:

- Begin to build an application, a New York Times news reading application creatively named **RNNYT (React Native – New York Times)**
- Integrate some of the most popular and interesting native components from React Native
- Enrich the app using some native APIs provided by React Native

The list of React Native components, their respective props, and the native APIs is extensive. We will not go over every single one, but we will go through enough to give a clear idea of what topics are available and how to interact with native components. If you wish to learn more about a component that is not covered, take a look at the React Native documentation.

Native components

Most React Native components are cross-platform; they work on both iOS and Android operating systems. However, there are a few components that are restricted to one platform or the other. The convention is to suffix platform-specific component names with the name of the platform. For example, TabBarIOS is an iOS-only navigational component. The dominant reason that this component and other platform-specific components are limited to one platform has to do with the accepted user interface conventions on that platform. In this case, a tabbed navigational interface is very common on iOS applications, but is not considered a best practice on Android.

Before we dive in, let's set up our new project. We'll follow the same procedure outlined in Chapter 2, *Saying Hello World in React Native*. In the terminal, we will run the following command:

```
react-native init RNNYT
```

Since our application is becoming more complex than the one discussed in Chapter 2, *Saying Hello World in React Native*, we'll add some directories to our project to store all of our new components. First, we'll create an src folder in the root of our project for all of our JavaScript files. Within that folder, we will create a components folder for storing components we'll create throughout this chapter. We'll also create a styles folder where we'll store global styles, as shown in the following screenshot:

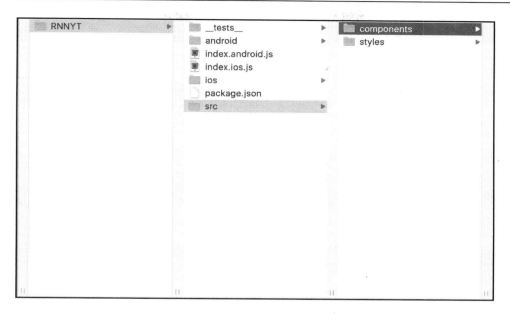

Text

In a React Native application, text content cannot be placed just anywhere within JSX like in React web applications. Instead, text content must reside within a Text component. This was a deliberate choice made by the creators of React Native to make styling text more efficient and predictable.

Since we are creating a news application, we can revisit some of the custom components we made for the Web in Chapter 1, *Building a Foundation in React*, and ensure that they are React Native-compatible. But first, in order to make the text throughout our RNNYT application uniform, we'll create a component called AppText in a new file called src/components/AppText.js, as shown in the following code snippet:

```
import React, { PropTypes } from 'react';
import { Text } from 'react-native';
import * as globalStyles from '../styles/global';

const AppText = ({ children, style, ...rest }) => (
  <Text style={[globalStyles.COMMON_STYLES.text, style]} {...rest}>
    {children}
  </Text>
);

AppText.propTypes = {
```

```
    style: Text.propTypes.style,
    children: PropTypes.node
};
```

```
export default AppText;
```

First, we import `React` and `PropTypes` from the `react` module, just as we would in a React web application:

```
import React, { PropTypes } from 'react';
```

Unlike native web components, such as h1 or p, React Native components must be imported from the `react-native` library:

```
import { Text } from 'react-native';
```

Next, we'll create a file for global styles that can be imported throughout the application, `src/styles/global.js`:

```
import { StyleSheet } from 'react-native';

export const BG_COLOR = '#343336';
export const BAR_COLOR = '#4e4d52';
export const TEXT_COLOR = '#e5dbda';
export const HEADER_TEXT_COLOR = '#fff';
export const MUTED_COLOR = '#8e8786';
export const LINK_COLOR = '#48e9d9';
export const ACCENT_COLORS = ['#d31d65', '#751c53', '#c248c0', '#7d6e8b',
'#bbc6f7'];

export const COMMON_STYLES = StyleSheet.create({
  text: {
    color: TEXT_COLOR,
    fontFamily: 'Helvetica Neue'
  }
});
```

We'll then import these styles in the `AppText` component's file:

```
import * as globalStyles from '../styles/global';
```

The `AppText` component itself is a simple functional component that just wraps `children` in a React Native `Text` component:

```
const AppText = ({ children, style, ...rest }) => (
  <Text style={[globalStyles.COMMON_STYLES.text, style]} {...rest}>
    {children}
  </Text>
);
```

To complete the component, we'll add prop type validation and export the component:

```
AppText.propTypes = {
  style: Text.propTypes.style,
  children: PropTypes.node
};

export default AppText;
```

Now that we have this `AppText` component, we can replace h1 in the `Title` component from `Chapter 1`, *Building a Foundation in React,* and add some additional styles. We'll do this in a new file, `src/components/Title.js`, as shown in the following code snippet:

```
import React, { PropTypes } from 'react';
import {
  StyleSheet,
  Text
} from 'react-native';
import AppText from './AppText';
import * as globalStyles from '../styles/global';

const Title = ({ style, children }) => (
  <AppText style={[styles.title, style]}>
    {children}
  </AppText>
);

Title.propTypes = {
  style: Text.propTypes.style,
  children: PropTypes.node
};

const styles = StyleSheet.create({
  title: {
    fontFamily: 'HelveticaNeue-CondensedBold',
    fontSize: 18,
    color: globalStyles.HEADER_TEXT_COLOR,
    backgroundColor: `${globalStyles.BG_COLOR}99`
  }
```

```
});

export default Title;
```

We can use this same pattern of composition to create an additional SmallText component that can be used to display deemphasized text. You'll notice that the contents of src/components/SmallText.js are much the same as Title.js, just with different styles:

```
import React, { PropTypes } from 'react';
import {
  StyleSheet,
  Text
} from 'react-native';
import AppText from './AppText';

const SmallText = ({ children, style, ...rest }) => (
  <AppText style={[styles.small, style]} {...rest}>
    {children}
  </AppText>
);

SmallText.propTypes = {
  children: PropTypes.node,
  style: Text.propTypes.style
};

const styles = StyleSheet.create({
  small: {
    fontSize: 11
  }
});

export default SmallText;
```

Props

As we see in the AppText component we created in the preceding code snippet, the Text component accepts a style prop. Given that the Text component is the only component that can have text content, it is also the only component whose style object can contain text-related styles, such as fontSize or color, as mentioned in the last chapter. Take a look at the following code snippet:

```
<Text
  style={{
    fontSize: 12,
```

```
    color: 'red'
  }}
>
  Hello World!
</Text>
```

The `Text` component also has a prop `numberOfLines` (number) that allows you to specify the number of lines to display before the text is truncated with an ellipsis:

```
<Text
  numberOfLines={4}
>
  This text will be truncated if it is greater than 4 lines long.
</Text>
```

On iOS, a `Text` component will by default use the user's preferences to scale font sizes. This is generally a desirable feature, but it can be disabled by setting the `allowFontScaling` (Boolean) prop to `false`:

```
<Text
  allowFontScaling={false}
>
  This font will not be scaled by user's preferences.
</Text>
```

Finally, if we wish to make some text within our application act as a link that can be touched or pressed, and respond in some way, we can take advantage of a prop called `onPress` (function). This prop is React Native's way of exposing and abstracting a simple interaction from the more complex gesture recognition system. The function passed to this prop is called when the user presses on the enclosed text. It could be used, for instance, to navigate to another part of the application. Take a look at the following code snippet:

```
<Text
  onPress={navigateToSettings}
>
  Settings
</Text>
```

View

The `View` component is perhaps the most basic and fundamental component provided by React Native. The best analogy in React for the Web is a `div` element. It is a generic container that is primarily only used for grouping or laying out children. In other words, it has no real semantic or functional purpose other than styling and grouping. All components (including the `View` component itself) can be nested within a `View` for creating complex layouts.

It is also fundamental in that many of the properties and styles that `View` supports are also supported by other components. In this section, we'll cover many of those properties, but for other components, we'll only note how the accepted properties differ from those of `View`.

Let's create a `Byline` component, in `src/components/Byline.js`, groups some of our new text wrapper components into visual rows:

```
import React, { PropTypes } from 'react';
import {
  StyleSheet,
  View
} from 'react-native';
import SmallText from './SmallText';
import * as globalStyles from '../styles/global';

const Byline = ({ date, author, location }) => (
  <View>
    <View style={styles.row}>
      <SmallText>
        {date.toLocaleDateString()}
      </SmallText>
      <SmallText>
        {author}
      </SmallText>
    </View>

    {location ? (
      <View style={styles.row}>
        <SmallText style={styles.location}>
          {location}
        </SmallText>
      </View>
    ) : null}
  </View>
);
```

```
Byline.propTypes = {
  date: PropTypes.instanceOf(Date).isRequired,
  author: PropTypes.string.isRequired,
  location: PropTypes.string
};

const styles = StyleSheet.create({
  row: {
    flexDirection: 'row',
    justifyContent: 'space-between',
    marginBottom: 5
  },
  location: {
    color: globalStyles.MUTED_COLOR
  }
});

export default Byline;
```

Here we are adding the `View` component to the `react-native` import:

```
import {
  StyleSheet,
  View
} from 'react-native';
```

We then use that component to group and lay out a visual row of `SmallText` components showing a news article's author and date of publication:

```
<View style={styles.row}>
  <SmallText>
    {date.toLocaleDateString()}
  </SmallText>
  <SmallText>
    {author}
  </SmallText>
</View>
```

We create an optional second row to display the article's location using a ternary expression:

```
{location ? (
  <View style={styles.row}>
    <SmallText style={styles.location}>
      {location}
    </SmallText>
  </View>
) : null}
```

Finally, we use a third `View` component to group together these two rows:

```
<View>
  <View style={styles.row}>
    <SmallText>
      {date.toLocaleDateString()}
    </SmallText>
    <SmallText>
      {author}
    </SmallText>
  </View>

  {location ? (
    <View style={styles.row}>
      <SmallText style={styles.location}>
        {location}
      </SmallText>
    </View>
  ) : null}
</View>
```

Props

As we saw in Chapter 3, *Styling and Layout in React Native*, the `View` component accepts a style prop that is either a single `style` object, a `StyleSheet` reference, or an array of `style` objects, where the latter objects are merged into the former. Take a look at the following code snippet:

```
<View
  style={[styles.base, { backgroundColor: 'green' }]}
>
```

There are a set of properties that describe whether and how to make a given component accessible to various accessibility devices such as screen readers. First, there is an accessible prop that accepts a Boolean. This prop indicates whether or not the `View` should be considered accessible. If it is set to `true`, several other properties are looked at. For instance, `accessibilityLabel` (string) indicates text that should be read by a screen reader when it reaches this `View`. If not specified, the screen reader will default to the text contained inside the `View`, as shown in the following code snippet:

```
<View
  accessible // Since this is a Boolean, it's presence is interpreted as
true
  accessibilityLabel="News item" // Screen reader text for this View
>
```

A `View` also has a set of properties that can be used to make performance improvements. Many of these are platform-specific. As an example, there is a `shouldRasterizeIOS` (Boolean) property that tells iOS whether or not it should turn the contents of the view into an image for faster animations under some circumstances. One optimization prop that is cross-platform is the `removeClippedSubviews` (Boolean) property that tells React whether or not it should remove (not render) any children that are not shown on screen. If there are many such components, enabling this property could speed up rendering time dramatically:

```
<View
    shouldRasterizeIOS // only recognized if running on iOS device
    removeClippedSubviews
>
```

Finally, there are a number of event listener props that allow us to respond to user interaction or other application events. Two in the former category are `onAccessibilityTap` (function) and `onMagicTap` (function), which are functions that respond to accessibility device *taps*, but only if the accessible prop has been set to `true`. In the latter group, the `onLayout` (function) property accepts a function that is invoked whenever the layout of the `View` changes, as shown in the following code snippet:

```
<View
    onAccessibilityTap={(evt) => console.log('Accessibility tapped!')}
    onMagicTap={(evt) => console.log('Magic tapped!')}
    onLayout={(evt) => console.log('The layout has changed!')}
>
```

In the web world, we might expect a property such as `onClick` to be among the list of accepted event listeners. Clearly, the notion of *clicking* is not present in a mobile application, but there are other reasons why an analogous event listener is not an accepted property of the `View` component.

In order to make applications look and feel native, the interface needs to both give the user feedback when they interact and give them the ability to cancel that interaction. To enable this, native environments have a rich and complex gesture architecture. We, as React Native developers, can tap into that gesture architecture if we need to respond to intricate or nonstandard gestures through a series of properties. The `onStartShouldSetResponder` (function) prop is called at the start of a touch gesture and is used to determine whether or not a `View` should become a responder to the gesture. If that function returns true, React Native will call props such as `onResponderMove` (function), which is called when a user's finger is moving across the `View`.

This gesture responder system is necessarily complex since users can interact with mobile devices in a multitude of ways. However, most interactions we care about are far simpler than the complex gestures this system enables. For this reason, React Native provides some abstractions for simple gestures in the form of touchable components that we will discuss later in this chapter. For a more in depth discussion of the gesture responder architecture, see Chapter 8, *Animation and Gestures in React Native*.

Image

Now that we've completed our `Title` and `Byline` components, our next challenge will be to create a `Thumbnail` component that displays an image for the news item. We will do this by using an `Image` component, which, as we saw in the previous chapter, is analogous to the HTML `img` tag. Since our `Thumbnail` component will be relatively simple and won't need lifecycle methods, we can once again use React's functional component syntax, as shown in the following code snippet:

```
import React, { PropTypes } from 'react';
import {
  StyleSheet,
  Image
} from 'react-native';

const Thumbnail = ({ url }) => {
  return (
    <Image
      style={[styles.image]}
      source={{
        uri: url
      }}
    />
  );
};

Thumbnail.propTypes = {
  url: PropTypes.string.isRequired
};

const styles = StyleSheet.create({
  image: {
    height: 100,
    justifyContent: 'flex-end'
  }
});
```

```
export default Thumbnail;
```

In our application, we want to layer the title of the article on top of the thumbnail image. To use images as backgrounds like this, we simply add the foreground components as children:

```
import React, { PropTypes } from 'react';
import {
  StyleSheet,
  Image
} from 'react-native';
import Title from './Title';

const Thumbnail = ({ url, titleText }) => {
  return (
    <Image
      style={[styles.image]}
      source={{
        uri: url
      }}
    >
      <Title style={styles.title}>{titleText}</Title>
    </Image>
  );
};

Thumbnail.propTypes = {
  url: PropTypes.string.isRequired,
  titleText: PropTypes.string
};

const styles = StyleSheet.create({
  image: {
    height: 100,
    justifyContent: 'flex-end'
  },
  title: {
    padding: 5
  }
});

export default Thumbnail;
```

We also want to add a colored border to the bottom of the thumbnail. In order to do this, we will need to wrap the component in a `View` and give the wrapper a border, as shown in the following code snippet:

```
import React, { PropTypes } from 'react';
import {
  StyleSheet,
  Image,
  View
} from 'react-native';
import Title from './Title';

const Thumbnail = ({ url, titleText, accentColor, style }) => {
  const imageStyle = {
    backgroundColor: `${accentColor}77` // adds some transparency to the
color
  };

  return (
    <View style={[styles.container, { borderColor: accentColor }, style]}>
      <Image
        style={[styles.image]}
        source={{
          uri: url
        }}
      >
        <Title style={styles.title}>{titleText}</Title>
      </Image>
    </View>
  );
};

Thumbnail.propTypes = {
  style: View.propTypes.style,
  url: PropTypes.string.isRequired,
  titleText: PropTypes.string,
  accentColor: PropTypes.string.isRequired
};

const styles = StyleSheet.create({
  container: {
    borderBottomWidth: 3,
    borderStyle: 'solid'
  },
  image: {
    height: 100,
    justifyContent: 'flex-end'
  },
```

```
  title: {
    padding: 5
  }
});
```

```
export default Thumbnail;
```

Finally, in some circumstances, an article might not have an image. In that case, we'll simply use a `View` that is the correct size. The following is the final component that we'll create in `src/components/Thumbnail.js`:

```jsx
import React, { PropTypes } from 'react';
import {
  StyleSheet,
  Image,
  View
} from 'react-native';
import Title from './Title';

const Thumbnail = ({ style, titleText, accentColor, url }) => {
  const imageStyle = {
    backgroundColor: `${accentColor}77` // adds some transparency to the
color
  };
  const TitleComponent = <Title style={styles.title}>{titleText}</Title>;

  return (
    <View style={[styles.container, { borderColor: accentColor }, style]}>
      {url.length > 0 ? (
        <Image
          style={[styles.image, imageStyle]}
          source={{
            uri: url
          }}
        >
          {TitleComponent}
        </Image>
      ) : (
        <View
          style={[styles.image, imageStyle]}
        >
          {TitleComponent}
        </View>
      )}
    </View>
  );
};
```

```
Thumbnail.propTypes = {
  style: View.propTypes.style,
  url: PropTypes.string.isRequired,
  accentColor: PropTypes.string.isRequired,
  titleText: PropTypes.string
};

const styles = StyleSheet.create({
  container: {
    borderBottomWidth: 3,
    borderStyle: 'solid'
  },
  image: {
    height: 100,
    justifyContent: 'flex-end'
  },
  title: {
    padding: 5
  }
});

export default Thumbnail;
```

Props

In the previous chapter, we learned about the source (object) prop and how it is used to choose what image is displayed within the Image component. We also looked at how the Image component allows for some additional style types in its style (object) prop. While these are enough to get us started, there are a number of other properties accepted by the Image component that we can use to further customize it.

On iOS, you can define a prop defaultSource (object) that takes the same form as the regular source property, but is used as a placeholder image until the main image has loaded, as shown in the following code snippet:

```
<Image
  defaultSource={require('defaultImage.png')}
/>
```

iOS also gives you the ability to easily apply a blur filter to the image by using the blurRadius (number) property:

```
<Image
  blurRadius={10}
/>
```

There are also a number of event listener properties that the `Image` component exposes. The `onLoad` (function) prop is called when the image is loaded successfully. On iOS, you can also specify an `onProgress` (function) that will be called as the image download progresses. This could be used to show a loading bar as the image is being downloaded:

```
<Image
  onLoad={this.hideProgressBar}
  onProgress={this.updateProgressBar}
/>
```

Static methods

In addition to properties, some React Native components provide static methods that can be used to perform tasks that are tangentially related to the contents of the component. `Image` is one such component.

There is a static method `prefetch` that allows you to preload a remote image (by its URL). This can provide a better user experience by allowing you as a developer to anticipate when an image is about to come into view and reducing the amount of time the user sees a blank or placeholder image:

```
import { Image } from 'react-native';

Image.prefetch('http://example.com/large-image.jpg');
```

In addition to `prefetch`, there is also a `getSize` static method that will allow us to get the dimensions of an image source before displaying it. Unlike `prefetch`, which is only for remote images, `getSize` can be used for both local and remote images.

Touchable

When developing React applications for the Web, we can attach `onClick` listeners to almost any native HTML element. In React Native, however, we typically limit the equivalent **press** events to a series of components that we call `touchable` components. These components are designed to simplify how we as developers interact with the gesture system by solving two main issues that contribute to applications not feeling `native`. First, they provide the user with some sort of visual feedback when interacting with the application. Second, they provide the ability to cancel a gesture if the user scrolls away from the original press.

The base `touchable` component, `TouchableWithoutFeedback`, is actually one that is not used often for reasons that may seem obvious from the preceding paragraph. This component gives access to press events, but does not provide any visual feedback. A developer could justify using this component if he/her were implementing his/her own feedback system, but generally we will avoid using this component.

There is also a `TouchableNativeFeedback` component that provides a native feedback experience on Android only. The `TouchableHighlight` component gives feedback on both platforms by altering the `View` hierarchy. This can work in some cases, but in others can cause unexpected layout changes. Finally, the component we'll use most often for capturing and responding to press events is the `TouchableOpacity` component. This component provides visual feedback by simply modifying the opacity of all of its children when it is pressed.

To make use of this component, you simply need to wrap components that should be pressable. For our application, let's say we want to respond in some way whenever each `NewsItem` component is pressed. Here is how we might add a touchable component to enable that behavior in `src/components/NewsItem.js`:

```
import React, { Component, PropTypes } from 'react';
import {
    View,
    TouchableOpacity,
    StyleSheet
} from 'react-native';
import Byline from './Byline';
import AppText from './AppText';
import Thumbnail from './Thumbnail';
import * as globalStyles from '../styles/global';

export default class NewsItem extends Component {

  render() {
    const {
      style,
      imageUrl,
      title,
      author,
      date,
      location,
      description,
    } = this.props;
    const accentColor = globalStyles.ACCENT_COLORS[
      this.props.index % globalStyles.ACCENT_COLORS.length
    ];
```

```
    return (
      <TouchableOpacity
        style={style}
      >
        <View>
          <Thumbnail
            url={imageUrl}
            titleText={title}
            accentColor={accentColor}
            style={styles.thumbnail}
          />
          <View style={styles.content}>
            <Byline
              author={author}
              date={date}
              location={location}
            />
            <AppText>
              {description}
            </AppText>
          </View>
        </View>
      </TouchableOpacity>
    );
  }
}

NewsItem.propTypes = {
  imageUrl: PropTypes.string,
  title: PropTypes.string.isRequired,
  description: PropTypes.string,
  date: PropTypes.instanceOf(Date).isRequired,
  author: PropTypes.string.isRequired,
  location: PropTypes.string,
  index: PropTypes.number.isRequired,
  onPress: PropTypes.func.isRequired,
  style: View.propTypes.style
};

const styles = StyleSheet.create({
  thumbnail: {
    marginBottom: 5
  },
  content: {
    paddingHorizontal: 5
  }
});
```

Once again, all we've done is add the `TouchableOpacity` component to our React Native `import` statement and then use it as the outermost element in the render method's `return` statement. This by itself will cause the component to respond to touch visually by changing the opacity of `NewsItem` when it is pressed, but we have not yet actually done anything in response to that event.

Props

The most important props for a `touchable` component are, as you might expect, event listener functions. The most basic and commonly used of these is the `onPress` (function) prop. Using this property, we can define what to do when the user presses our component. If, however, we want to get more specific about the timing of our response, `touchable` components also have an `onPressIn` (function) prop, which is called as the user begins the press, and an `onPressOut` (function) prop, which is called when the user is lifting his/her finger at the end of a press:

```
<TouchableOpacity
  onPressIn={() => console.log('Press started')}
  onPressOut={() => console.log('Press ending')}
  onPress={() => console.log('Press complete')}
>
```

In addition to regular presses, we can also listen for long presses and respond differently. Imagine we want to open a context menu of some sort when a user presses our `NewsItem` component and holds. In order to do that, we would need to define the `onLongPress` (function) prop, as shown in the following code snippet:

```
<TouchableOpacity
  onLongPress={this.openContextMenu}
>
```

We can also build in a delay between when the press occurs and when our listener function is called by using the `delayPressIn` (number), `delayPressOut` (number), and `delayLongPress` (number), which are all defined as a number of milliseconds, as shown in the following code snippet:

```
<TouchableOpacity
  onLongPress={this.openContextMenu} // Called 1 second after long press
  delayLongPress={1000}
>
```

Finally, touchable components have a prop called `hitSlop` (object) that allows us to define how far away from our component a press event can start. This is useful if a component is small and may be difficult for a user to easily target with his/her finger. Creating a larger `hitSlop` can account for the impreciseness of our human user. Take a look at the following code snippet:

```
<TouchableOpacity
  hitSlop={{
    top: 10, // distance from the top of the component that press can start
    left: 5,
    right: 5,
    bottom: 10
  }}
>
```

ListView

At this point, we've more or less created a single `NewsItem` component. The next step for us is to create a `NewsFeed` component that will contain a list of `NewsItems`. The core of our feed will be another React Native component called `ListView`. The `ListView` component is unique among components we've talked about so far in that, instead of giving it `children` components, we give it an array, or list, of JavaScript objects as well as a function to render those individual objects. The internal workings of the component determine when and where to display and use them.

Following is the basic outline of our new `NewsFeed` component in `src/components/NewsFeed.js`:

```
import React, { PropTypes, Component } from 'react';
import {
  ListView,
  StyleSheet,
  View
} from 'react-native';
import * as globalStyles from '../styles/global';

export default class NewsFeed extends Component {

  render() {
    return (
      <View style={globalStyles.COMMON_STYLES.pageContainer}>
        <ListView />
      </View>
    );
```

```
    }

  }
```

Next, let's define `propTypes` for the `NewsFeed` component. This is pretty straightforward because we know that our `ListView` will need a list of news item objects. We'll also accept a `listStyle` prop, which allows the nested `ListView` component to be styled:

```
NewsFeed.propTypes = {
  news: PropTypes.arrayOf(PropTypes.object),
  listStyles: View.propTypes.style
};
```

DataSource

In order to get these news item JavaScript objects into our `ListView`, we need to create a `DataSource`. The `DataSource` includes not only the raw data, but also a method to tell when that underlying data has changed, which helps `ListView` render more efficiently. Typically, we will create the `DataSource` for our component's `ListView` within the constructor:

```
constructor(props) {
  super(props);
  this.ds = new ListView.DataSource({
    rowHasChanged: (row1, row2) => row1.title !== row2.title
  });
  this.state = {
    dataSource: this.ds.cloneWithRows(props.news)
  };
}
```

First, we instantiate our `DataSource` of `NewsFeed` and give it a function, `rowHasChanged`, that tells it how to compare two rows to tell if they have changed. In our function, we simply compare the title; if a row's title has changed, then the entire row has changed, so `ListView` should re-render it:

```
this.ds = new ListView.DataSource({
  rowHasChanged: (row1, row2) => row1.title !== row2.title
});
```

On the next line, we give the new data source the raw data and store the result in our component's state so that we can access it at render time:

```
this.state = {
  dataSource: this.ds.cloneWithRows(props.news)
};
```

renderRow

We also need to define within our component a method that tells `ListView` how to render each individual row. In our `NewsFeed` component, this method is pretty simple:

```
renderRow(rowData, ...rest) {
  const index = parseInt(rest[1], 10);
  return (
    <NewsItem
      style={styles.newsItem}
      index={index}
      {...rowData}
    />
  );
}
```

Notice that here we are using the JavaScript spread operator to set all of the entries of the `rowData` object, a single news item, as props on the `NewsItem`. This is equivalent to doing the following:

```
<NewsItem
  imageUrl={rowData.imageUrl}
  title={rowData.title}
  description={rowData.description}
  date={rowData.date}
  author={rowData.author}
  location={rowData.location}
/>
```

Props

Now that we've created a `DataSource` and a method for rendering rows, we need to add them to the `dataSource` (object) and `renderRow` (function) props of the `ListView` component, respectively. Additionally, we'll pass the `listStyle` prop to the `ListView` component:

```
render() {
```

```
    return (
      <View style={globalStyles.COMMON_STYLES.pageContainer}>
        <ListView
          dataSource={this.state.dataSource}
          renderRow={this.renderRow}
          style={this.props.listStyles}
        />
      </View>
    );
  }
}
```

We'll also add the enableEmptySections (Boolean) prop to ListView. This property says that empty list sections should still be rendered:

```
<View style={globalStyles.COMMON_STYLES.pageContainer}>
  <ListView
    enableEmptySections
    dataSource={this.state.dataSource}
    renderRow={this.renderRow}
    style={this.props.listStyles}
  />
</View>
```

In addition to these required props, there are many others we can use to fine tune a ListView. Not only can we tell ListView how to render its rows, we can also tell it how to render a header, footer, and row separators through the renderHeader (function), renderFooter (function), and renderSeparator (function) props. Each of these functions should return a renderable React element.

Many of the props available for a ListView are related to tuning the component's performance. These properties will be covered in more depth in Chapter 11, *Preparing for Production*.

Let's take a look at our NewsFeed component so far:

```
import React, { PropTypes, Component } from 'react';
import {
  ListView,
  StyleSheet,
  View
} from 'react-native';
import * as globalStyles from '../styles/global';

export default class NewsFeed extends Component {

  constructor(props) {
    super(props);
```

```
    this.ds = new ListView.DataSource({
      rowHasChanged: (row1, row2) => row1.title !== row2.title
    });
    this.state = {
      dataSource: this.ds.cloneWithRows(props.news)
    };
  }

  renderRow(rowData, ...rest) {
    const index = parseInt(rest[1], 10);
    return (
      <NewsItem
        style={styles.newsItem}
        index={index}
        {...rowData}
      />
    );
  }

  render() {
    return (
      <View style={globalStyles.COMMON_STYLES.pageContainer}>
        <ListView
          enableEmptySections
          dataSource={this.state.dataSource}
          renderRow={this.renderRow}
          style={this.props.listStyles}
        />
      </View>
    );
  }
}

NewsFeed.propTypes = {
  news: PropTypes.arrayOf(PropTypes.object),
  listStyles: View.propTypes.style
};

NewsFeed.defaultProps = {
  news: [
    {
      title: 'React Native',
      imageUrl: 'https://facebook.github.io/react/img/logo_og.png',
      description: 'Build Native Mobile Apps using JavaScript and React',
      date: new Date(),
      author: 'Facebook',
      location: 'Menlo Park, California',
```

```
        url: 'https://facebook.github.io/react-native'
    },
    {
      title: 'Packt Publishing',
      imageUrl:
  'https://www.packtpub.com/sites/default/files/packt_logo.png',
      description: 'Stay Relevant',
      date: new Date(),
      author: 'Packt Publishing',
      location: 'Birmingham, UK',
      url: 'https://www.packtpub.com/'
    }
  ]
};

const styles = StyleSheet.create({
  newsItem: {
    marginBottom: 20
  }
});
```

Notice that, since we have not yet brought real data into our application (we'll cover this in Chapter 6, *Integrating with the NYT API and Redux*), we've created mock data and added it as defaultProps on the NewsFeed component:

```
NewsFeed.defaultProps = {
  news: [
    {
      title: 'React Native',
      imageUrl: 'https://facebook.github.io/react/img/logo_og.png',
      description: 'Build Native Mobile Apps using JavaScript and React',
      date: new Date(),
      author: 'Facebook',
      location: 'Menlo Park, California',
      url: 'https://facebook.github.io/react-native'
    },
    {
      title: 'Packt Publishing',
      imageUrl:
  'https://www.packtpub.com/sites/default/files/packt_logo.png',
      description: 'Stay Relevant',
      date: new Date(),
      author: 'Packt Publishing',
      location: 'Birmingham, UK',
      url: 'https://www.packtpub.com/'
    }
  ]
};
```

Modal

Now that we have the ability to listen for user presses on our `NewsItem` component, let's respond to that event by showing them the full news article. The first step in this process is creating an area in our application where we can display the content. Normally, we would use routing and navigation to go to a new part of our application, but since we haven't learned about those things yet, we'll use a new component called a `Modal`.

The `Modal` component does a full-screen takeover to display its children on top of any other content on the page. This sounds like it could be a good solution for showing our news article. A visibility of `Modal` can be toggled, so we can include it within our `NewsFeed` component, but only make it visible when a user presses on a news item:

```
import React, { PropTypes, Component } from 'react';
import {
  ListView,
  StyleSheet,
  View,
  Modal
} from 'react-native';
import * as globalStyles from '../styles/global';

export default class NewsFeed extends Component {

  constructor(props) {
    super(props);
    this.ds = new ListView.DataSource({
      rowHasChanged: (row1, row2) => row1.title !== row2.title
    });
    this.state = {
      dataSource: this.ds.cloneWithRows(props.news)
    };
  }

  renderModal() {
    return (
      <Modal>
      </Modal>
    );
  }

  renderRow(rowData, ...rest) {
    const index = parseInt(rest[1], 10);
    return (
      <NewsItem
        style={styles.newsItem}
```

```
            index={index}
            {...rowData}
        />
      );
    }

    render() {
      return (
        <View style={globalStyles.COMMON_STYLES.pageContainer}>
          <ListView
            enableEmptySections
            dataSource={this.state.dataSource}
            renderRow={this.renderRow}
            style={this.props.listStyles}
          />
          {this.renderModal()}
        </View>
      );
    }

}
```

Now we've added the `Modal` to the `NewsFeed` component and rendered it. Notice that this time we split the rendering of the `Modal` into a helper method:

```
renderModal() {
  return (
    <Modal>
    </Modal>
  );
}
```

We then called that helper method as part of the main render method:

```
{this.renderModal()}
```

Props

In order to toggle the modal open and close, we can use the `visible` prop of `Modal` (Boolean). If this property is `true`, then the modal becomes visible to the user, and if it is `false`, then it is hidden. In order to keep track of whether or not we want the modal to be showing, we'll use the `NewsFeed` component's state. First, we'll need to initialize this state in the component's constructor:

```
constructor(props) {
  super(props);
```

```
this.ds = new ListView.DataSource({
  rowHasChanged: (row1, row2) => row1.title !== row2.title
});
this.state = {
  dataSource: this.ds.cloneWithRows(props.news),
  modalVisible: false
};
}
```

Since we initially want the modal to be hidden, we initialize a state value `modalVisible` to `false`. The next thing we need to do is to add this state value as a prop on the `Modal` itself:

```
renderModal() {
  return (
    <Modal
      visible={this.state.modalVisible}
    >
    </Modal>
  );
}
```

Finally, we need to change the state value when the user presses on the `NewsItem`. In order to do that, we'll create an event listener function in the `NewsFeed` component:

```
onModalOpen() {
  this.setState({
    modalVisible: true
  });
}
```

Because we're using the ES2015 class syntax, we need to bind the `this` context to the event listeners in the component's constructor:

```
constructor(props) {
  super(props);
  this.ds = new ListView.DataSource({
    rowHasChanged: (row1, row2) => row1.title !== row2.title
  });
  this.state = {
    dataSource: this.ds.cloneWithRows(props.news),
    modalVisible: false
  };

  this.onModalOpen = this.onModalOpen.bind(this);
}
```

Next, we'll pass this handler down as an `onPress` prop to the `NewsItem` components in the `renderRow` method:

```
renderRow(rowData, ...rest) {
  const index = parseInt(rest[1], 10);
  return (
    <NewsItem
      onPress={() => this.onModalOpen()}
      style={styles.newsItem}
      index={index}
      {...rowData}
    />
  );
}
```

As it happens, a `renderRow` method of `ListView` also needs to be bound if we wish to access the component's `this` context, so we'll add that to the constructor, as shown in the following code:

```
constructor(props) {
  super(props);
  this.ds = new ListView.DataSource({
    rowHasChanged: (row1, row2) => row1.title !== row2.title
  });
  this.state = {
    dataSource: this.ds.cloneWithRows(props.news),
    modalVisible: false
  };

  this.renderRow = this.renderRow.bind(this);
  this.onModalOpen = this.onModalOpen.bind(this);
}
```

Finally, we need to make use of this new prop in the `NewsItem` component. We'll do this by adding it to prop type validation and attaching it to that component's `TouchableOpacity`:

```
import React, { Component, PropTypes } from 'react';
import {
    View,
    TouchableOpacity,
    StyleSheet
} from 'react-native';
import Byline from './Byline';
import AppText from './AppText';
import Thumbnail from './Thumbnail';
import * as globalStyles from '../styles/global';
```

```
export default class NewsItem extends Component {

  render() {
    const {
      style,
      imageUrl,
      title,
      author,
      date,
      location,
      description,
      onPress
    } = this.props;
    const accentColor = globalStyles.ACCENT_COLORS[
      this.props.index % globalStyles.ACCENT_COLORS.length
    ];
    return (
      <TouchableOpacity
        style={style}
        onPress={onPress}
      >
        <View>
          <Thumbnail
            url={imageUrl}
            titleText={title}
            accentColor={accentColor}
            style={styles.thumbnail}
          />
          <View style={styles.content}>
            <Byline
              author={author}
              date={date}
              location={location}
            />
            <AppText>
              {description}
            </AppText>
          </View>
        </View>
      </TouchableOpacity>
    );
  }
}

NewsItem.propTypes = {
  imageUrl: PropTypes.string,
  title: PropTypes.string.isRequired,
  description: PropTypes.string,
```

```
    date: PropTypes.instanceOf(Date).isRequired,
    author: PropTypes.string.isRequired,
    location: PropTypes.string,
    index: PropTypes.number.isRequired,
    onPress: PropTypes.func.isRequired,
    style: View.propTypes.style
};

const styles = StyleSheet.create({
  thumbnail: {
    marginBottom: 5
  },
  content: {
    paddingHorizontal: 5
  }
});
```

Now that we've created the ability to open the modal, we also need to create the ability to close the modal. The first way we can do this is by defining the Modal prop onRequestClose (function). This function is called when the user uses some native means to attempt to close the modal, for instance, when the user hits the native back button on an Android device. Since it is a required property on Android, the general best practice is to define this property. In order to do that, we'll create a new event listener method within our NewsFeed component:

```
onModalClose() {
  this.setState({
    modalVisible: false
  });
}
```

We'll then add the new event listener as a prop on our Modal:

```
renderModal() {
  return (
    <Modal
      visible={this.state.modalVisible}
      onRequestClose={this.onModalClose}
    >
    </Modal>
  );
}
```

Because this method is an event listener, we will also need to bind the `this` context once again in our constructor:

```
constructor(props) {
  super(props);
  this.ds = new ListView.DataSource({
    rowHasChanged: (row1, row2) => row1.title !== row2.title
  });
  this.state = {
    dataSource: this.ds.cloneWithRows(props.news),
    modalVisible: false
  };

  this.renderRow = this.renderRow.bind(this);
  this.onModalClose = this.onModalClose.bind(this);
  this.onModalOpen = this.onModalOpen.bind(this);
}
```

It is generally a good idea to also provide the user with a button, or `TouchableOpacity`, which allows them to close it without using some native means, so let's add that to our `Modal` as well. The content that we want to show inside the `Modal` component is added as children:

```
renderModal() {
  return (
    <Modal
      visible={this.state.modalVisible}
      onRequestClose={this.onModalClose}
    >
      <View style={styles.modalContent}>
        <TouchableOpacity
          onPress={this.onModalClose}
          style={styles.closeButton}
        >
          <SmallText>Close</SmallText>
        </TouchableOpacity>
      </View>
    </Modal>
  );
}
```

For this, we'll need to add `TouchableOpacity` to the imports:

```
import {
  ListView,
  StyleSheet,
  View,
```

```
    Modal,
    TouchableOpacity
} from 'react-native';
```

We'll also need to add some styles for the new Modal content:

```
const styles = StyleSheet.create({
  newsItem: {
    marginBottom: 20
  },
  modalContent: {
    flex: 1,
    justifyContent: 'center',
    paddingTop: 20,
    backgroundColor: globalStyles.BG_COLOR
  },
  closeButton: {
    paddingVertical: 5,
    paddingHorizontal: 10,
    flexDirection: 'row'
  }
});
```

By default, the Modal will instantly be visible when the visible prop is set to true. This can be a jolting experience and is not especially desirable. To mitigate this, we can set an animationType (string) prop on our modal to have it animate in from the bottom of the application. We'll use the 'slide' animation, as shown in the following code:

```
<Modal
  animationType="slide"
  visible={this.state.modalVisible}
  onRequestClose={this.onModalClose}
>
```

WebView

We have now created a place to put the article, but we now need a means to show it. Rather than pulling the text of the entire article into our application, which has questionable legality, we will take the user to the original website where the article was posted by using a WebView component. A WebView is simply a limited native browser that we can embed within our application and control.

The first thing we'll need to do is add a `WebView` inside of our `NewsFeed` component's `Modal`:

```
renderModal() {
  return (
    <Modal
      animationType="slide"
      visible={this.state.modalVisible}
      onRequestClose={this.onModalClose}
    >
      <View style={styles.modalContent}>
        <TouchableOpacity
          onPress={this.onModalClose}
          style={styles.closeButton}
        >
          <SmallText>Close</SmallText>
        </TouchableOpacity>
        <WebView />
      </View>
    </Modal>
  );
}
```

Props

In order to tell our `WebView` what to show, we'll need to define its `source` (object) prop. Here, we can tell it to open some web page or any arbitrary HTML string that we pass in, as shown in the following code:

```
<WebView
  source={{uri: 'http://example.com'}} // Open a webpage
/>

<WebView
  source={{html: '<html><head></head><body><h1>Hello
World!</h1></body></html>'}} // Open static HTML
/>
```

In our case, we want to render a web page from the article's URL. We'll assume that the URL of the current article is stored in the `NewsFeed` component's state:

```
renderModal() {
  return (
    <Modal
      animationType="slide"
      visible={this.state.modalVisible}
```

```
          onRequestClose={this.onModalClose}
      >
        <View style={styles.modalContent}>
          <TouchableOpacity
            onPress={this.onModalClose}
            style={styles.closeButton}
          >
            <SmallText>Close</SmallText>
          </TouchableOpacity>
          <WebView
            source={{ uri: this.state.modalUrl }}
          />
        </View>
      </Modal>
    );
  }
```

A `WebView` can be styled just like a regular `View` component, using the `style` (object) prop. We can also tell the `WebView` to ensure the contents of the web page fit nicely inside of the `View` by setting the `scalesPageToFit` (Boolean) prop:

```
<WebView
  scalesPageToFit
  source={{ uri: this.state.modalUrl }}
/>
```

In order for this to work, we will need to set the `modalUrl` in the `NewsFeed` state. We will do this by adding it to the `onModalOpen` method, as shown in the following code:

```
onModalOpen(url) {
  this.setState({
    modalVisible: true,
    modalUrl: url
  });
}
```

Then, we need to pass in this argument from the `NewsItem`:

```
renderRow(rowData, ...rest) {
  const index = parseInt(rest[1], 10);
  return (
    <NewsItem
      onPress={() => this.onModalOpen(rowData.url)}
      style={styles.newsItem}
      index={index}
      {...rowData}
    />
  );
```

```
}
```

There are also a number of event listener props for the `WebView` component. The first group is called at various times while a page is loading: `onLoadStart` (function) is called when the site begins to load, `onLoad` (function) is called when the site is loaded successfully, `onError` (function) is called when the site fails to load, and `onLoadEnd` (function) is called when the load ends either way.

There is also a special `onNavigationStateChange` (function) prop that is called when the user navigates within the web page by, for instance, by clicking a link on that page. We can use this function to optionally show a back button or other navigational components. Take a look at the following code:

```
<WebView
  onNavigationStateChange={(navState) => {
    if (navState.canGoBack) {
      this.showBackButton();
    }
  }}
/>
```

TabBarIOS

Now that we've created our `NewsFeed`, it is a good time to take this custom React Native component and actually place it into an application. The first thing we'll do is create a **Home Screen** for our application that will be displayed when the application is first opened. We'll do this by creating a new component in our `components` directory called `HomeScreen`. We're going to be making use of an iOS-only component (`TabBarIOS`) in the `HomeScreen`, so we'll name the file `HomeScreen.ios.js`. The extension tells the React Native packager that this component should only be included in the iOS version of the application.

The `HomeScreen` will use a new React Native component called `TabBarIOS` to display our `NewsFeed` component (under a **Featured** tab) as well as **Search** and **Bookmarks** components under different tabs, as shown in the following screenshot:

The `TabBarIOS` component is a simple navigational component that allows the user to navigate to different parts of the application by pressing the icon associated with that area. We'll begin to build our `HomeScreen` component by importing the `component` and adding it to the `render` method, as shown in the following code snippet:

```
import React, { Component } from 'react';
import {
  TabBarIOS,
  Text
} from 'react-native';
import NewsFeed from './NewsFeed';
import * as globalStyles from '../styles/global';

export default class HomeScreen extends Component {

  render() {
    return (
      <TabBarIOS>
      </TabBarIOS>
    );
  }
}
```

Notice we're also importing the `Text` and `NewsFeed` components because we'll be using those as well.

Props

In order to style the `TabBarIOS` component, we can use the `tintColor` (string), `barTintColor` (string), and `translucent` (Boolean) props:

```
render() {
  return (
    <TabBarIOS
      barTintColor={globalStyles.BAR_COLOR}
      tintColor={globalStyles.LINK_COLOR}
      translucent={false}
    >
    </TabBarIOS>
  );
}
```

TabBarIOS.Item

Each tab in our tab bar is created by using `TabBarIOS.Item`. Within these elements, we place the components we wish to be rendered when that tab is selected. We're going to be making three tabs, so we'll use three `TabBarIOS.Item` elements:

```
render() {
  return (
    <TabBarIOS>
      <TabBarIOS.Item>
        <NewsFeed />
      </TabBarIOS.Item>
      <TabBarIOS.Item>
        <Search />
      </TabBarIOS.Item>
      <TabBarIOS.Item>
        <Text>Bookmarks</Text>
      </TabBarIOS.Item>
    </TabBarIOS>
  );
}
```

Now we've created three tabs. The first contains our newly created `NewsFeed` component and the other two, for now, only contain some text that describes what we will eventually put in them.

Props

In order to know which tab to display, we'll need to use the `TabBarIOS.Item` prop `selected` (Boolean). First we'll store the name of the selected tab in state and initialize it as the `newsFeed` tab in our constructor:

```
constructor(props) {
  super(props);
  this.state = {
    tab: 'newsFeed'
  };
}
```

Next, each tab will assign its selected prop based on the name that is stored in the state of `HomeScreen`:

```
render() {
  return (
    <TabBarIOS>
```

```
      <TabBarIOS.Item
        selected={this.state.tab === 'newsFeed'}
      >
        <NewsFeed />
      </TabBarIOS.Item>
      <TabBarIOS.Item
        selected={this.state.tab === 'search'}
      >
        <Search />
      </TabBarIOS.Item>
      <TabBarIOS.Item
        selected={this.state.tab === 'bookmarks'}
      >
        <Text>Bookmarks</Text>
      </TabBarIOS.Item>
    </TabBarIOS>
  );
}
```

Now, when the HomeScreen is first loaded, the NewsFeed tab will properly be showing, but we also need to give the user the ability to change the tab. We do this by using the TabBarIOS.Item prop onPress (function). Each tab will simply update the component's state when it is pressed. Take a look at the following code snippet:

```
render() {
  return (
    <TabBarIOS>
      <TabBarIOS.Item
        selected={this.state.tab === 'newsFeed'}
        onPress={() => this.setState({ tab: 'newsFeed' })}
      >
        <NewsFeed />
      </TabBarIOS.Item>
      <TabBarIOS.Item
        selected={this.state.tab === 'search'}
        onPress={() => this.setState({ tab: 'search' })}
      >
        <Search />
      </TabBarIOS.Item>
      <TabBarIOS.Item
        selected={this.state.tab === 'bookmarks'}
        onPress={() => this.setState({ tab: 'bookmarks' })}
      >
        <Text>Bookmarks</Text>
      </TabBarIOS.Item>
    </TabBarIOS>
  );
}
```

Finally, we need to tell `TabBarIOS.Items` what icons and labels to show. We can do this in one of two ways. The first is we could use custom icon images and label text by using the `icon` (object) and `title` (string) props, respectively. Alternatively, we can use one of the built-in system icons by specifying the `systemIcon` (string) prop instead, which is what we'll do on our `HomeScreen`. We're using the `featured` system icon for the news feed tab because there is no built-in **news** system icon, as shown in the following code snippet:

```
render() {
  return (
    <TabBarIOS>
      <TabBarIOS.Item
        systemIcon={'featured'}
        selected={this.state.tab === 'newsFeed'}
        onPress={() => this.setState({ tab: 'newsFeed' })}
      >
        <NewsFeed />
      </TabBarIOS.Item>
      <TabBarIOS.Item
        systemIcon={'search'}
        selected={this.state.tab === 'search'}
        onPress={() => this.setState({ tab: 'search' })}
      >
        <Search />
      </TabBarIOS.Item>
      <TabBarIOS.Item
        systemIcon={'bookmarks'}
        selected={this.state.tab === 'bookmarks'}
        onPress={() => this.setState({ tab: 'bookmarks' })}
      >
        <Text>Bookmarks</Text>
      </TabBarIOS.Item>
    </TabBarIOS>
  );
}
```

The `TabBarIOS.Item` also gives us the ability to show a **badge** (string or number) on it. A badge is usually used to draw a user's attention to some part of the application. In our application, if we wanted to notify the user that there were four new articles in the **Featured** tab that they have yet to see, we could add a badge to that tab, as shown in the following code snippet:

```
<TabBarIOS.Item
  badge={4}
  systemIcon={'featured'}
  selected={this.state.tab === 'newsFeed'}
  onPress={() => this.setState({ tab: 'newsFeed' })}
```

```
>
  <NewsFeed />
</TabBarIOS.Item>
```

Take a look at the following screenshot:

Now that we have a complete `HomeScreen` component, the final step is to add this to our project's entry point `index.ios.js`. We'll do that by removing most of what is there and simply passing our `HomeScreen` to the `AppRegistry`:

```
import {
  AppRegistry
} from 'react-native';
import HomeScreen from './src/components/HomeScreen';

AppRegistry.registerComponent('RNNYT', () => HomeScreen);
```

And, just like that, we have a working application! Before we claim victory, let's add a few more components.

TextInput

Let's begin to create what will become our `Search` component. As part of this component, we will need a way to accept user input. The primary way we do this in React Native applications is by using a `TextInput` component. This component is analogous to an HTML input component with a `type="text"` attribute.

First, we'll create a new component, `Search.js`, in the `components` directory and import the `TextInput` component:

```
import React, { Component } from 'react';
import {
  View,
  TextInput
} from 'react-native';

export default class Search extends Component {

  render() {
```

```
    return (
      <View>
        <View>
          <TextInput />
        </View>
      </View>
    );
  }
}
```

Props

Though it may not seem it, `TextInput` is actually one of the most sophisticated components we'll look at in this chapter. Most of its sophistication comes from the sheer number of props it exposes to the developer.

Similar to a `Text` or other components we have looked at, a `TextInput` can receive a `style` (object) prop. In our `Search` component, we'll add some basic styles to the `TextInput` element in order to make it visible in our application. We'll also add some basic styles to the surrounding `Views`:

```
import React, { Component } from 'react';
import {
  View,
  TextInput,
  StyleSheet
} from 'react-native';
import * as globalStyles from '../styles/global';

export default class Search extends Component {

  render() {
    return (
      <View style={globalStyles.COMMON_STYLES.pageContainer}>
        <View style={styles.search}>
          <TextInput
            style={styles.input}
          />
        </View>
      </View>
    );
  }
}

const styles = StyleSheet.create({
  input: {
```

```
      height: 35,
      color: globalStyles.TEXT_COLOR,
      paddingHorizontal: 5,
      flex: 1
    },
    search: {
      borderColor: globalStyles.MUTED_COLOR,
      flexDirection: 'row',
      alignItems: 'center',
      borderRadius: 5,
      borderWidth: 1,
      marginTop: 10,
      marginBottom: 5
    }
});
```

In order to capture the user's input, we typically use the parent component's state (in this case, the Search component). We will use the TextInput event listener prop onChangeText (function), which is called every time the user taps a key, to update the component's state:

```
render() {
  return (
    <View style={globalStyles.COMMON_STYLES.pageContainer}>
      <View style={styles.search}>
        <TextInput
          style={styles.input}
          onChangeText={text => this.setState({ searchText: text })}
        />
      </View>
    </View>
  );
}
```

We then need to keep the TextInput value (string) prop in sync with the parent component's state. The value prop is what the user sees displayed within the TextInput, so it is important that this matches what the user has typed, as shown in the following code snippet:

```
<TextInput
  style={styles.input}
  onChangeText={text => this.setState({ searchText: text })}
  value={this.state.searchText}
/>
```

In order to use state, we also need to initialize it in the constructor:

```
constructor(props) {
  super(props);
  this.state = {
    searchText: ''
  };
}
```

We can add placeholder text, which appears before the user begins to input text and prompts them as to what the text input expects, by using the `placeholder` (string) prop. We can also style this placeholder text by using the `placeholderTextColor` (string) prop, as shown in the following code snippet:

```
<TextInput
  style={styles.input}
  onChangeText={text => this.setState({ searchText: text })}
  value={this.state.searchText}
  placeholder={'Search'}
  placeholderTextColor={globalStyles.MUTED_COLOR}
/>
```

Now that we have a functioning `Search` component, we'll add this component to `HomeScreen`:

```
import React, { Component } from 'react';
import {
  TabBarIOS,
  Text,
  Alert,
  Vibration,
  StatusBar
} from 'react-native';
import NewsFeed from './NewsFeed';
import Search from './Search';
import * as globalStyles from '../styles/global';

// Set the status bar for iOS to light
StatusBar.setBarStyle('light-content');

export default class HomeScreen extends Component {

  constructor(props) {
    super(props);
    this.state = {
      tab: 'newsFeed'
    };
```

```
    }

    showBookmarkAlert() {
      Vibration.vibrate();
      Alert.alert(
        'Coming Soon!',
        'We're hard at work on this feature, check back in the near future.',
        [
          { text: 'OK', onPress: () => console.log('User pressed OK') }
        ]
      );
    }

    render() {
      return (
        <TabBarIOS
          barTintColor={globalStyles.BAR_COLOR}
          tintColor={globalStyles.LINK_COLOR}
          translucent={false}
        >
          <TabBarIOS.Item
            systemIcon={'featured'}
            selected={this.state.tab === 'newsFeed'}
            onPress={() => this.setState({ tab: 'newsFeed' })}
          >
            <NewsFeed />
          </TabBarIOS.Item>
          <TabBarIOS.Item
            systemIcon={'search'}
            selected={this.state.tab === 'search'}
            onPress={() => this.setState({ tab: 'search' })}
          >
            <Search />
          </TabBarIOS.Item>
          <TabBarIOS.Item
            systemIcon={'bookmarks'}
            selected={this.state.tab === 'bookmarks'}
            onPress={() => this.showBookmarkAlert()}
          >
            <Text>Bookmarks</Text>
          </TabBarIOS.Item>
        </TabBarIOS>
      );
    }
  }
```

One of the interesting and more useful props available to the `TextInput` component is the ability to change the default keyboard the user sees when they focus on the input. For instance, if `TextInput` is used to collect the user's phone number, we can set the `keyboardType` (string) prop to `"phone-pad"`:

```
<TextInput
  keyboardType="email-address" // Uses a keyboard optimized for email
address entry
/>
```

If `TextInput` is being used for secure information (that is a password), we can set the `secureTextEntry` (Boolean) to true and the input will be obscured:

```
<TextInput
  secureTextEntry // Obscure password input
/>
```

If we wish to capture many lines of input, rather than just a few words, we can set the `multiline` (Boolean) prop to `true` and use the `numberOfLines` (Number) prop to specify exactly how many lines to allow, as shown in the following code snippet:

```
<TextInput
  multiline // Allow multiple lines of text input
  numberOfLines={3} // Limit the number of line to 3
/>
```

There is also a whole slew of event listener functions in addition to `onChange`, that allow us to tap into different parts of the `TextInput` lifecycle. These include `onFocus` (function), `onBlur` (function), `onSelectionChange` (function), and many more.

Other input components

In addition to the `TextInput` component, there are a number of other input components that can be used to capture different types of user inputs. We won't be using them yet in our application, but it behooves you to know what they are and when to use them.

A `Slider` component can be used to capture number within a finite range. For instance, this could be used to select a **percent satisfaction** (a number between 0 and 1) on a user feedback survey. Take a look at the following screenshot:

The `Switch` component is used to capture a Boolean, on or off, choice. This type of input could be used to opt out of push notifications within our application. Take a look at the following screenshot:

The `Picker` component is an interesting one in that, though it is used for both platforms, its appearance is completely different on iOS and Android. This component is analogous to an HTML select component and is used for selecting from a list of discrete options. For instance, this type of input would be used to select the country in which the user lives.

Native APIs

Some native functionality does not fit nicely into a component. For these things, React Native also exposes several Native APIs that can be used in an application. Some of these we've talked about already in previous chapters. For instance, in Chapter 3, *Styling and Layout in React Native*, we introduced the `StyleSheet` API, which allows us to create stylesheets for our components. Others we'll cover in depth in future chapters on animation, fetching data, and performance optimization. Aside from these, there are a few that are of interest to us and our application right now.

ActionSheetIOS

In iOS applications, we often show context menus in the form of **action sheets**. These provide the user with nested options for a particular item on screen. In our application, we will use the `ActionSheetIOS` API to show the user a context menu that allows them to bookmark a `NewsItem` when they long press on the `NewsItem` itself, as shown in the following screenshot:

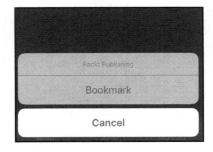

In order to do this, the first thing we'll need to do is create a listener for the long press event, bind it to the this context in the constructor of the `NewsItem`, and attach it to the `TouchableOpacity` element of `NewsItem`, as shown in the following code:

```
export default class NewsItem extends Component {

  constructor(props) {
    super(props);

    this.onLongPress = this.onLongPress.bind(this);
  }

  onLongPress() {
    // Open action sheet
  }
  render() {
    const {
      style,
      imageUrl,
      title,
      author,
      date,
      location,
      description,
      onPress
    } = this.props;
    const accentColor = globalStyles.ACCENT_COLORS[
      this.props.index % globalStyles.ACCENT_COLORS.length
    ];
    return (
      <TouchableOpacity
        style={style}
        onPress={onPress}
        onLongPress={this.onLongPress}
      >
        <View>
          <Thumbnail
            url={imageUrl}
            titleText={title}
            accentColor={accentColor}
            style={styles.thumbnail}
          />
          <View style={styles.content}>
            <Byline
              author={author}
              date={date}
              location={location}
```

```
            />
            <AppText>
              {description}
            </AppText>
          </View>
        </View>
      </TouchableOpacity>
    );
  }
}
```

Next, we need to import the `ActionSheetIOS` API and use its `showActionSheetWithOptions` method to open the context menu:

```
import {
    View,
    TouchableOpacity,
    StyleSheet,
    ActionSheetIOS
} from 'react-native';
```

Here, we'll modify our newly created `onLongPress` method:

```
onLongPress() {
  ActionSheetIOS.showActionSheetWithOptions({
    options: ['Bookmark', 'Cancel'],
    cancelButtonIndex: 1,
    title: this.props.title
  }, buttonIndex => console.log('Button selected', buttonIndex));
}
```

As we can see, the `showActionSheetWithOptions` method takes two arguments. The first argument is a JavaScript object with several entries:

```
{
  options: ['Bookmark', 'Cancel'],
  cancelButtonIndex: 1,
  title: this.props.title
}
```

The options value is an array of strings that will be displayed on the buttons that make up the action sheet. Here, we are specifying that we want two buttons, the first says `Bookmark` and the second `Cancel`:

```
options: ['Bookmark', 'Cancel']
```

We can also tell the action sheet which button is used for canceling the interaction so that it can treat it different visually. In the case of cancel buttons, iOS separates them from the other buttons. Our cancel button is at index 1 in the array:

```
cancelButtonIndex: 1
```

Finally, we can optionally add a title to the action sheet that is displayed in order to give the user some direction. In this case, the title of the article provides sufficient context:

```
title: this.props.title
```

The second argument the `showActionSheetWithOptions` method takes is a callback function invoked when the user presses a button on the action sheet. The callback receives one argument, the index of the button that was selected. Since we have not yet created the ability to bookmark articles, we'll just log the selected index to the console:

```
(buttonIndex) => console.log('Button selected', buttonIndex)
```

The `ActionSheetIOS` API comes with another method, `showShareActionSheetWithOptions`, which can be used to show the native sharing menu of iOS. This allows users to share content from within an app to social media platforms, such as Facebook or Twitter, to printers, text message, and much more.

Alert

The `Alert` API is a cross-platform API used to create a pop-up alert dialog. An alert's function is to bring the user's attention to something urgent. Since we have yet to implement the **Bookmark** tab of our application, let's use an alert to let the user know we are working hard to get this feature finished:

To implement this, we'll need to import the `Alert` API into our `HomeScreen` component:

```
import {
  TabBarIOS,
  Alert
} from 'react-native';
```

Next, we'll create a method within the `HomeScreen` component that will eventually be responsible for opening the alert:

```
showBookmarkAlert() {
  // Show alert here
}
```

Finally, we'll call the `showBookmarkAlert` method when the `bookmarks` tab is selected, instead of navigating to that tab:

```
<TabBarIOS.Item
  systemIcon={'bookmarks'}
  selected={this.state.tab === 'bookmarks'}
  onPress={() => this.showBookmarkAlert()}
>
  <Text>Bookmarks</Text>
</TabBarIOS.Item>
```

Now that we have the setup out of the way, we must implement the `showBookmarkAlert` method and use the `Alert` API, as shown in the following code snippet:

```
showBookmarkAlert() {
  Alert.alert(
    'Coming Soon!',
    'We're hard at work on this feature, check back in the near future.',
    [
      { text: 'OK', onPress: () => console.log('User pressed OK') }
    ]
  );
}
```

The first argument that `Alert.alert` takes is the string title of the alert. The second is a string message, which is displayed below the title in a slightly smaller font size. The third argument is an array of objects that represent the buttons shown at the bottom of the alert. Each button has a text value that is displayed on the button and an `onPress` value, which is a function called when the user selects the button. Since we aren't responding to the press in any way, we'll simply log to the console.

Vibration

If the alert wasn't enough to get the user's attention, React Native also allows us to access the hardware and make the mobile device vibrate by using the Vibration API. This is a very simple API and can be implemented in only a few lines of code. We'll use it to give the user a jolt at the same time we show the alert from the previous section.

The first thing we need to do is add the Vibration API to the import statement of HomeScreen:

```
import {
  TabBarIOS,
  Alert,
  Vibration
} from 'react-native';
```

Next, we'll simply call the API's vibrate method right before we open the alert:

```
showBookmarkAlert() {
  Vibration.vibrate();
  Alert.alert(
    'Coming Soon!',
    'We're hard at work on this feature, check back in the near future.',
    [
      { text: 'OK', onPress: () => console.log('User pressed OK') }
    ]
  );
}
```

And that's all there is to it! Note that, since your computer cannot vibrate, this will have no effect when running in the emulator.

StatusBar

The StatusBar API allows us to modify the operating system status bar displayed at the top of the screen. We've styled our application to have a dark theme. Since the default color of the status bar is also dark, it will probably be hard for users to read. We'll use the StatusBar API on the HomeScreen to make the status bar display in a lighter color.

First, we'll import the `StatusBar` API:

```
import {
  TabBarIOS,
  Text,
  Alert,
  Vibration,
  StatusBar
} from 'react-native';
```

Then we'll simply call the `setBarStyle` method, passing it the name of the theme we would like to use:

```
// Set the status bar for iOS to light
StatusBar.setBarStyle('light-content');
```

Now the status bar stands out on the screen, as shown in the following screenshot:

Summary

React Native, like React for the Web, comes bundled with many components and APIs that give us direct access to native interfaces and functionality. We can use these components and APIs in combination to make more complex components of our own and, eventually, an entire application.

We said this at the beginning of the chapter, but it bears repeating, this list of components, props, and APIs is by no means comprehensive. Some of the components and APIs that were left out will be introduced in later chapters, though some will not. To find a comprehensive list, refer to the React Native documentation.

Before we take our RNNYT application to the next level, we'll first spend the next chapter discussing data management strategies for React applications.

5

Flux and Redux

React, at it its core, is a user interface library. For an application of any sophistication, the user interface, or the *view-layer*, only constitutes about half of our concerns. What remains is what is often referred to as the data layer. This part of our application is responsible for fetching, persisting, and mutating data, and communicating mutations to the view layer for their display.

React itself, and, by proxy, React Native, has no opinions or prescriptions for handling data within an application. In theory, React could be used with any number of libraries or frameworks that provide a solution for data handling. In fact, when the library first came out, this was common. There were integrations with basically all of the major frameworks at the time (Backbone, Angular, Ember, and so on.) that used React in place of the framework's traditional view-layer.

As React became more popular, developers began looking for a data handling solution created with React in mind and shared some of the principles of the library itself. Around this time, developers began to turn to Facebook's homegrown internal application architecture called **Flux**.

Flux, in contrast to React, is not an implementation–it is an architecture. Much in the same way Model-View-Controller is an architecture implemented by Backbone or Angular, Flux provides a design pattern that must be implemented by an application or library developer. Flux began as a set of blog posts and conference talks where Facebook team members described the architecture and provided boilerplate implementation code suggesting how it might be done. It has grown from that point to a rich and diverse ecosystem of implementation libraries with slightly different abstractions and opinions, but all focusing around the central themes of unidirectional dataflow and the reduction of shared mutable state.

It may still be too early to say that there is a canonical Flux implementation, but much of the community, especially those involved in React Native development, seems to be coalescing around an implementation called **Redux**. Redux is not what some refer to as *pure* Flux, but it draws from its founding principles, and creates some abstractions that make the library arguably more useful in practice.

In this chapter, we'll cover the following:

- An in-depth explanation of the Flux architecture in its pure form
- Simple implementations of all the essential Flux components from scratch
- An introduction to the Redux library, its components, and core concepts
- Using Redux to create a simple application

 For some applications, Flux or Redux (or any formal data layer) might be considered over-engineering. In simple applications with few components and relatively static data, it may be easier to store the entire application's state inside of a top-level React component. When this approach starts to feel too complicated, it is probably time to graduate to Flux or Redux.

The Flux architecture

The Flux application architecture is the new paradigm for handling data within applications, developed as an alternative to traditional **Model-View-Controller** (**MVC**) architectures or derivatives thereof. Before we delve into learning the architecture and using it to build an application, let's discuss the motivations for creating Flux and why we are using it in our React Native applications.

Motivation

When Facebook introduced Flux, they contended that MVC architectures do not scale. The reason for this, their argument goes, is that large applications become less and less predictable as they scale under these architectures. This lack of predictability stems from opaque lines of communication between the various architecture components that often lead to unintended consequences when they are not fully understood.

The motivation of Flux, therefore, is to increase predictability in large applications, enabling developers to feel confident in making changes and to do so faster. There are two primary mechanisms introduced by Flux to achieve that end:

- Unidirectional dataflow
- Removal of shared mutable state

In MVC architectures, it is common for data to flow back and forth through the controller component: Data flows *into* the controller from views as the user interacts with the application, and data flows *out* of the controller to the view as the underlying data model is updated.

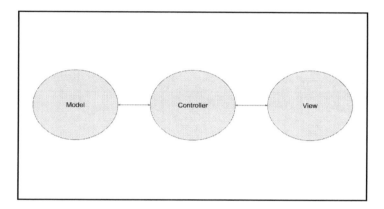

These multidirectional arrows can be hard to reason about, especially as your application grows and more models and views are introduced. Flux enforces unidirectional dataflow in order to combat this complexity. In other words, when we assemble the Flux architecture diagram, each arrow points in only one direction.

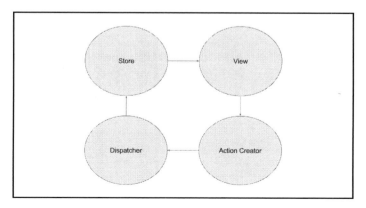

There is an oft-repeated quote among JavaScript developers that is usually attributed to Pete Hunt, who was heavily involved in the creation of React (though it probably predates his use of it at the *React.js Conference* in 2015, and is also derived from similar condemnations)–*shared mutable state is the root of all evil.* This is obviously a bit hyperbolic, but it probably strikes a nerve if you've spent any amount of time developing large JavaScript applications.

It is not uncommon for an application's state to be passed around from component to component. In JavaScript, this is problematic because objects, most often used to represent state, are mutable. Therefore, any component that receives a reference to the state object has the ability to update it. As one might imagine, tracking down which component is making the change is not always an easy task. The reality of shared mutable state is bugs that are hard to find and permanently eliminate.

Flux approaches this problem by encapsulating all state mutations into a single class of component: Stores. Some implementations take this even further by mandating that the state itself be made up of so called immutable objects, or, as we'll see in Redux, using the principles of functional programming. By centralizing all mutations, Flux provides developers with a clear place to look when a bug is discovered.

Saying that MVC does not scale is a bold claim, and not one we will take sides on in this book. Whether or not Flux is really an improvement over traditional MVC architectures is almost certainly subjective. The argument can be, and has been, made that MVC can in fact scale when implemented properly. However, there is still a very compelling reason to use Flux when creating React and React Native applications–the community support.

The React community has dedicated much effort to making Flux implementations that integrate with React extremely well. Using these implementations that have React in mind help us to write apps that are easy to reason about and scale quickly and effectively.

Implementing Flux

In order to learn how Flux works in practice, we'll be creating a simple application and implementing the Flux architecture within it. The app we'll be creating, **Countly**, is a tally counter application that can be used to count people entering and leaving an event venue.

From a high level, we can think of Flux as a cyclical pattern. The cycle generally starts in the view layer; in our case, these are React components. When a user interacts with our **view**, they generate what Flux calls an action using an **action creator**. This action is passed to the **dispatcher**, a singleton component that only allows one action to be processed at a time. The **dispatcher** sends, or dispatches, the action to each of the application's stores. Each **store** processes the action for itself and modifies its own internal state accordingly.

The **store** then broadcasts this change to subscribed views, which re-render in turn, completing the cycle.

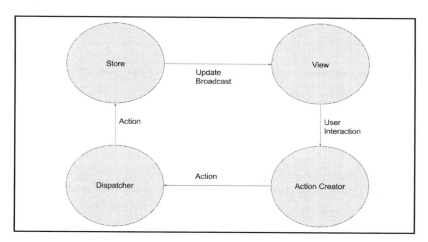

Creating our view

The first thing we'll need to do is create a new React Native project for Countly and create the view that will display the tally to the user. To make the project, we'll need to run this command:

```
react-native init Countly
```

As we discussed in previous chapters, this creates all of the boilerplate React Native files we'll need for our new app. In order to make our view, we'll work directly in the index.ios.js file. The view is very simple. It shows the current tally as well as buttons to increment, decrement, and zero-out the tally:

```
import React, { Component } from 'react';
import {
  AppRegistry,
  StyleSheet,
  Text,
```

```
  View,
  TouchableOpacity
} from 'react-native';

class Countly extends Component {

  render() {
    return (
      <View style={styles.container}>
        <Text style={styles.appName}>
          Countly
        </Text>
        <Text style={styles.tally}>
          Tally: 0
        </Text>
        <TouchableOpacity style={styles.button}>
          <Text style={styles.buttonText}>
            +
          </Text>
        </TouchableOpacity>
        <TouchableOpacity style={styles.button}>
          <Text style={styles.buttonText}>
            -
          </Text>
        </TouchableOpacity>
        <TouchableOpacity style={styles.button}>
          <Text style={styles.buttonText}>
            0
          </Text>
        </TouchableOpacity>
      </View>
    );
  }
}

const styles = StyleSheet.create({
  container: {
    flex: 1,
    justifyContent: 'center',
    alignItems: 'center',
    backgroundColor: '#F5FCFF'
  },
  appName: {
    fontSize: 20,
    textAlign: 'center',
    margin: 10
  },
  tally: {
```

```
      textAlign: 'center',
      color: '#333333',
      marginBottom: 20,
      fontSize: 25
    },
    button: {
      backgroundColor: 'blue',
      width: 100,
      marginBottom: 20,
      padding: 20
    },
    buttonText: {
      color: 'white',
      textAlign: 'center',
      fontSize: 20
    }
});
```

```
AppRegistry.registerComponent('Countly', () => Countly);
```

The first thing we do, as always, is import the `React` libraries and native components we need in our view:

```
import React, { Component } from 'react';
import {
  AppRegistry,
  StyleSheet,
  Text,
  View,
  TouchableOpacity
} from 'react-native';
```

Next, we create our `Countly` application component class, extending the React `Component` class. Inside the `Countly` component's `render()` method, we return the `Text` elements containing the tally, which is zero when the app first starts. We also return three `TouchableOpacity` elements, which act as buttons allowing the user to increment, decrement, and zero-out the count. For now, since we haven't defined the `onPress` property, these buttons do nothing:

```
class Countly extends Component {

  render() {
    return (
      <View style={styles.container}>
        <Text style={styles.appName}>
          Countly
        </Text>
```

```
          <Text style={styles.tally}>
            Tally: 0
          </Text>
          <TouchableOpacity style={styles.button}>
            <Text style={styles.buttonText}>
              +
            </Text>
          </TouchableOpacity>
          <TouchableOpacity style={styles.button}>
            <Text style={styles.buttonText}>
              -
            </Text>
          </TouchableOpacity>
          <TouchableOpacity style={styles.button}>
            <Text style={styles.buttonText}>
              0
            </Text>
          </TouchableOpacity>
        </View>
      );
    }
  }
```

We also create some basic styles to make our app palatable:

```
const styles = StyleSheet.create({
  container: {
    flex: 1,
    justifyContent: 'center',
    alignItems: 'center',
    backgroundColor: '#F5FCFF'
  },
  appName: {
    fontSize: 20,
    textAlign: 'center',
    margin: 10
  },
  tally: {
    textAlign: 'center',
    color: '#333333',
    marginBottom: 20,
    fontSize: 25
  },
  button: {
    backgroundColor: 'blue',
    width: 100,
    marginBottom: 20,
    padding: 20
```

```
  },
  buttonText: {
    color: 'white',
    textAlign: 'center',
    fontSize: 20
  }
});
```

Finally, we register the component using the `AppRegistry` API to initialize the application:

```
AppRegistry.registerComponent('Countly', () => Countly);
```

Now that we have our application's view assembled, we need to make the buttons respond to the user's selection. To do this, we turn to actions and action creators.

Actions and action creators

In Flux, an action is a JavaScript object that has both a type and, optionally, a payload of data. An action object is created as a result of user interaction (or some other event), and the type of the action is most often a constant string that reflects the interaction's intent. In our application, the action's type is enough information to deduce the effect on the application state, so our action objects will be very minimal:

```
{
  type: 'INCREMENT'
}
```

Now that we know what the medium of communication looks like, we need to construct the channel on which to send it. The first thing we need is a way for our view to create these actions, and we do that by making reusable functions, cleverly called **action creators**. In order to keep our app modular and organized, we'll put our action creators in a new file: `src/actions.js`:

```
export const increment = () => {
  const action = {
    type: 'INCREMENT'
  };
};

export const decrement = () => {
  const action = {
    type: 'DECREMENT'
  };
};

export const zero = () => {
```

```
  const action = {
    type: 'ZERO'
  };
};
```

Note that these action creators are not yet complete; they create the action object, but do nothing with it. We'll revisit this in the next section. For now, we need to wire these new action creators into our view. We'll do this by first importing them into our index.ios.js file:

```
import React, { Component } from 'react';
import {
  AppRegistry,
  StyleSheet,
  Text,
  View,
  TouchableOpacity
} from 'react-native';

import { increment, decrement, zero } from './src/actions';
```

Next, we need to call the action creator functions when the appropriate button is pressed by the user. We can easily do this by passing them as the onPress property for their respective TouchableOpacity:

```
<TouchableOpacity onPress={increment} style={styles.button}>
  <Text style={styles.buttonText}>
    +
  </Text>
</TouchableOpacity>
<TouchableOpacity onPress={decrement} style={styles.button}>
  <Text style={styles.buttonText}>
    -
  </Text>
</TouchableOpacity>
<TouchableOpacity onPress={zero} style={styles.button}>
  <Text style={styles.buttonText}>
    0
  </Text>
</TouchableOpacity>
```

Now that we've connected the view to the action creators, we need to complete them by building the next part of our data pipeline–the dispatcher.

Dispatcher

The dispatcher's role in a Flux application is to accept actions, one at a time, and hand them off to the stores. Though Facebook does not provide specific implementation details for much of Flux, they do have an open source dispatcher that developers tend to use when constructing their own Flux code.

However, in our application, we'll build a simple dispatcher ourselves in order to see how it works. The version found in Facebook's open source Flux repository is slightly more robust, and if we were creating this application for a production deployment, it would probably be a better choice.

The first thing we'll need to do is create a `src/Dispatcher.js` file and create the `Dispatcher` class in it:

```
class Dispatcher {

  dispatch(action) {
    // TODO: Pass to Stores
  }

}
```

For now, our `Dispatcher` has one method, `dispatch()`, which accepts an action object and will eventually pass that action along to stores. We can improve upon this a bit by enforcing the requirement that only one action be processed at a time. To do this, we'll define a property, `isDispatching`, that can be set at the beginning and end of our `dispatch()` function. If, however, the `Dispatcher` is already in the middle of a dispatch when the `dispatch()` method is called again, we'll throw an error:

```
class Dispatcher {

  constructor() {
    this.isDispatching = false;
  }

  dispatch(action) {
    if (this.isDispatching) {
      throw new Error('Cannot dispatch in the middle of a dispatch');
    }
    this.isDispatching = true;
    // TODO: Pass to Stores
    this.isDispatching = false;
  }

}
```

The one at a time rule of the dispatcher may seem odd at first glance. You may be asking yourself, won't this slow down our application? Well, there is actually a very good reason for this invariant to be in place. If an action is dispatched as the result of another action, we are in danger of, at the very least, having cascading effects throughout our application that are difficult to predict and follow. In the worst case, these may lead to circular cascading effects that cause an infinite dispatching loop and break our application. It's far better for us to disallow this behavior altogether.

Now that we have the skeleton for our dispatcher, we need to export it. Instead of exporting the class, though, we will actually export an instance of the class. We do this in order to create a singleton dispatcher that manages all the actions for our entire application:

```
export default new Dispatcher();
```

Finally, we need to draw a metaphorical line between the action creators and the dispatcher. To do this, we'll first import the new dispatcher instance into our `actions.js` file:

```
import Dispatcher from './Dispatcher';
```

Then, in each of the action creator functions, we'll send the action into the dispatcher's `dispatch()` method:

```
export const increment = () => {
  const action = {
    type: 'INCREMENT'
  };
  Dispatcher.dispatch(action);
};

export const decrement = () => {
  const action = {
    type: 'DECREMENT'
  };
  Dispatcher.dispatch(action);
};

export const zero = () => {
  const action = {
    type: 'ZERO'
  };
  Dispatcher.dispatch(action);
};
```

Now, to complete the dispatcher, we must connect it to the final piece of our Flux application–the store.

Stores

Stores have two responsibilities in a Flux application. First, as their name suggests, they are responsible for storing the application's state. In a traditional Flux application, stores are broken up by logical domain, each one responsible for a small part of the greater application. For example, in a social media application, one store might be responsible for the user's profile and another responsible for the user's posts.

Stores are also responsible for updating the application state as a result of actions received from the dispatcher. As we discussed earlier, this encapsulation of state and mutation logic helps reduce complexity by removing shared mutable state from all other parts of the application.

For our Countly application, we only need one store for keeping track of the tally. We'll call it `TallyStore`. In a new `src/TallyStore.js` file, the first thing we'll do is create a variable to store the application state in and give it an initial value:

```
let tally = 0;
```

This `tally` variable is considered a private variable that is within the closure of the store, but not exported for public consumption. Shielding this, and other variables and methods, from the rest of the application is one way that we can reduce the opportunity to mutate state outside this file.

Since we've deemed that the `tally` variable will not be accessible from the outside, we need to create a public getter function that allows other components to get the application's current state:

```
class TallyStore {
  getTally() {
    return tally;
  }
}

const instance = new TallyStore();
export default instance;
```

Note that, since the value of the `tally` variable is a primitive number and is, therefore, immutable, we can return it directly. If, however, our `tally` variable stored a mutable JavaScript object, we would need to return a copy of the object rather than the object itself. Doing so prevents developers of other components from accidentally mutating the application state:

```
const tally = {
  count: 0
```

```
};

class TallyStore {
  getTally() {
    return Object.assign({}, tally);
  }
}

const instance = new TallyStore();
export default instance;
```

Next, we need to create some private mutation methods that can modify the application's internal state:

```
var tally = {
  count: 0
};

const increment = () => {
  tally.count += 1;
};

const decrement = () => {
  tally.count -= 1;
};

const zero = () => {
  tally.count = 0;
};

class TallyStore {
  getTally() {
    return Object.assign({}, tally);
  }
}

const instance = new TallyStore();
export default instance;
```

Just like the private `tally` variable, these functions are private and they should not be used outside of this file.

We now need to create a function that receives an action and calls the appropriate internal function:

```
const handleAction = (action) => {
  switch (action.type) {
    case 'INCREMENT':
```

```
      increment();
      break;
    case 'DECREMENT':
      decrement();
      break;
    case 'ZERO':
      zero();
      break;
    default:
      // do nothing
  }
};
```

In order to connect the store to the dispatcher, we'll need to add some more code to our dispatcher. When the dispatcher receives an action, it needs to hand it off to each store in our application. To do this, the dispatcher will keep a registry of store action handlers and will call each during the dispatch.

First, we'll create an empty array in the dispatcher's constructor to hold the individual action handlers:

```
constructor() {
  this.isDispatching = false;
  this.actionHandlers = [];
}
```

Next, we'll create a register method that will allow stores to register their handleAction methods with the dispatcher:

```
register(actionHandler) {
  this.actionHandlers.push(actionHandler);
}
```

We will also need to modify the dispatcher's dispatch() method to actually call the registered action handlers:

```
dispatch(action) {
  if (this.isDispatching) {
    throw new Error('Cannot dispatch in the middle of a dispatch');
  }
  this.isDispatching = true;

  this.actionHandlers.forEach(handler => handler(action));

  this.isDispatching = false;
}
```

Finally, we'll need to register our tally store's action handler with the dispatcher in order for it to receive dispatched actions. To do this, we'll need to first import the dispatcher instance:

```
import Dispatcher from './Dispatcher';
```

Then, we'll need to register the handleAction function:

```
const handleAction = (action) => {
  switch (action.type) {
    case 'INCREMENT':
      increment();
      break;
    case 'DECREMENT':
      decrement();
      break;
    case 'ZERO':
      zero();
      break;
    default:
      // do nothing
  }
  instance.emitChange();
};

Dispatcher.register(handleAction);
```

To complete the Flux data flow cycle, the last step involves getting the updated data from the store back to the view.

Rendering updated data

Views that are connected to the stateful part of our application, the stores, are typically called controller views, or sometimes containers. These views are special in that they fetch data from stores and store them in their own internal state. Getting the initial data from the store into the controller view's state is pretty straightforward, we'll just add it in the constructor. First, we'll need to import the TallyStore into the index.ios.js file:

```
import React, { Component } from 'react';
import {
  AppRegistry,
  StyleSheet,
  Text,
  View,
  TouchableOpacity
} from 'react-native';
```

```
import { increment, decrement, zero } from './src/actions';
import TallyStore from './src/TallyStore';
```

Here is the `constructor` of our `Countly` React component:

```
constructor(props) {
  super(props);
  this.state = {
    tally: TallyStore.getTally()
  };
}
```

This will work for getting initial data, but as soon as the store updates itself, the data in the view's `state` will be stale and out of sync with the underlying store data. In order for the view to stay in sync with the store, we need the controller view to be notified whenever the stores it cares about change.

The way this is most often achieved is to make the store a simple event emitter that emits a change event when its contents have been updated. A controller view can then subscribe to the stores they are interested in. Event emitters are commonplace in JavaScript, in fact, Node's standard library comes with one built in. As it happens, React Native also comes with an `EventEmitter` that we will use to enhance our `TallyStore`.

We'll need to first import the `EventEmitter` module:

```
import EventEmitter from 'EventEmitter';
import Dispatcher from './Dispatcher';
```

Then, we need to merge its methods with the store's public API:

```
class TallyStore extends EventEmitter {
  getTally() {
    return Object.assign({}, tally);
  }
}
```

Next, we'll add some public functions to our store that allow controller views to subscribe and unsubscribe to changes. These methods will abstract the underlying `EventEmitter` methods:

```
class TallyStore extends EventEmitter {
  getTally() {
    return Object.assign({}, tally);
  }
  addChangeListener(callback) {
    this.addListener('CHANGE', callback);
  }
```

```
  removeChangeListener(callback) {
    this.removeListener('CHANGE', callback);
  }
  emitChange() {
    this.emit('CHANGE');
  }
}
```

Finally, we will emit the change event whenever the `handleAction` function is called:

```
const handleAction = (action) => {
  switch (action.type) {
    case 'INCREMENT':
      increment();
      break;
    case 'DECREMENT':
      decrement();
      break;
    case 'ZERO':
      zero();
      break;
    default:
      // do nothing
  }
  instance.emitChange();
};
```

Now that our store is prepared for subscribers, we will need to add the Countly controller view as a subscriber to the tally store's changes. We do this in the `componentDidMount` lifecycle method. Likewise, we'll have the view unsubscribe in its `componentWillUnmount` lifecycle method. We'll also need to create a method on our view that will update its internal `state` as a result of the change:

```
constructor(props) {
  super(props);
  this.state = {
    tally: TallyStore.getTally()
  };
  this.updateState = this.updateState.bind(this);
}

componentDidMount() {
  TallyStore.addChangeListener(this.updateState);
}

componentWillUnmount() {
  TallyStore.removeChangeListener(this.updateState);
```

```
  }

  updateState() {
    this.setState({
      tally: TallyStore.getTally()
    });
  }
```

And now the final step–Using the real data in our `render()` method!

```
render() {
  return (
    <View style={styles.container}>
      <Text style={styles.appName}>
        Countly
      </Text>
      <Text style={styles.tally}>
        Tally: {this.state.tally.count}
      </Text>
      <TouchableOpacity onPress={increment} style={styles.button}>
        <Text style={styles.buttonText}>
          +
        </Text>
      </TouchableOpacity>
      <TouchableOpacity onPress={decrement} style={styles.button}>
        <Text style={styles.buttonText}>
          −
        </Text>
      </TouchableOpacity>
      <TouchableOpacity onPress={zero} style={styles.button}>
        <Text style={styles.buttonText}>
          0
        </Text>
      </TouchableOpacity>
    </View>
  );
}
```

We've now created a complete application with both a view layer in React Native, and a data layer in our Flux implementation. We could use our home-grown Flux implementation in our production application, but it would probably be wise for us to instead turn to a community-supported flavor of Flux called Redux.

Getting started with Redux

Redux is an implementation library for data handling in client applications that was inspired, in large part, by Flux. It draws on the ideas of Flux and adds in immutability and the principles of functional programming in an attempt to bring sanity to frontend applications that, as a category, are growing in complexity on a regular basis.

While the motivations behind Redux are very much in line with those of Flux, the approach that it takes is slightly different. To understand Redux, you must first understand the three principles that guide the framework.

Principles of Redux

The first principle of Redux is that all application state is contained within a single store, which is most often a JavaScript object. Remember that, in Flux, we could have many disparate stores, each responsible for its own logical domain. Redux uses a single store instead, but has **reducer functions** that are responsible for managing smaller parts of the greater state.

There are many benefits to having a single store. Perhaps one of the more compelling is the ability to easily serialize and then download the state for later use. Once we have a saved copy of the application's state, we can later load the application under those exact conditions, or rehydrate the state. This is helpful for development as well as for debugging problem states.

The second principle of Redux is that the application's state is immutable. This means that at no point should the object representing the state be modified in any way by any component. In our implementation of Flux, we reduced and encapsulated the mutability of state by only allowing the stores to mutate their own data. In Redux, we mandate that the state is never mutated. Instead, we use reducer functions to create a new state object when an action is dispatched, leaving the old state unmodified.

The third and final principle of the Redux framework is that all functions that compute the new state (the so called reducer functions) must be **pure functions**. Pure functions are functions that produce no side-effects and are deterministic—for a given set of inputs, the output will always be the same. Side-effects include API calls, but they also include the mutation of inputs. Because Redux reducers are pure, or side-effect free, the dispatcher needed to coordinate action dispatching in Flux can be removed. Pure reducers with deterministic results can also enable advanced debugging techniques, such as time-travelling between states.

Installing Redux

In order to start using Redux in our application, we'll need to first install the package. Redux, like other dependencies we've used so far, can be installed as a Node module using npm. In our Countly React Native project directory, we'll run the install command, saving the package and version information in the `package.json` file:

```
npm install redux --save
```

Implementing Redux

We will now modify our Countly application so that it can use Redux. This will involve refactoring some components and removing others. First, lets look at the core of the Redux framework, the store.

Refactoring the store

Remembering that Redux only has a single store for all of the application state, the first thing we'll do is change the name of our `TallyStore.js` file to simply `store.js`. Inside the store file, we'll need to make two large changes:

- Convert our `handleAction` function to a Redux reducer
- Use the Redux `createStore` utility to initialize the store

Reducer

In Redux, a reducer is a pure function that takes the previous state and an action as input and returns the new state. In our Flux application, the closest analogous function is the `handleAction` function in the store:

```
const handleAction = (action) => {
  switch (action.type) {
    case 'INCREMENT':
      increment();
      break;
    case 'DECREMENT':
      decrement();
      break;
    case 'ZERO':
      zero();
      break;
    default:
```

```
        // do nothing
    }
    instance.emitChange();
};
```

In order to convert this function to a Redux reducer, we'll need to make a few changes. First, we'll change the name of the function to something more appropriate, such as `countReducer`:

```
const countReducer = (action) => {
```

We'll also need to change the function's signature. Every Redux reducer receives two parameters—The current `state` and the dispatched action:

```
const countReducer = (state, action) => {
```

Next, we need to make this a pure function that returns the new state instead of mutating some external state object. In order to do this, we'll have to get rid of the mutational functions `increment`, `decrement`, and `zero`. In replacing them, we may be tempted to modify the state according to the action type and then return it:

```
case 'INCREMENT':
  state.count = state.count + 1;
  return state;
```

This, however, would be wrong. Remember, the second principle of Redux states that the application state must not be mutated. Therefore, we must create a new object and return that instead:

```
case 'INCREMENT':
  return {
    count: state.count + 1
  };
```

We will also need to remove the line where we emit changes. We *must* remove it because emitting a change is a side-effect that would cause our reducer function to be impure. We *can* remove it because Redux has a built-in mechanism for emitting state changes that is external to the reducer functions. Our new reducer now looks like this:

```
const countReducer = (state, action) => {
  switch (action.type) {
    case 'INCREMENT':
      return {
        count: state.count + 1
      };
    case 'DECREMENT':
      return {
```

```
      count: state.count - 1
    };
  case 'ZERO':
    return {
      count: 0
    };
  default:
    // Do nothing
  }
};
```

This is nearly complete, but there are a few more changes we'll need to make. A Redux reducer is called every time an action is dispatched, even if that reducer doesn't need to make any changes for that particular action. We need to handle this situation and return the state unmodified if an unrecognized action makes its way into `countReducer`. We'll do this by updating the `default` case in our switch statement:

```
default:
  return state;
```

Finally, when the reducer is first called, the state will not yet be defined, so we will need to initialize it. We will do this by repurposing the tally object, calling it `initialState`, and then using the ES2015 default argument syntax.

```
const initialState = {
  count: 0
};

const countReducer = (state = initialState, action) => {
```

We now have a complete Redux reducer.

```
const initialState = {
  count: 0
};

const countReducer = (state = initialState, action) => {
  switch (action.type) {
    case 'INCREMENT':
      return {
        count: state.count + 1
      };
    case 'DECREMENT':
      return {
        count: state.count - 1
      };
    case 'ZERO':
```

```
      return {
        count: 0
      };
    default:
      return state;
  }
};
```

Creating the store

In order to create a store from our reducer, we will use the Redux utility `createStore`. This is a function that takes in a reducer and returns an object with several methods that allow interaction with the store. Remember, since there is only a single store in Redux applications, the `createStore` function should only ever be called once in an application.

The methods that the created store will have are as follows:

- `dispatch(action)`: This is used to dispatch an action directly to the store (remember, there is no dispatcher in Redux).
- `getState()`: This returns the current application state. It can be used by controller views when the store is updated.
- `subscribe(listener)`: This is used to subscribe to store updates by controller views.

We'll look at each of these methods in depth as we use them in other components. For now, to complete our store, we simply need to import the `createStore` function from the Redux package and also export our newly created store:

```
import { createStore } from 'redux';

const initialState = {
  count: 0
};

const countReducer = (state = initialState, action) => {
  switch (action.type) {
    case 'INCREMENT':
      return {
        count: state.count + 1
      };
    case 'DECREMENT':
      return {
        count: state.count - 1
      };
    case 'ZERO':
```

```
      return {
        count: 0
      };
    default:
      return state;
  }
}
```

```
export default createStore(countReducer);
```

Multiple reducers

Countly is a simple application, and thus does not need more than a single reducer. In any useful application, the application's state will likely be much more complex. Rather than writing a single large reducer function that handles all actions and all parts of the state, we can use Redux's `combineReducers` function to create one large reducer from many smaller reducers.

To do this, we will typically modularize the reducers, organizing them into separate files. The name of each reducer will correspond to the key for the part of the state object it is managing. Here is an example of a hypothetical, more complicated store:

```
import { combineReducers, createStore } from 'redux';

//count Reducer
import count from 'reducers/count';
//metadata Reducer
import metadata from 'reducers/metadata';

const reducer = combineReducers({
  count,
  metadata
});

export default createStore(reducer);
```

In this application, the state will be organized into two sections, one with a key of `count`, which is managed by the `count` reducer, and one with a key of `metadata` managed by the `metadata` reducer.

Action creators

When introducing Redux, we mentioned that there is no dispatcher like the one that we used in our Flux implementation. This difference has implications on our action creators. In Redux, rather than having action creators that both create an action object and dispatch it to the dispatcher, our action creators will simply create the action and return it. The component that creates the action will directly dispatch the action to the store.

Let's start by refactoring our action creators, contained in the `actions.js` file:

```
export const increment = () => {
  const action = {
    type: 'INCREMENT'
  };
  return action;
};

export const decrement = () => {
  const action = {
    type: 'DECREMENT'
  };
  return action;
};

export const zero = () => {
  const action = {
    type: 'ZERO'
  };
  return action;
};
```

We now need to refactor our controller view component in `index.ios.js` to take on the responsibility of not only calling the action creators, but also dispatching the created action to the store.

To do this, we'll need to import the store, in addition to the action creators:

```
import { increment, decrement, zero } from './src/actions';
import store from './src/store';
```

We'll then need to replace the `onPress` functions with new ones that create actions, and also dispatch those actions to the store by calling the store's `dispatch()` method. For simplicity, we'll do this by using anonymous ES2015 arrow functions:

```
render() {
  return (
    <View style={styles.container}>
```

```
    <Text style={styles.appName}>
      Countly
    </Text>
    <Text style={styles.tally}>
      Tally: {this.state.tally.count}
    </Text>
    <TouchableOpacity onPress={() => store.dispatch(increment())}
style={styles.button}>
        <Text style={styles.buttonText}>
          +
        </Text>
    </TouchableOpacity>
    <TouchableOpacity onPress={() => store.dispatch(decrement())}
style={styles.button}>
        <Text style={styles.buttonText}>
          -
        </Text>
    </TouchableOpacity>
    <TouchableOpacity onPress={() => store.dispatch(zero())}
style={styles.button}>
        <Text style={styles.buttonText}>
          0
        </Text>
    </TouchableOpacity>
    </View>
  );
}
```

Subscribing to the store

The final stage of our Redux refactor is subscribing our controller view to changes to the application state that happen in the store. The first thing we'll need to do is to up the way we fetch the application state from the store by using the Redux store `getState()` method:

```
class Countly extends Component {
  constructor(props) {
    super(props);
    this.state = {
      tally: store.getState()
    };
    this.updateState = this.updateState.bind(this);
  }

  ...

  updateState() {
    this.setState({
```

```
      tally: store.getState()
    });
  }
```

Next, we'll need to replace the subscribing and unsubscribing methods of our
`EventEmitter` based store with the corresponding Redux store calls. The subscribe portion
is a direct translation because, as we noted earlier, a Redux Store has a `subscribe` method
that behaves similarly to the `addEventListener` method we used in Flux. However, there
is no `unsubscribe` method. Instead, `subscribe` returns a function that, when called,
unsubscribes the listener from the store. We'll need to store this `unsubscribe` function in
the component's state so that it can be called on unmount:

```
componentDidMount() {
  this.setState({
    unsubscribe: store.subscribe(this.updateState)
  });
}

componentWillUnmount() {
  this.state.unsubscribe();
}
```

Finally, setting state is generally discouraged in the `componentDidMount` lifecycle method,
so we'll move the subscription to the constructor:

```
constructor(props) {
  super(props);
  this.updateState = this.updateState.bind(this);
  this.state = {
    tally: store.getState(),
    unsubscribe: store.subscribe(this.updateState)
  };
}
```

We now have a complete Redux application, but we're not going to stop there. Next, we'll
look at how we can use the **React-Redux** package to integrate with Redux using less code.

React-Redux

As we've now seen, we can create an entire Redux application using only the Redux package. However, most people using Redux in React applications use the React-Redux package as well. The React-Redux package provides both some convenient abstractions that make interacting with the store directly less of a concern for the application developer, and an easy way of separating presentational components from container components (what we've been calling controller views).

Installing React-Redux

Just as we did with the Redux package itself, we'll use npm to install React-Redux and save the dependency in our package.json:

```
npm install react-redux --save
```

React context and providers

In addition to props, there is another way parent elements can pass values down to children elements in React that we have not discussed up to this point. It is called **context**, and it works in much the same way as props, except that it does not have to be explicitly passed down. Instead, if an element provides its children with context, any child, no matter how far down the tree, can have access to it.

The React context API is considered experimental and is subject to change, which is why we have not explored it in any depth thus far, but some libraries use it to create what are called **provider** components. These provider components wrap an entire application, and provide context to any other React component in the application that cares to tune in.

React-Redux uses this pattern to provide the store as context to any container (controller view) component that needs access to the application state. In order to take advantage of this, we'll need to import the Provider component from React-Redux and give it to the store as a prop:

```
import React, { Component } from 'react';
import {
  AppRegistry,
  StyleSheet,
  Text,
  View,
  TouchableOpacity
} from 'react-native';
```

```
import { Provider } from 'react-redux';

import store from './src/store';

class Countly extends Component {

  render() {
    return (
      <Provider store={store}>
        ...
      </Provider>
    );
  }
}

AppRegistry.registerComponent('Countly', () => Countly);
```

Container and presentational components

In Redux, we generally call the controller view components, those that are aware of the store and action creators, **container components**. Those that do not need this information and are only concerned with presentation are called **presentational components**. React-Redux provides a simple utility for efficiently separating these concerns called `connect`. In order to demonstrate how this works, we'll abstract out a presentational component called `Counter` from the Countly application, and then use `connect` to wrap it into a container component.

First, we'll create a new file called `src/Counter.js` and move the bulk of our Countly component's render function to this new presentational component.

```
import React, { PropTypes } from 'react';
import {
  StyleSheet,
  View,
  Text,
  TouchableOpacity
} from 'react-native';

const Counter = props => (
  <View style={styles.container}>
    <Text style={styles.appName}>
      Countly
    </Text>
    <Text style={styles.tally}>
      Tally: {props.count}
    </Text>
  </View>
```

```
        <TouchableOpacity onPress={props.increment} style={styles.button}>
          <Text style={styles.buttonText}>
            +
          </Text>
        </TouchableOpacity>
        <TouchableOpacity onPress={props.decrement} style={styles.button}>
          <Text style={styles.buttonText}>
            ─
          </Text>
        </TouchableOpacity>
        <TouchableOpacity onPress={props.zero} style={styles.button}>
          <Text style={styles.buttonText}>
            0
          </Text>
        </TouchableOpacity>
      </View>
  );

Counter.propTypes = {
  count: PropTypes.number,
  increment: PropTypes.func,
  decrement: PropTypes.func,
  zero: PropTypes.func
};

const styles = StyleSheet.create({
  container: {
    flex: 1,
    justifyContent: 'center',
    alignItems: 'center',
    backgroundColor: '#F5FCFF'
  },
  appName: {
    fontSize: 20,
    textAlign: 'center',
    margin: 10
  },
  tally: {
    textAlign: 'center',
    color: '#333333',
    marginBottom: 20,
    fontSize: 25
  },
  button: {
    backgroundColor: 'blue',
    width: 100,
    marginBottom: 20,
    padding: 20
```

```
    },
    buttonText: {
      color: 'white',
      textAlign: 'center',
      fontSize: 20
    }
});
export default Counter;
```

Note that this is now a simple, functional component with no reference to the store or any action creators. It is solely concerned with the presentation of the props passed in by its parent. We can see that the new component expects four props in particular:

```
Counter.propTypes = {
  count: PropTypes.number,
  increment: PropTypes.func,
  decrement: PropTypes.func,
  zero: PropTypes.func
};
```

In order to get these props into our new presentational component, we'll return to index.ios.js and use connect to create a container component from the Counter component. We'll need to import the Counter component as well as the connect function:

```
import React from 'react';
import {
  AppRegistry
} from 'react-native';
import { Provider, connect } from 'react-redux';

import store from './src/store';
import Counter from './src/Counter';
import { increment, decrement, zero } from './src/actions';
```

The connect method takes several arguments, but most often we'll only need the first two. The first argument is a function that maps the application state to a JavaScript object that is passed into the presentational component as props. For our Counter component, that function would look like this:

```
const mapStateToProps = state => ({
  count: state.count
});
```

The second argument that the `connect` function needs is a function that maps the store's `dispatch()` method to `props`. This is how we pass in action creators to our presentational component:

```
const mapDispatchToProps = dispatch => ({
  increment: () => dispatch(increment()),
  decrement: () => dispatch(decrement()),
  zero: () => dispatch(zero())
});
```

Now that we have these two functions, we can call `connect`. The return value of `connect` is a new function that, when passed a presentational component, returns a wrapped container component with all of the connections to the store and action creators wired up:

```
const CounterContainer = connect(
  mapStateToProps,
  mapDispatchToProps
)(Counter);
```

We can actually make this even simpler. If the second argument is an object instead of a function, `connect` will assume that each entry is an action creator and will wrap them in `dispatch` automatically. This allows us to pass our imported actions directly rather than having to create a mapping function:

```
import * as actions from './src/actions';

const CounterContainer = connect(
  mapStateToProps,
  actions
)(Counter);
```

We can now use the `CounterContainer` in the Countly application component's `render()` method and remove all the logic that previously connected it to the store. Here is the completed `index.ios.js` file:

```
import React from 'react';
import {
  AppRegistry
} from 'react-native';
import { Provider, connect } from 'react-redux';

import store from './src/store';
import Counter from './src/Counter';
import * as actions from './src/actions';

const mapStateToProps = state => ({
  count: state.count
```

```
});

const CounterContainer = connect(
  mapStateToProps,
  actions
)(Counter);

const Countly = () => (
  <Provider store={store}>
    <CounterContainer />
  </Provider>
);

AppRegistry.registerComponent('Countly', () => Countly);
```

Middleware

Redux by itself is optimized for a synchronous workflow. Actions are dispatched synchronously and the view layer is updated accordingly. In real applications, we know that some things cannot be done synchronously. Common activities, such as fetching data from a server, are done asynchronously. To accommodate asynchronous actions, as well as other custom actions, Redux provides a middleware architecture.

In Redux, middleware is injected between the dispatching of an action and its arrival at the reducer. The Redux-promise middleware is one middleware option that can be used to handle asynchronous action creators that return a JavaScript promise as the action's payload. Here is an example of what an asynchronous action creator might look like:

```
const loadCounts = async () => {
  const response = await fetch('http://example.com/counts');
  const counts = await response.json();
  return {
    type: 'RECEIVE_COUNTS',
    payload: {
      news: json
    }
  };
};
```

Here, we are using the proposed ES2017 async, await syntax to create the promise. The middleware will resolve the promise and then dispatch the action to the store upon completion. In order to make this work, we need to set up the middleware in the store. If we needed asynchronous actions in our Countly application, we could add them to the project by first installing the package:

```
npm install redux-promise --save
```

We then need to add it to `store.js` by using the `applyMiddleware` function from the Redux library:

```javascript
import { createStore, applyMiddleware } from 'redux';
import promise from 'redux-promise;

const initialState = {
  count: 0
};

const countReducer = (state = initialState, action) => {
  switch (action.type) {
    case 'INCREMENT':
      return {
        count: state.count + 1
      };
    case 'DECREMENT':
      return {
        count: state.count - 1
      };
    case 'ZERO':
      return {
        count: 0
      };
    default:
      return state;
  }
};

const middleware = applyMiddleware(promise);

export default createStore(countReducer, middleware);
```

Here we simply pass our newly applied middleware to the `createStore` function, and now our application is prepared to handle asynchronous actions.

Middleware is commonly used for asynchronous processing, but it can also be used for things such as logging and optimistic updating.

Summary

Redux is an implementation library for handling data in client applications that is based on an architecture called Flux, pioneered by Facebook. Redux is the most common way of handling data in a React Native application as its motivation, goals, and principles are closely aligned with those of React itself. Now that we know what Redux is and how to use it in a React Native application, lets use it to enhance our New York Times feed reader application.

6
Integrating with the NYT API and Redux

With a solid background of Flux and Redux, it's time to apply these concepts to the RNNYT application we started in Chapter 4, *Starting our Project with React Native Components*. In this chapter, we'll apply Redux and related Redux technologies to a React Native application. We'll start off with a simple, synchronous implementation using mock NYT API data that flows through our application using Redux and some helper libraries. Later on in the chapter, we'll reconfigure our app to talk directly to the NYT API using the fetch API and Redux middleware to support a real-world, asynchronous flow.

In this chapter, we'll cover the following:

- Review how to make requests to the NYT API, and understand the shape of that data
- Install dependencies for using Redux with React Native
- Refactor our app to use Redux with mock NYT data and synchronous actions
- Implement selectors using Reselect
- Review Redux asynchronous data flow and utilize the fetch API and the Redux-promise middleware to talk directly with the NYT API
- Add pull to refresh support

Understanding the NYT API data

Before going too far into the detail of our Redux refactoring endeavor, let's first review the data we'll ultimately be consuming from the NYT API. The NYT API offers a few options, including books, movie reviews, event listings, and so forth. We'll be using the `Top Stories` (V2) API. It provides a list of articles in both JSON and JSONP format across a variety of *sections*, including world, national, opinion, and so forth. But given that this is a book about technology, we're going to use the technology section. To make a request to the NYT API technology section, you'll need to form an http get request:

```
https://api.nytimes.com/svc/topstories/v2/technology.json?api-key=your-api-key
```

The portion of the URI following `v2/` is where you specify both the section and the format. In our case, we're interested in *technology* in JSON format, thus `technology.json`. Additionally, you must append your API key in the query string. You can register for an API key by going to `http://developer.nytimes.com/signup`. Once you have your key, you can give the NYT API a test run in your browser. Refer to the following screenshot:

> I recommend visiting the Chrome Web Store and installing **Postman**. It's a great tool for testing out RESTful interfaces.

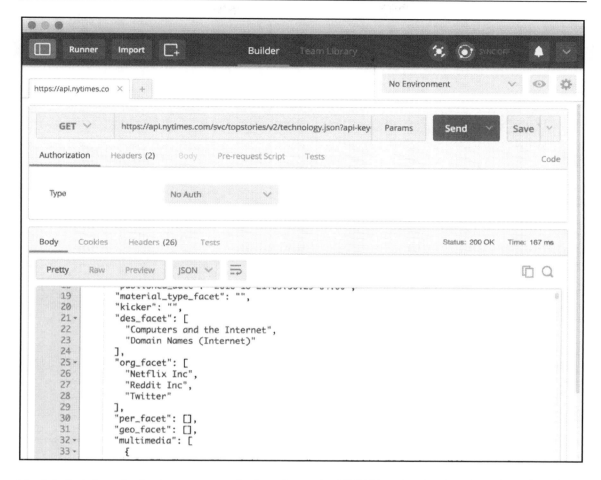

Next, let's take a look at some sample data from the NYT Top Stories V2 API. I've placed
. . . to denote areas where I've truncated the payload:

```
{
  "status": "OK",
  "copyright": "Copyright (c) All Rights Reserved.",
  "section": "technology",
  "last_updated": "2016-05-21T07:22:06-05:00",
  "num_results": 30,
  "results": [
    {
      "section": "Technology",
      "subsection": "",
      "title": "Title of the article",
      "abstract": "Lorem ipsum dolor sit amet, consectetur adipiscing elit.
```

```
      Pellentesque dictum.",
          "url":
"http://www.nytimes.com/2016/05/20/technology/url-to-article.html",
          "byline": "By FIRSTNAME LASTNAME",
          "item_type": "Article",
          "updated_date": "2016-05-19T20:38:45-5:00",
          "created_date": "2016-05-19T20:38:46-5:00",
     *    "published_date": "2016-05-20T00:00:00-5:00",
          "material_type_facet": "News",
          "kicker": "",
          "des_facet": [
            "Description Facet 1",
            "Description Facet 2"
          ],
          "org_facet": [
            "Packt Publishing",
            "Another Company Name"
          ],
          "per_facet": [
            "Masiello, Eric",
            "Friedman, Jacob"
          ],
          "geo_facet": [
            "China"
          ],
          "multimedia": [
            {
              "url": "https://static01.nyt.com/images/2016/05/20/image.jpg",
              "format": "Standard Thumbnail",
              "height": 75,
              "width": 75,
              "type": "image",
              "subtype": "photo",
              "caption": "Caption text",
              "copyright": "Photographer-Name/Copyright-Holder"
            },
            ...
          ]
        }
        ...
      ]
    }
```

There's quite a bit here, but we're only really concerned with a few key pieces of data. At the top of the response, there's a property called results. This contains a list of objects representing the top stories. Within each of the top story objects, we'll utilize the abstract byline, published_date, title, and url properties for our app. We'll also want to expose a location and display an image with each article. The location is available via the `geo_facet` property, and the image can be extracted from multimedia. `geo_facet` and multimedia will require a little bit more massaging than the other properties since the actual values exist within nested lists. But before we start transforming any data, let's configure our app to work with Redux.

Wiring up our Redux data flow

Now that we've had a look at what this data will look like, let's start writing some code. From the terminal, navigate to the root directory of RNNYT and run the following:

```
npm install redux react-redux redux-logger --save
```

We already discussed redux and react-redux at length in `Chapter 5`, *Flux and Redux*. **redux-logger** is a popular Redux middleware useful for observing changes to your app's Redux state tree from your browser's console. You may find it useful as you work through this chapter or future chapters.

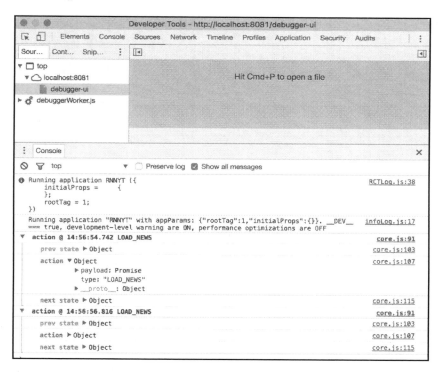

Next, let's reorganize our files and folders to match one of the more conventional project structures seen in Redux applications. Create the following directories within your `src` directory:

- `actions`
- `config`
- `containers`
- `reducers`
- `util`

Each folder will house different parts of our application.

> We've opted to organize our code by *role*. That is to say, we'll be grouping all our action creators in the `actions` folder, containers in the `containers` folder, and so forth. This is a pretty common way of organizing Redux projects, and is what you'll likely encounter in other React and Redux tutorials. Since our app will end up being relatively small, this structure will suit us fine. However, a common criticism levelled against a role-based file structure is that, as your app grows, the organization doesn't scale because it requires you to dip in and out of many folders just to set up a new feature.
> An alternative way to organize your code is by *domain* or *feature*. This might give you a folder structure that looks like this:
> ```
> global/
>   Button.js
>   PrimaryButton.js
> news/
>   components/
>     NewsFeed.js
>     NewsItem.js
>     Search.js
>   actions.js
>   actionTypes.js
>   index.js
>   reducers.js
>   selectors.js
> createStore.js
> index.js
> ```
> This is just a hypothetical example of how you might organize your code. The key takeaway is that everything related to the `news` feature exists under the `news` directory. If you were to create an entirely new feature,

say onboarding (as we'll do in Chapter 8, *Animation and Gestures in React Native*), you would create a new directory called onboarding that maintains all of its components, containers, reducers, actions, and so on. However, when organizing by role, all the onboarding components would be commingled with news and other components under a generic components folder.

Creating the Redux state tree

When creating a Redux application, I find it useful to start by creating a single Redux state tree and then growing the code from there. We can define the shape of our state tree by answering the question, what data will I need to expose to my application? Since this is an application for displaying news, a news property containing a list of news articles would be an obvious choice. Looking beyond the primary news tab, we also have **Search** and **Bookmarks** tabs. We're going to save **Bookmarks** for a later chapter, but we will flesh out **Search** in this chapter. **Search** will require the same news data from our state tree, but it will also need to know what the user is searching for so it can filter the results. Since our app will do the filtering in JavaScript, we can track the value of the search filter with another property we'll call searchTerm. With that, let's create a file inside src called createStore.js with the following code:

```
import { createStore, applyMiddleware, combineReducers } from 'redux';
import createLogger from 'redux-logger';
import newsFeedReducer from './reducers/newsFeedReducer';
import searchTermReducer from './reducers/searchTermReducer';

const logger = createLogger();

export default (initialState = {}) => (
  createStore(
    combineReducers({
      news: newsFeedReducer,
      searchTerm: searchTermReducer
    }),
    initialState,
    applyMiddleware(logger)
  )
);
```

We import the required libraries at the top of the file, including two files we have yet to define–newsFeedReducer and searchTermReducer. We'll create both of these shortly. For the time being, let's just pretend they exist. On line six, we call createLogger() to create our logger middleware (you may optionally pass in a configuration, but we'll stick with the default). Then we export an anonymous function that we'll use in another part of our application shortly. The anonymous function allows us to pass in an initial state to hydrate our application. When executed, this function creates the store with the two state properties we discussed earlier–news and searchTerm and then applies the logger middleware.

The next thing we need to do is create our action creators. But before we do that, let's create our action types. Inside the actions directory, create a file called actionTypes.js with these two values:

```
export const LOAD_NEWS = 'LOAD_NEWS';
export const SEARCH_NEWS = 'SEARCH_NEWS';
```

These two values represent the only two actions that our app needs at the moment. To keep things simple for now, our initial pass at transforming our app into a Redux application will utilize an entirely synchronous data flow. That is to say, we won't make any Ajax requests to the actual NYT API. Instead we'll use hardcoded mock data. Later, once we've got everything working, we'll update our code to actually call the NYT API. With that said, create a file in your src directory called mockData.json. Since we don't need every property from the NYT API, our mock data will only include the properties we're using:

```
{
  "results": [
    {
      "title": "React Native",
      "abstract": "Build Native Mobile Apps using JavaScript and React",
      "url": "https://facebook.github.io/react-native",
      "byline": "By Facebook",
      "published_date": "2016-05-20T00:00:00-5:00",
      "geo_facet": [
        "Menlo Park, California"
      ],
      "multimedia": [
        {
          "url": "https://facebook.github.io/react/img/logo_og.png",
          "format": "thumbLarge"
        }
      ]
    },
    {
      "title": "Packt Publishing",
      "abstract": "Stay Relevant",
```

```
      "url": "https://www.packtpub.com/",
      "byline": "By Packt Publishing",
      "published_date": "2016-05-20T00:00:00-5:00",
      "geo_facet": [
        "Birmingham, UK"
      ],
      "multimedia": [
        {
          "url":
"https://www.packtpub.com/sites/default/files/packt_logo.png",
          "format": "thumbLarge"
        }
      ]
    }
  ]
}
```

Next, create a file named newsActions.js inside the actions directory:

```
import { LOAD_NEWS, SEARCH_NEWS } from './actionTypes';
import mockData from '../mockData.json';

export const loadNews = () => ({
  type: LOAD_NEWS,
  payload: mockData
});

export const searchNews = searchTerm => ({
  type: SEARCH_NEWS,
  payload: searchTerm
});
```

There are only two actions—loadNews and searchNews. For now, loadNews just returns our static mock data. searchNews simply takes whatever search term we pass it as a parameter and forwards it along to the reducers as the payload.

Speaking of reducers, let's create those next. Inside the reducers directory, create two files—newsFeedReducer.js and searchTermReducer.js. As far as reducers go, these two are pretty straightforward. newsFeedReducer imports the LOAD_NEWS action. If the action type matches, we simply return the results array from the action payload. Take a look at the following code:

```
import { LOAD_NEWS } from '../actions/actionTypes';

export default (state = [], action = {}) => {
  switch (action.type) {
    case LOAD_NEWS:
```

```
      return action.payload.results || [];
    default:
      return state;
  }
};
```

`searchTermReducer` operates in much the same way. In this case, however, the `searchTerm` contained within our state tree is just a string, so we'll return the entire payload:

```
import { SEARCH_NEWS } from '../actions/actionTypes';

export default (state = '', action = {}) => {
  switch (action.type) {
    case SEARCH_NEWS:
      return action.payload;
    default:
      return state;
  }
};
```

Wiring up Redux data to our app

At this point, we have an entirely synchronous data flow configured using Redux. Now all we need to do is hook it up to our views. As we discussed in the previous chapter, this is where containers come in. In this chapter, we're going to create two containers—one for our `NewsFeed` and one for `Search`. Let's start by creating the `NewsFeedContainer`. Create a file called `NewsFeedContainer.js` inside the `containers` directory:

```
import { connect } from 'react-redux';
import { bindActionCreators } from 'redux';
import { loadNews } from '../actions/newsActions';
import NewsFeed from '../components/NewsFeed';

const mapStateToProps = state => ({
  news: state.news
});

const mapDispatchToProps = dispatch => (
  bindActionCreators({
    loadNews
  }, dispatch)
);

export default connect(mapStateToProps, mapDispatchToProps)(NewsFeed);
```

Here we have a pretty standard container. The `mapStateToProps` method exposes our state tree's news property as a prop to `NewsFeed` called news. Additionally, we expose the `loadNews` action creator as a prop via `mapDispatchToProps`.

Next, create a file inside `src` called `App.js`. The `App` component will become our new root view. It will wrap the `HomeScreen` component and expose the Redux state tree to our app via the `Provider` component:

```
import React from 'react';
import { Provider } from 'react-redux';
import HomeScreen from './components/HomeScreen';
import createStore from './createStore';

const store = createStore();

export default () => (
  <Provider store={store}>
    <HomeScreen />
  </Provider>
);
```

We need to make a few more modifications to bring everything together. Inside `HomeScreen.ios.js`, find this line of code:

```
import NewsFeed from './NewsFeed';
```

Replace it with this:

```
import NewsFeedContainer from '../containers/NewsFeedContainer';
```

Also, replace the `<NewsFeed />` element with `<NewsFeedContainer />` inside the `render` method.

Inside `NewsFeed`, we need to call the `loadNews` action creator in order for our data to begin flowing through our app. Add these three methods to the `NewsFeed` component:

```
componentWillMount() {
  this.refresh();
}

componentWillReceiveProps(nextProps) {
  this.setState({
    dataSource: this.state.dataSource.cloneWithRows(nextProps.news)
  });
}

refresh() {
```

```
  if (this.props.loadNews) {
    this.props.loadNews();
  }
}
```

Additionally, inside the constructor, add the following line of code:

```
this.refresh = this.refresh.bind(this);
```

Then update `propTypes`:

```
NewsFeed.propTypes = {
  news: PropTypes.arrayOf(PropTypes.object),
  listStyles: View.propTypes.style,
  loadNews: PropTypes.func
};
```

Now, when the `NewsFeed` component mounts, it will automatically call `refresh`, which executes the `loadNews` action creator if it's available. Additionally, whenever new props are passed into `NewsFeed`, it will update `dataSource` to match the newly passed-in news prop.

Finally, update `index.ios.js` so that it imports the `App` component instead of the `HomeScreen` component:

```
import {
  AppRegistry
} from 'react-native';
import App from './src/App';

AppRegistry.registerComponent('RNNYT', () => App);
```

Now, if you were to run the app inside the simulator, you might expect everything to just start working. However, what you'll actually see is a big red error message. So what gives?

Refactoring and reshaping

In the last section, we refactored our application to use Redux to handle our data flow. When we first began building this application in Chapter 4, *Starting our Project with React Native Components*, we relied on the `defaultProps` of `NewsFeed` to provide mock data to our application. But our app no longer relies on `defaultProps` because we're now passing news from the Redux state tree via the `NewsFeedContainer`.

But more importantly, the shape of the data we're passing to NewsFeed no longer matches what we originally designed. For example, instead of a description, we have an abstract. Instead of an author, we have a byline. This leaves us with two options. We can update our components to match the data format offered by the NYT API, or we can transform, or reshape, the data we get from the NYT API to match what our components expect. The path we'll follow involves a bit of both.

Refactoring the components

For starters, let's simplify things a bit. Our data is now sourced from mockData.json (and soon from the NYT API). So with that, we can remove NewsFeed defaultProps.

In NewsItem.js, we'll make one adjustment to the propTypes. Instead of date being a JavaScript Date object, we'll just expect it to be a string. Everything else can stay the same:

```
NewsItem.propTypes = {
    imageUrl: PropTypes.string,
    title: PropTypes.string.isRequired,
    description: PropTypes.string,
    date: PropTypes.string.isRequired,
    author: PropTypes.string.isRequired,
    location: PropTypes.string,
    index: PropTypes.number.isRequired,
    onPress: PropTypes.func.isRequired,
    style: View.propTypes.style
};
```

Since the Byline component is ultimately the one that uses the date prop, we should update it as well:

```
Byline.propTypes = {
    date: PropTypes.string.isRequired,
    author: PropTypes.string.isRequired,
    location: PropTypes.string
};
```

Finally, inside the ByLine render method, replace {date.toLocaleDateString()} with just {date}.

Reshaping the data

At this point, we've done all the necessary refactoring of our components, and can begin transforming the data. There are a few different approaches we can take. We could create some custom middleware that sits between the action creators and reducers, and watches for the LOAD_NEWS action. When the middleware sees this action, it could take the raw data from the NYT payload, transform it, and then simply pass it along to the Redux state tree already fully transformed and ready for consumption by our app. Or, we can let the raw data remain unaltered in the state tree and instead transform it in transit from the state tree to our components. Either approach would work, but for this app, we're going to take the latter approach.

Create a file called dataTransformations.js inside the util directory. What we need to do is create a suite of functions that will take the raw NYT data as input and transform it into an array of objects that match the shape expected by the NewsItem component:

```
import moment from 'moment';

const getMultimediaUrlByFormat = (multimedia, format) => {
  if (!multimedia) {
    return '';
  }
  const matchingFormat = multimedia.find(media => media.format === format);
  if (!matchingFormat) {
    return '';
  }
  return matchingFormat.url;
};

export const reshapeNewsData = news => (
  news.map(({ abstract, byline, geo_facet, multimedia, published_date,
title, url }) => ({
    description: abstract || '',
    author: byline ? byline.replace('By ', '') : '',
    location: geo_facet.length > 0 ? geo_facet[0] : '',
    imageUrl: getMultimediaUrlByFormat(multimedia, 'thumbLarge'),
    date: moment(published_date).format('MMM Do YYYY'),
    title,
    url
  }))
);
```

This module exposes the function `reshapeNewsData`. All it does is take the raw news, map over the objects in the array, and return a new array of objects with the properties expected by our components. `reshapeNewsData` uses an additional helper function, `getMultimediaUrlByFormat`, which is used to extract the `imageUrl` of the multimedia property with `thumbLarge` as the format. Additionally, we'll use the moment library to format the date we get from the API into a more human digestible format.

Now, to actually utilize this method, open up `NewsFeedContainer.js`. At the top of the file, add the following:

```
import { reshapeNewsData } from '../util/dataTransformations';
```

Then, update `mapStateToProps` to utilize our transformation utility:

```
const mapStateToProps = state => ({
  news: reshapeNewsData(state.news)
});
```

Finally, if you refresh the app in the simulator, you'll see our mock news displaying as intended!

Adding a searchable news feed

With our `NewsFeed` component fully wired up to a synchronous Redux data flow, we're ready to expand upon our application's features. Currently, the `Search` component doesn't do much other than display a `TextInput`. We'd like it to initially display nothing, but then, as the user beings to type into the `TextInput`, we'll filter the news list, returning only the results that contain the search string in either the description, title, or author values. As we stated earlier, we'll store whatever the user searches for in the state tree as `searchTerm`. The `Search` component will then be passed a collection of matching news items via the `SearchContainer`. `Search` will, in turn, pass that collection down to a child `NewsFeed` element to render the matching results. Taking a step back, this means that the `Search` component's content is derived from two parts of our Redux state tree: news and `searchTerm`.

Introducing Reselect

Redux has amassed a large following over the past year or so. As such, the community of JavaScript libraries supporting Redux has also grown. One popular library, **Reselect**, is designed to compute derived data from a Redux store using a concept known as **selectors**. Selectors are methods that take one or more parts of a Redux state as input and from these compute an output that's appropriate for your components. Reselect is designed for efficiency. It will only compute new output if the input values have changed. This makes Reselect a perfect candidate for exactly what we're trying to accomplish with our Search component.

Before shifting into the Search component, let's look back at some of our existing code. Right now, NewsFeedContainer contains the following function:

```
const mapStateToProps = state => ({
  news: reshapeNewsData(state.news)
});
```

Whenever state is updated, reshapeNewsData is executed. While this certainly gets the job done, this operation could be costly. Since reselect memoizes its selectors, we could utilize it instead and not have to worry about needlessly executing reshapeNewsData when our data hasn't even changed.

Let's install reselect and refactor our existing code to use memoized selectors of reselect:

```
npm install reselect --save
```

Next, create a new directory named selectors within your src directory. In there, add the file newsSelectors.js with the following content:

```
import { createSelector } from 'reselect';
import { reshapeNewsData } from '../util/dataTransformations';

const newsSelector = state => state.news;

const reshapeNewsSelector = createSelector(
  [newsSelector],
  reshapeNewsData
);

export const allNewsSelector = createSelector(
  [reshapeNewsSelector],
  newsItems => newsItems
);
```

Reselect works off two types of `selectors`—**basic input selectors** and **memoized selectors**. Input selectors simply read data from the Redux state. It's important that these input selectors do not in any way transform the data. They are then used as inputs to the more advanced memoized selectors, which are created using `createSelector`. In `newsSelectors.js` we have one input selector called `newsSelector` that simply returns the news portion of our Redux state tree. From there, we create two memoized selectors–`reshapeNewsSelector` and `allNewsSelector`. Memoized selectors take two arguments. The first is an array of inputs or memoized selectors. The values returned from each of these selectors are passed as arguments to the result function. This result function is responsible for the actual data transformation. In the case of `reshapeNewsSelector`, there is only one input selector-`newsSelector`. The input `newsSelector` simply returns `state.news`. Therefore, `state.news` is passed into `reshapeNewsData` as input. We then use `reshapeNewsSelector` as an input selector to `allNewsSelector`. The transformed output of `reshapeNewsSelector` becomes input to the result function of `allNewsSelector`. The result function of `allNewsSelector` simply returns the entire transformed list without modification (`newsItems => newsItems`). Having these two memoized selectors probably feels redundant at the moment. However, later on we'll reuse `reshapeNewsSelector`, making it more useful as a standalone memoized selector.

The only thing that remains is to update `NewsFeedContainer`. Remove the line of code where we import `reshapeNewsData`, and replace it with the following:

```
import { allNewsSelector } from '../selectors/newsSelectors';
```

Then, update `mapStateToProps` to the following (note that we pass it all of state, not just `state.news`):

```
const mapStateToProps = state => ({
  news: allNewsSelector(state)
});
```

Perfect. Now everything should be back to a working state using `reselect`. This sets us up nicely for the next part–adding search to our application.

Adding search

We already have all the Redux state setup that's necessary for search. All that's left to do is to create a `SearchContainer`, update the `Search` component to display the filtered news, and create the necessary selector for filtering the data. Let's begin by creating a function that filters the news.

Open up `dataTransformations.js` and add the following function:

```
export const filterNewsBySearchTerm = (newsItems, searchTerm) => {
  // returns an empty list if you haven't typed anything
  if (searchTerm.length === 0) {
    return [];
  }
  return newsItems.filter(({ description, author, title }) => (
    description.toLowerCase().indexOf(searchTerm) > -1 ||
    author.toLowerCase().indexOf(searchTerm) > -1 ||
    title.toLowerCase().indexOf(searchTerm) > -1
  ));
};
```

Similar to `reshapeNewsData`, `filterNewsBySearchTerm` will be used by a selector. It will take the pre-transformed data as input, along with the search term. If the search term is empty, `filterNewsBySearchTerm` returns an empty list. Otherwise, it filters the news by looking for a string match in the description, author, or title.

Next, inside `newsSelectors.js`, replace the `dataTransformations` import statement with the following:

```
import { reshapeNewsData, filterNewsBySearchTerm } from
'../util/dataTransformations';
```

Then add these selectors to the end of the file:

```
const searchTermSelector = state => state.searchTerm;

const caseInsensitiveSearchTermSelector = createSelector(
  searchTermSelector,
  searchTerm => searchTerm.toLowerCase()
);

export const searchNewsSelector = createSelector(
  [reshapeNewsSelector, caseInsensitiveSearchTermSelector],
  filterNewsBySearchTerm
);
```

`searchTermSelector` is a basic input selector responsible for simply returning the current value of `searchTerm` from the Redux state tree. `caseInsensitiveSearchTermSelector` takes `searchTermSelector` as an input and transforms it to a lowercase string for case-insensitive searching. Finally, `searchNewsSelector` takes two inputs–our previous `reshapeNewsSelector` and `caseInsensitiveSearchTermSelector`. These are passed as arguments to the `filterNewsBySearchTerm` function. The returning value from `filterNewsBySearchTerm` will ultimately be the data exposed to the `SearchContainer`.

Speaking of `SearchContainer`, let's create that next. Inside the `containers` directory, create `SearchContainer.js`:

```
import { connect } from 'react-redux';
import { bindActionCreators } from 'redux';
import { searchNews } from '../actions/newsActions';
import Search from '../components/Search';
import { searchNewsSelector } from '../selectors/newsSelectors';

const mapStateToProps = state => ({
  filteredNews: searchNewsSelector(state)
});

const mapDispatchToProps = dispatch => (
  bindActionCreators({
    searchNews
  }, dispatch)
);

export default connect(mapStateToProps, mapDispatchToProps)(Search);
```

`SearchContainer` operates much the same as `NewsFeedContainer`. However, in this case we'll expose two props to the `Search` component–`filteredNews` and the action creator `searchNews`.

Next, we'll update `Search`. Open up `Search.js` and import `PropTypes` from React, along with the `NewsFeed` component. Then, update the `Search` component to match the following while keeping the existing styles intact:

```
import React, { Component, PropTypes } from 'react';
import {
  View,
  TextInput,
  StyleSheet
} from 'react-native';
import NewsFeed from './NewsFeed';
import * as globalStyles from '../styles/global';

export default class Search extends Component {

  constructor(props) {
    super(props);
    this.state = {
      searchText: ''
    };
    this.searchNews = this.searchNews.bind(this);
  }
```

```
  searchNews(text) {
    this.setState({ searchText: text });
    this.props.searchNews(text);
  }

  render() {
    return (
      <View style={globalStyles.COMMON_STYLES.pageContainer}>
        <View style={styles.search}>
          <TextInput
            style={styles.input}
            onChangeText={this.searchNews}
            value={this.state.searchText}
            placeholder={'Search'}
            placeholderTextColor={globalStyles.MUTED_COLOR}
          />
        </View>
        <NewsFeed news={this.props.filteredNews} listStyles={{{}}} />
      </View>
    );
  }
}

Search.propTypes = {
  filteredNews: PropTypes.arrayOf(PropTypes.object),
  searchNews: PropTypes.func.isRequired
};
```

We've created a method called `searchNews` to replace the inline `onChangeText` handler of `TextInput`. On top of updating the component's internal state, it will pass the search text along to the Redux state tree via the `searchNews` action creator. Additionally, the `NewsFeed` component will accept `filteredNews` passed down by the `SearchContainer` as its news.

Finally, to bring it all together, open up `HomeScreen.ios.js` and import `SearchContainer` in lieu of the `Search` component:

```
import SearchContainer from '../containers/SearchContainer';
```

Then, replace `<Search />` with `<SearchContainer />`. With that final change, you now have a functioning search tab!

Wiring up the NYT API with asynchronous requests

The final piece of our Redux workflow requires that we actually hook up our app to the real NYT API. If you haven't done so already, you'll need to register for the NYT API. Visit http ://developer.nytimes.com/ and register for an NYT API key. Once you have your API key, create a file inside the config directory called nytApiKey.js:

```
const NYT_API_KEY = 'YOUR_API_KEY_GOES_HERE';
export default NYT_API_KEY;
```

Up to this point, we've used an entirely synchronous Redux workflow. However, with the help of middleware, we can return actions from action creators that, instead of data, contain promises. fetch is a JavaScript polyfill provided by React Native for managing Ajax requests as promises. fetch, combined with the Redux-promise middleware, will easily allow us to request data from the NYT API without needing to heavily refactor our code.

Begin by installing the Redux-promise middleware:

```
npm install redux-promise --save
```

Next, open newsActions.js. Remove mockData and instead import your API key:

```
import NYT_API_KEY from '../config/nytApiKey';
```

Then, replace the loadNews action creator with the following:

```
export const loadNews = () => {
  const req =
fetch(`https://api.nytimes.com/svc/topstories/v2/technology.json?api-key=${
NYT_API_KEY}`);
  return {
    type: LOAD_NEWS,
    payload: req.then(response => response.json())
  };
};
```

The updated `loadNews` action creator begins by creating a promise called `req`. `req` is then set as the `payload` of the returned Redux action. The Redux-promise middleware will intercept this action and resolve the promise automatically before it ever hits the reducers. Take a look at the following diagram:

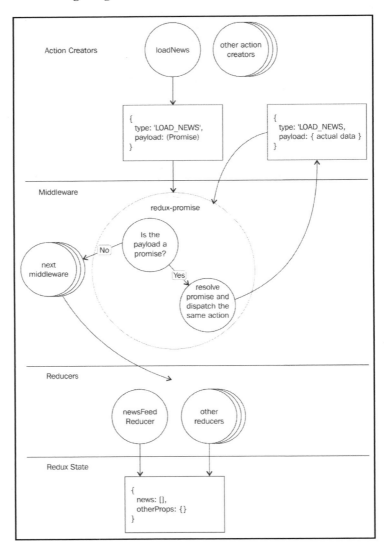

The previous diagram illustrates how the Redux-promise middleware works. Actions are dispatched from our action creators. All actions are then passed through any middleware we have installed. Once the action reaches the Redux-promise middleware, it will inspect its `payload` property to see if it's a promise. If it's not, it will just forward the action along to the next middleware, and then ultimately out to the reducers. If the `payload` property is a promise, Redux-promise stops the action from moving forward and instead waits for the promise to resolve. If the promise resolves successfully, Redux-promise will take the original action and replace the old promise payload with the actual data returned from the promise. Then it simply re-dispatches the updated action. The action will flow through the middleware chain again. However, when the action hits the Redux-promise middleware this time, the `payload` is no longer a promise, and thus simply passes through the middleware and off to the reducers.

Now all that's left is to make our store aware of the Redux–promise middleware. In `createStore.js`, add the following `import` statement:

```
import promiseMiddleware from 'redux-promise';
```

Then, update the `applyMiddleware` call, adding `promiseMiddleware` as a parameter, as shown in the following code snippet:

```
export default (initialState = {}) => (
  createStore(
    combineReducers({
      news: newsFeedReducer,
      searchTerm: searchTermReducer
    }),
    initialState,
    applyMiddleware(logger, promiseMiddleware)
  )
);
```

Now, if you refresh your app one more time, you'll see live data from the NYT API that is fully searchable!

Redux-promise is just one of many middleware libraries out there for adding asynchronous support to Redux. It works great as an introductory tool because it's so simple. However, if your application requires more advanced behavior, you may want to explore other Redux middleware, such as Redux **Thunk** or Redux **Saga**.
Refer to the following links:
https://github.com/gaearon/redux-thunk
https://github.com/yelouafi/redux-saga

Fixing iOS transport security

While our `NewsFeed` and `Search` are displaying live data as expected, if you click on any of the `NewItem` elements to expose the `Modal`, you'll likely encounter an error. As of version 0.28, the React Native CLI is a bit less promiscuous with iOS security. Apple very much wants all connections within the apps running on its platform to be secure. In our case, we're trying to load a webpage from the NY Times over an insecure HTTP request. We can easily create an exception for our app by modifying the `Info.plist` file found inside the `ios/RNNYT` directory. Open up `Info.plist` and locate `NSAppTransportSecurity`. Currently, there's an exception being made only for localhost. Update `Info.plist` to add a `nytimes.com` exception, as shown in the following code:

```
<key>NSAppTransportSecurity</key>
    <!--See
http://ste.vn/2015/06/10/configuring-app-transport-security-ios-9-osx-10-11
/ -->
    <dict>
        <key>NSExceptionDomains</key>
        <dict>
            <key>localhost</key>
            <dict>
                <key>NSTemporaryExceptionAllowsInsecureHTTPLoads</key>
                <true/>
            </dict>
            <key>nytimes.com</key>
            <dict>
                <key>NSIncludesSubdomains</key>
                <true/>
                <key>NSTemporaryExceptionAllowsInsecureHTTPLoads</key>
                <true/>
            </dict>
        </dict>
    </dict>
```

If you're currently running your app in the simulator, you'll need to stop it and redeploy it for the changes to take effect. If you run into any issues, check your console. It's very easy to accidentally include too many or too few `<dict></dict>` tags within `Info.plist`.

Adding pull to refresh and a loading spinner

Just as a final touch, let's improve the user experience by adding **pull to refresh** and a loading spinner to the `NewsFeed`. Thankfully React Native makes this super easy. Inside `NewsFeed.js`, import `RefreshControl` and `ActivityIndicator`, as shown in the following code snippet:

```
import {
  ListView,
  StyleSheet,
  View,
  Modal,
  TouchableOpacity,
  WebView,
  RefreshControl,
  ActivityIndicator
} from 'react-native';
```

Next, we'll need to add two new properties to the state of `NewsFeed`--refreshing and `initialLoading`. `refreshing` will be used by `RefreshControl` to track whether `NewsFeed` is still loading after a pull to refresh. `initialLoading` will be used to display a loading icon (`ActivityIndicator`) while we're waiting for the data to initially load. Take a look at the following code snippet:

```
this.state = {
  dataSource: this.ds.cloneWithRows(props.news),
  initialLoading: true,
  modalVisible: false,
  refreshing: false
};
```

Whenever we've received data back from the NYT API, we'll need to set `initialLoading` to `false`:

```
componentWillReceiveProps(nextProps) {
  this.setState({
    dataSource: this.state.dataSource.cloneWithRows(nextProps.news),
    initialLoading: false
  });
}
```

We only want to show the `ActivityIndicator` if we're loading the `NewsFeed` from the primary tab. We can control this via a prop.

Update `propTypes` of `NewsFeed` to add the `showLoadingSpinner` prop and add a `defaultProp`, setting it to `true`:

```
NewsFeed.propTypes = {
  news: PropTypes.arrayOf(PropTypes.object),
  listStyles: View.propTypes.style,
  loadNews: PropTypes.func,
  showLoadingSpinner: PropTypes.bool
};

NewsFeed.defaultProps = {
  showLoadingSpinner: true
};
```

Next, update the `render` method:

```
render() {
  const {
    listStyles = globalStyles.COMMON_STYLES.pageContainer,
    showLoadingSpinner
  } = this.props;
  const { initialLoading, refreshing, dataSource } = this.state;

  return (
    (initialLoading && showLoadingSpinner
      ? (
        <View style={[listStyles, styles.loadingContainer]}>
          <ActivityIndicator
            animating
            size="small"
            {...this.props}
          />
        </View>
      ) : (
        <View style={styles.container}>
          <ListView
            refreshControl={
              <RefreshControl
                refreshing={refreshing}
                onRefresh={this.refresh}
              />
            }
            enableEmptySections
            dataSource={dataSource}
            renderRow={this.renderRow}
            style={listStyles}
          />
          {this.renderModal()}
```

```
      </View>
    )
  )
);
}
```

Next, add the container and `loadingContainer` styles to the `StyleSheet`:

```
const styles = StyleSheet.create({
  newsItem: {
    marginBottom: 20
  },
  container: {
    flex: 1
  },
  loadingContainer: {
    alignItems: 'center',
    justifyContent: 'center'
  },
  modalContent: {
    flex: 1,
    justifyContent: 'center',
    paddingTop: 20,
    backgroundColor: globalStyles.BG_COLOR
  },
  closeButton: {
    paddingVertical: 5,
    paddingHorizontal: 10,
    flexDirection: 'row'
  }
});
```

Finally, update the `Search` component so that it sets `showLoadingSpinner` for the `NewsFeed` to `false`:

```
<NewsFeed
  news={this.props.filteredNews}
  listStyles={{}}
  showLoadingSpinner={false}
/>
```

Pull to refresh is also pretty straightforward. The `RefreshControl` invokes our component's refresh method, which calls the `loadNews` action creator. The NYT `Top Stories` API doesn't update too frequently, so don't be alarmed if the data doesn't seem to change after pulling to refresh. But otherwise, you're all done!

Summary

In this chapter, we applied our knowledge of Redux to our RNNYT app. We also tackled real-world scenarios, such as reshaping/transforming data, creating derived data with Reselect, and resolving asynchronous actions using middleware. We even improved the user experience by adding a loading icon and pull to refresh capability. With all this in place, users can now navigate to the **Search** tab to seek out specific news items. Currently, all navigation within the app is handled by the `TabBarIOS` component. In the next chapter, we'll expand upon our app's navigation capabilities by reviewing some of React Native's navigation APIs.

7
Navigation and Advanced APIs

The React Native framework is certainly young and many of its APIs are still evolving and settling in (we're not even upto version 1.0.0!), but nothing demonstrates this quite as well as navigation. Even though we've built a simple application without using a navigation API, navigating between scenes is pretty fundamental to a mobile application, especially as it grows. Because it is so fundamental and, to be frank, complex, it has gone through several drafts. At the time of writing, there are still multiple supported navigation APIs that a React Native developer has to choose from.

In this chapter, we will untangle navigation libraries by looking at the differences and use cases for each. We will also implement some formal navigation into our news reader application. Finally, we will look at a few other advanced React Native APIs that can be used to take our relatively simple application to the next level.

Specifically, we'll cover:

- The React Native navigation landscape, from a high level
- Implementing the `Navigator` API
- Implementing the `NavigationExperimental` API
- Using advanced React Native APIs such as `AsyncStorage` and `NetInfo`

Navigation landscape

React Native was first released with two competing navigation APIs. Facebook was internally experimenting with two different approaches to navigation when it was time to open source the library, so, rather than choose one over the other, both were included. As time went on, it was discovered that there were some pain points with those initial APIs and use cases, so a new navigation API that was more versatile and extensible was crafted. In addition to these official APIs, other community members, who wanted to create navigation APIs that reflected those used in React for the Web, created a number of projects on top of the React Native modules.

This is where we are today, with so many navigation options it could make your head spin. Fear not, for we will delve into each of these and give you the information you need to pick the best navigation strategy for your project.

NavigatorIOS

The NavigatorIOS component is built on top of the native iOS navigational components. This means that all navigational animations are run on the main, native thread and do not require input from JavaScript. For this reason, NavigatorIOS will typically have the best performance characteristics of all the navigation options, at least for now.

 Though it is true that NavigatorIOS currently has an advantage in the performance department, there is active work being done in React Native to offload more animations in more parts of the framework to native threads. This will likely lead to a narrowing of this performance gap, to the point where it is irrelevant in the near future.

There are some fairly obvious drawbacks to the NavigatorIOS API. The first of these is right there in the name: iOS. This component and navigation strategy is not cross-platform compatible, so if your application will target both iOS and Android, this is a non-starter. There has also been some indication that NavigatorIOS will not be developed further by the core React Native team.

For these reasons and more, it would be best to steer clear of this component for most use cases. One could imagine a simple iOS-only application developed to be used for a short period of time where NavigatorIOS would suffice, but even then, justifying it would be a stretch.

Navigator

The Navigator component is the other original React Native navigation API. It was designed to be a JavaScript implementation of basically the same API as NavigatorIOS. The obvious advantage that this component has over NavigatorIOS is that it works on both iOS and Android. Until recently, this was the recommended solution for navigation in React Native applications.

In addition to the fact that it can be less performant than native alternatives, again, this is poised to change, there are other reasons why we might consider other navigation APIs. The Navigator component was designed to have an API similar to NavigatorIOS and, because of this, does not fit perfectly into the React and Redux paradigm.

For starters, API of the Navigator for changing scenes is imperative. In order to navigate, we have to pass around a reference to the component to other components. This is contrary to the React philosophy of declaratively defined UI components and can feel awkward lumped into an application built with this philosophy.

Second, the Navigator and NavigatorIOS components store all of the application's navigation state internally. In a Redux application, we learned that all application states should be stored in the store. With the navigation state confined to the Navigator component, the store is no longer the source of truth for what is happening in the application.

Finally, while the Navigator and NavigatorIOS components support simple forms of push and pop navigation, they do not support more advanced navigational structures such as tabbed or drawer navigation. In an application that has these more advanced patterns, using Navigator forces you to store navigational state not in just one component, but in multiple (that is, TabBarIOS).

These drawbacks are not especially apparent if the application is very simple. However, as our applications grow larger and the navigation state becomes more complex, they become a little painful. At some point, the React Native team determined that there must be a better way.

NavigationExperimental

NavigationExperimental is the cutting-edge navigational API that the React Native team has indicated is the future of navigation for the library. As its name suggests, it is neither complete nor stable. This means that we must use it with caution, realizing it will likely change over time. Though the API may change in some ways, what likely won't change is the approach NavigationExperimental takes and how this approach differs from the other available options.

NavigationExperimental was designed with two primary and related goals in mind. First, the components are not stateful, such as Navigator and NavigatorIOS; second, its API is declarative unlike the imperative API of the other navigators. The first goal is intended at making NavigationExperimental work well with Flux or Redux architectures that require the application state be kept outside the React components. The second goal is aimed to make NavigationExperimental feel more natural in React, which is largely defined by declarative component definitions.

A result of achieving these goals is an API that is much more flexible and customizable than other available options. This flexibility comes with a steeper learning curve, which makes NavigationExperimental less intuitive than other forms of navigation. Also, where the other navigators are primarily a single React component, NavigationExperimental is a collection of components and utilities that are used in tandem.

Choosing a navigator

As much as we'd like to give a definitive answer to the question: *What navigation API should I use in my new app?* At the moment, there is no obvious choice. Instead, there are pros and cons to each that must be weighed in the context of the application itself.

The case for NavigatorIOS is hard to make and gets harder by the day. The strongest argument against it is that it precludes cross-platform applications or would require two implementations of navigation. In the past, the superior animation performance of this native-built component might have been a reason to use it, but this difference is now negligible in most scenarios and that trend will continue as React Native offloads more types of animation to native threads. However, if this performance boost is deemed important to your application, there are external libraries that implement a similar API using all native components on both platforms and may be worth investigating.

For simple applications, such as an application for which even Flux or Redux would be considered over-engineering or an application that has a simple navigational structure, it is still probably a good idea to use the `Navigator` API. `Navigator` is cross-platform-compatible, relatively easy to use, and perhaps most importantly stable. There are drawbacks, but for simple applications, these can largely be overlooked.

For big applications with complex state and navigational structures, it is worth learning and implementing `NavigationExperimental`, especially if starting from scratch. Yes, this will likely mean at least some refactoring when upgrading React Native until the API completely stabilizes. On the bright side, there has been some indication that these changes will not be large from here on out and that stability is not far off. The declarative nature of `NavigationExperimental` allows for rich navigational structures that can be managed independently of the components used to display the interface.

Finally, there is another option. In all of the commotion over the official navigational APIs, numerous external libraries have also emerged. These libraries are generally built on top of React Native navigational libraries and seek to either make the implementation process simpler, make navigation in mobile applications more similar to web navigational patterns that most React developers are familiar with, or create stabilized APIs with similar principles to `NavigationExperimental`. These libraries are too numerous to examine in any depth, nor is there a clear leader among the pack. However, they may be worth further investigation before deciding on a navigation solution for a new application.

In this chapter, we will first use `Navigator` to add a simple introduction screen to our news reader application. Then, we will refactor the application to have the navigational state managed separately from the navigational components by implementing `NavigationExperimental`.

Using Navigator

In this section, we're going to add a simple introduction screen to our application that is presented to the user before the news feed. When they tap the screen, it will navigate to the home screen that we currently have in the application, as shown in the following screenshot:

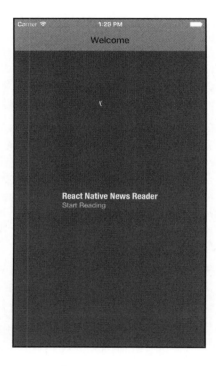

The first thing we'll do is create a simple new component for this intro screen in a new `src/components/IntroScreen.js` file:

```
import React, { PropTypes } from 'react';
import {
  View,
  TouchableOpacity,
  StatusBar,
  StyleSheet
} from 'react-native';
import Title from './Title';
import AppText from './AppText';
import * as globalStyles from '../styles/global';

// Set the status bar for iOS to light
```

```
StatusBar.setBarStyle('light-content');

const IntroScreen = ({ onPress }) => (
  <View style={[globalStyles.COMMON_STYLES.pageContainer,
styles.container]}>
    <TouchableOpacity
      onPress={onPress}
    >
      <Title>React Native News Reader</Title>
      <AppText>
        Start Reading
      </AppText>
    </TouchableOpacity>
  </View>
);

IntroScreen.propTypes = {
  onPress: PropTypes.func.isRequired
};

const styles = StyleSheet.create({
  container: {
    marginBottom: 0,
    justifyContent: 'center',
    alignItems: 'center'
  }
});

export default IntroScreen;
```

`IntroScreen` is a straightforward component that simply displays some text and performs an action when the text is pressed:

```
<TouchableOpacity
  onPress={onPress}
>
  <Title>React Native News Reader</Title>
  <AppText>
    Start Reading
  </AppText>
</TouchableOpacity>
```

The Navigator component

Now we have two independent screens, the IntroScreen and the HomeScreen, and we need the ability to navigate between them. If we look into the application's entry point, the App.js file, we see that currently the HomeScreen component is at the top level of our application, as shown in the following code snippet:

```
export default () => (
  <Provider store={store}>
    <HomeScreen />
  </Provider>
);
```

This raises an important issue: when we introduce formal navigation into a project, the navigation component is typically the top-level component (or near it) for the entire application. The navigator is responsible for determining at the highest level what components are displayed to the user, so it makes intuitive sense that it should manage individual screens as its children.

Therefore, our next step is to create a new Nav component and add it to the App.js file in place of the HomeScreen component. The Nav component will then display IntroScreen and HomeScreen when appropriate. The first step is to import the Navigator, HomeScreen, and the new IntroScreen modules, along with some other components that we will be using, into a new src/components/Nav.js file:

```
import React, { Component } from 'react';
import { Navigator, TouchableOpacity, StyleSheet } from 'react-native';

import HomeScreen from './HomeScreen';
import IntroScreen from './IntroScreen';

import Title from './Title';
import SmallText from './SmallText';

import * as globalStyles from '../styles/global';
```

The `Navigator` component uses route objects to describe what screens to show. Route objects are largely up to us as implementers to design. For our application we have two routes: one for the `IntroScreen` and another for the `HomeScreen`. We will define these routes at the top of the `Nav.js` file:

```
const HOME_ROUTE = { title: 'RNNYT' };
const INTRO_ROUTE = { title: 'Welcome' };
```

We will now create the `Nav` component class and, in its `render` method, simply return a `Navigator` component with two props. The `initialState` property tells the `Navigator` which route to display when the `App` component is first rendered. The `renderScene` property takes a function that tells the `Navigator` how to render a scene from currently active route objects, as shown in the following code snippet:

```
export default class Nav extends Component {

  render() {
    return (
      <Navigator
        initialRoute={INTRO_ROUTE}
        renderScene={this.renderScene}
      />
    );
  }

}
```

Here we define the `renderScene` method that tells our `Navigator` how to render the routes into React components. Take a look at the following code snippet:

```
renderScene(route, navigator) {
  if (route === INTRO_ROUTE) {
    return (
      <IntroScreen
        onPress={() => navigator.push(HOME_ROUTE)}
      />
    );
  }
  return <HomeScreen />;
}
```

Notice that the `renderScene` function gets not only the current route as an argument, but also a reference to the `Navigator` component itself. This is necessary because new scenes are navigated to by using an imperative API of the `Navigator`. We make use of this by passing the `IntroScene` component an `onPress` function property. This function passes the `HomeScreen` route to the `push` method of the `Navigator`:

```
onPress={() => navigator.push(HOME_ROUTE)}
```

The `Navigator` manages its state as a stack data structure where scenes can be pushed and popped. Pushing scenes goes forward and popping goes back to the previous scene on the stack. In addition to these operations, the `Navigator` can also reset the entire stack, replace the current top scene, and more. In our simple, linear navigational structure, we only need a small subset of these methods.

If our application has many scenes, we can imagine the `renderScene` method getting large if we were to follow the same approach outlined in the previous section. To make scene rendering more generic, we'll include a component to render and props to pass to it within the route objects:

```
const HOME_ROUTE = {
  title: 'RNNYT',
  component: HomeScreen
};
const INTRO_ROUTE = {
  title: 'Welcome',
  component: IntroScreen,
  props: {
    nextScene: HOME_ROUTE
  }
};
```

We can now refactor the `renderScene` method to use these new routes:

```
renderScene(route, navigator) {
  return (
    <route.component
      {...route.props}
    />
  );
}
```

Now, however, we've lost the ability to navigate to the next scene because we are not passing an `onPress` property to the `IntroScreen`. To remedy this, a common solution is to pass a reference to the navigator to all the scene components. This is where `Navigator` starts to become a bit messy, but for our application it is still not too bad. First, we'll pass the navigator reference to all the components rendered:

```
renderScene(route, navigator) {
  return (
    <route.component
      {...route.props}
      navigator={navigator}
    />
  );
}
```

And then we will refactor the `IntroScreen` component to use the reference directly, along with its new `nextScene` prop:

```
const IntroScreen = ({ navigator, nextScene }) => (
  <View style={[globalStyles.COMMON_STYLES.pageContainer,
styles.container]}>
    <TouchableOpacity
      onPress={() => navigator.push(nextScene)}
    >
      <Title>React Native News Reader</Title>
      <AppText>
        Start Reading
      </AppText>
    </TouchableOpacity>
  </View>
);


IntroScreen.propTypes = {
  navigator: PropTypes.shape({
    push: PropTypes.func
  }).isRequired,
  nextScene: PropTypes.objectOf(PropTypes.any)
};
```

This is all that is required for simple navigation. However, if we look at the earlier screenshot, one thing is missing: a navigation bar.

Navigation bar

We now have the ability to navigate forward-push onto the navigation stack, but what if we want to go back? A common way to handle this in mobile applications is to use a top navigation bar that displays a title, Back button, or other menu buttons, as shown in the following screenshot:

The `Navigator` API has a `Navigator.NavigationBar` component, which can be passed into the `Navigator` as a prop for this purpose. We'll first create a method for rendering a `NavigationBar` in the `Nav` component (`src/components/Nav.js`):

```
renderNavigationBar() {
  return (
    <Navigator.NavigationBar
      style={styles.navbar}
    />
  );
}
```

We will need to add some styles to `NavigationBar` to make it match the look and feel of our application, so at the bottom of the `Nav.js` file we'll add a `StyleSheet`:

```
const styles = StyleSheet.create({
  navbar: {
    backgroundColor: globalStyles.MUTED_COLOR
  }
});
```

Additionally, we'll need to update the `pageContainer` style in the global styles file (`src/styles/global.js`) to add some margin to the top of our screens and get out of the way of the new `NavigationBar`:

```
pageContainer: {
  backgroundColor: BG_COLOR,
```

```
    flex: 1,
    marginTop: 50,
    paddingTop: 20,
    marginBottom: 48,
    marginHorizontal: 0,
    paddingHorizontal: 10
  }
```

Next, we need to tell the `NavigationBar` what to render on the left-hand side, right-hand side, and for the title. We do this by passing the `NavigationBar` component a property called `routeMapper`. This object has three keys `LeftButton`, `RightButton`, and `Title`. The value for each of these keys is a function that receives the current route and returns the appropriate component, as shown in the following code snippet:

```
renderNavigationBar() {
  return (
    <Navigator.NavigationBar
      routeMapper={{
        LeftButton: this.renderLeftButton,
        RightButton: () => null,
        Title: this.renderTitle
      }}
      style={styles.navbar}
    />
  );
}
```

For our application, we will never show a button on the right-hand side of the `NavigationBar`, so that function will simply return `null` no matter what the current route is:

```
RightButton: () => null
```

For the left-hand side, we want to show a **Back** button, but only when there is more than one route on the Navigator's internal navigation stack. Luckily for us, `routeMapper` functions receive, in addition to the current route, a reference to the navigator as well as the current route's index. Since the first route on the stack has `index` 0, we only want to render a **Back** button when the `index` is not 0, as shown in the following code snippet:

```
renderLeftButton(route, navigator, index) {
  if (index === 0) {
    return null;
  }
  return (
    <TouchableOpacity
      style={styles.leftButton}
```

```
      onPress={() => navigator.pop()}
    >
      <SmallText>Back</SmallText>
    </TouchableOpacity>
  );
}
```

Here, we use another of the Navigator's methods: pop. This method pops a scene from the Navigator component's internal stack. In other words, this allows the user to go back. Take a look at the following code snippet:

```
onPress={() => navigator.pop()}
```

Finally, we'll use the title stored in the route to render a Title component in the center of the NavigationBar:

```
renderTitle(route) {
  return (
    <Title style={styles.title}>
      {route.title}
    </Title>
  );
}
```

We'll also need to add styles for both the left button and the title:

```
const styles = StyleSheet.create({
  navbar: {
    backgroundColor: globalStyles.MUTED_COLOR
  },
  leftButton: {
    padding: 12
  },
  title: {
    padding: 8,
    backgroundColor: globalStyles.MUTED_COLOR
  }
});
```

Now that we have a completed renderNavigationBar method, we need to use it to create a NavigationBar for our Navigator component:

```
render() {
  return (
    <Navigator
      initialRoute={INTRO_ROUTE}
      renderScene={this.renderScene}
      navigationBar={this.renderNavigationBar()}
```

```
      />
  );
}
```

We've now completed our Nav component, which will act as the manager for navigation in our application. Here it is in full:

```
import React, { Component } from 'react';
import { Navigator, TouchableOpacity, StyleSheet } from 'react-native';

import HomeScreen from './HomeScreen';
import IntroScreen from './IntroScreen';

import Title from './Title';
import SmallText from './SmallText';

import * as globalStyles from '../styles/global';

const HOME_ROUTE = {
  title: 'RNNYT',
  component: HomeScreen
};
const INTRO_ROUTE = {
  title: 'Welcome',
  component: IntroScreen,
  props: {
    nextScene: HOME_ROUTE
  }
};

export default class Nav extends Component {

  renderScene(route, navigator) {
    return (
      <route.component
        {...route.props}
        navigator={navigator}
      />
    );
  }

  renderLeftButton(route, navigator, index) {
    if (index === 0) {
      return null;
    }
    return (
      <TouchableOpacity
        style={styles.leftButton}
```

```
            onPress={() => navigator.pop()}
          >
            <SmallText>Back</SmallText>
          </TouchableOpacity>
        );
      }

      renderTitle(route) {
        return (
          <Title style={styles.title}>
            {route.title}
          </Title>
        );
      }

      renderNavigationBar() {
        return (
          <Navigator.NavigationBar
            routeMapper={{
              LeftButton: this.renderLeftButton,
              RightButton: () => null,
              Title: this.renderTitle
            }}
            style={styles.navbar}
          />
        );
      }

      render() {
        return (
          <Navigator
            initialRoute={INTRO_ROUTE}
            renderScene={this.renderScene}
            navigationBar={this.renderNavigationBar()}
          />
        );
      }

    }

const styles = StyleSheet.create({
  navbar: {
    backgroundColor: globalStyles.MUTED_COLOR
  },
  leftButton: {
    padding: 12
  },
  title: {
```

```
    padding: 8,
    backgroundColor: globalStyles.MUTED_COLOR
  }
});
```

`Navigator` works well in this scenario and might continue to work well in a simple linear navigation structure. However, the navigation in our application is not as simple as we've made it out to be and, thus, we may decide to look for other alternatives.

Advanced navigation with NavigationExperimental

While the navigation we implemented in the previous section is rather simple, the navigational structure of our entire application is actually less so. Not only do we navigate between the intro and home screens, but we also navigate between tabs and show modals for individual articles. With this in mind, where do we go to find out exactly where a user is in the application?

The answer to this question currently is that there is no one place to look. The navigational state is stored within the `Navigator` component, the `HomeScreen` component, and within the `NewsFeed` components. As our application gets larger, this opaque and disparate method of storing navigational state will become increasingly painful.

Our goal in this section is to use the components and utilities of the `NavigationExperimental` API to extract this navigational state from components and insert it into our Redux store. In doing so we'll need to remove `Navigator` and refactor `HomeScreen` and `NewsFeed` to once again attain declarative view definitions.

Representing the navigation state

When using the `Navigator`, all of the navigational state is contained and managed within that React component. When using `NavigationExperimental`, we take control of the navigational state and therefore need to decide how it should be represented. Some of the representation is dictated by the `NavigationExperimental` API, but some is up to the application developer.

We'll start by looking at the navigational state object for the very simple, two-scene example from the previous section:

```
{
  index: 0,
  routes: [
    { key: 'intro' }
  ]
}
```

The `routes` array is the navigation stack where each object in the array represents a scene on the stack. The `index` points to the scene in the `routes` stack that is currently visible. When the application first loads, there is a single scene on the stack (the intro screen), which is located at `index` 0. When the user navigates to the next scene (the home screen), a navigational `push` operation is performed by pushing a scene object into the `routes` array and incrementing the `index`:

```
{
  index: 1,
  routes: [
    { key: 'intro' },
    { key: 'home' }
  ]
}
```

The shape we are using for the state so far is one mandated by the `NavigationExperimental` API. The navigational state must have an `index` and `routes` array. Each `route` object within the array must also have a unique `key` string. It is common practice to append a timestamp or some other random number to the route's name in order to ensure that it is unique. However, in our application there are only two scenes and they will not appear on the stack more than once, so this is not necessary.

The rest of the data inside of the `route` objects is up to us as application developers to decide on. Adhering to the pattern established in the `Navigator` section, we'll also include a title as well as the scene's React component:

```
{
  index: 1,
  routes: [
    { key: 'intro', title: 'Welcome', component: IntroScreen },
    { key: 'home', title: 'RNNYT', component: HomeScreen }
  ]
}
```

This state representation is adequate for replacing the `Navigator` in our application. The next step is to create a Redux reducer to manage this state and Redux actions to manipulate it.

Managing the navigation state

First, we'll need to make some actions that can be used to manipulate the navigation state in our application. These actions will mimic the two `Navigator` methods from the previous section: `push` (to advance to a scene) and `pop` (to go back). We'll create a new `src/actions/navigationActions.js` file and create our actions in there:

```
import {
  NAVIGATION_PUSH,
  NAVIGATION_POP
} from './actionTypes';

export const push = key => ({
  type: NAVIGATION_PUSH,
  payload: key
});

export const pop = () => ({
  type: NAVIGATION_POP
});
```

For the `push` action, we specify the scene to add to the navigation stack by using the unique route key, which is added to the action's `payload`:

```
export const push = key => ({
  type: NAVIGATION_PUSH,
  payload: key
});
```

We'll also need to add these new action types to the `actionTypes.js` file:

```
export const LOAD_NEWS = 'LOAD_NEWS';
export const SEARCH_NEWS = 'SEARCH_NEWS';

export const NAVIGATION_PUSH = 'NAVIGATION_PUSH';
export const NAVIGATION_POP = 'NAVIGATION_POP';
```

Next, we need to create the reducer that listens for these actions. In a new
`src/reducers/navigationReducer.js` file, we'll start by creating an initial application
state object based on the preceding discussion:

```
import HomeScreen from '../components/HomeScreen';
import IntroScreen from '../components/IntroScreen';

const routes = {
  home: {
    key: 'home',
    title: 'RNNYT',
    component: HomeScreen
  },
  intro: {
    key: 'intro',
    title: 'Welcome',
    component: IntroScreen
  }
};
const initialState = {
  index: 0,
  routes: [
    routes.intro
  ]
};
```

Here, we've created a map of route objects and initialized the navigation state with only the
intro route on the stack. Next, we'll define the `reduce` method to produce a new navigation
state object when a `NAVIGATION_PUSH` or `NAVIGATION_POP` action is dispatched. To do this
we'll use a utility from the `NavigationExperimental` library called `StateUtils`:

```
import { NavigationExperimental } from 'react-native';
import {
  NAVIGATION_PUSH,
  NAVIGATION_POP
} from '../actions/actionTypes';
import HomeScreen from '../components/HomeScreen';
import IntroScreen from '../components/IntroScreen';

const { StateUtils } = NavigationExperimental;
```

The `StateUtils` module comes with several functions for working with navigation state
objects. It has both `push` and `pop` functions, in addition to many that we can use directly to
modify the navigation state of our application in the ways described in the previous section;
this is shown in the following code snippet:

```
export default (state = initialState, action = {}) => {
```

```
    if (action.type === NAVIGATION_PUSH) {
      return StateUtils.push(state, routes[action.payload]);
    } else if (action.type === NAVIGATION_POP) {
      return StateUtils.pop(state);
    }
    return state;
};
```

Finally, we must register this new reducer in the Redux store. This means updating `createStore.js`:

```
import { createStore, applyMiddleware, combineReducers } from 'redux';
import createLogger from 'redux-logger';
import newsFeedReducer from './reducers/newsFeedReducer';
import navigationReducer from './reducers/navigationReducer';
import searchTermReducer from './reducers/searchTermReducer';
import promiseMiddleware from 'redux-promise';

const logger = createLogger();

export default (initialState = {}) => {
  return createStore(combineReducers({
      news: newsFeedReducer,
      searchTerm: searchTermReducer,
      navigation: navigationReducer
    }),
    initialState,
    applyMiddleware(logger, promiseMiddleware)
  );
};
```

Now that we have the ability to manage the navigational state on our own, we must create a container component to use this information.

The CardStack component

The first step to incorporating the new navigation store into our application is to refactor the Nav component from the previous section. Rather than using the stateful Navigator component, we'll instead make this a simple presentational component using the NavigationExperimental API. Within the refactored Nav component, we will be using a NavigationExperimental component called the CardStack.

As was mentioned before, the NavigationExperimental API actually includes several components. The core component of the NavigationExperimental API is called NavigationTransitioner. NavigationTransitioner is an extremely powerful and flexible component that can be used with many different navigational patterns. As we have heard before, this power and flexibility comes with a steep learning curve. Luckily, the CardStack is a wrapper around this component that simplifies implementation of the most common stack-based navigational patterns.

Let's start by removing the Navigator-based functionality from the current Nav component and importing CardStack from NavigationExperimental:

```
import React, { Component, PropTypes } from 'react';
import {
  StyleSheet,
  NavigationExperimental
} from 'react-native';

import * as globalStyles from '../styles/global';

const { CardStack } = NavigationExperimental;

export default class Nav extends Component {

}

Nav.propTypes = {
  push: PropTypes.func.isRequired,
  pop: PropTypes.func.isRequired,
  navigation: PropTypes.objectOf(PropTypes.any)
};

const styles = StyleSheet.create({
});
```

Notice that we have added propTypes to the new Nav component. It will now receive the navigation state object, which will eventually come from the Redux store, and two action creator functions: push and pop:

```
Nav.propTypes = {
  push: PropTypes.func.isRequired,
  pop: PropTypes.func.isRequired,
  navigation: PropTypes.objectOf(PropTypes.any)
};
```

The first method we'll add to the refactored `Nav` component is the `render` method. This method will simply return a `CardStack` component:

```
render() {
  return (
    <CardStack
      onNavigateBack={this.props.pop}
      navigationState={this.props.navigation}
      renderScene={this.renderScene}
      style={styles.cardStack}
    />
  );
}
```

We pass the `pop` action to the `onNavigationBack` prop and pass along the `navigation` state to the `navigationState` prop. We also add some simple styles, so we'll need to add to the `StyleSheet` in this file:

```
const styles = StyleSheet.create({
  cardStack: {
    flex: 1
  }
});
```

We also need to create the `renderScene` method that gets passed into the `CardStack`. It will resemble the one created in the last section, but it will access the route from the `sceneProps` argument passed in from `CardStack` and it will use the `push` and `pop` methods from the component's props. Since the new `renderScene` method will need access to props, we'll need to bind `this` context in the `Nav` component's constructor:

```
constructor(props, context) {
  super(props, context);

  this.renderScene = this.renderScene.bind(this);
}

renderScene(sceneProps) {
  const route = sceneProps.scene.route;
  return (
    <route.component
      {...route.props}
      push={this.props.push}
      pop={this.props.pop}
    />
  );
}
```

Here we will pass the push and pop actions to each scene rendered by the Nav. This means we'll have to update the way the IntroScreen navigates. It will now need to call this passed in push prop with the key of the next scene ('home'):

```
const IntroScreen = ({ push }) => (
  <View style={[globalStyles.COMMON_STYLES.pageContainer,
styles.container]}>
    <TouchableOpacity
      onPress={() => push('home')}
    >
      <Title>React Native News Reader</Title>
      <AppText>
        Start Reading
      </AppText>
    </TouchableOpacity>
  </View>
);

IntroScreen.propTypes = {
  push: PropTypes.func.isRequired
};
```

Now that we have refactored the Nav component to use the CardStack component, which does not keep track of the navigational state internally, we need to create a container component that connects the Nav component to the Redux store and the application's navigational state. We will do this in a new file, src/containers/NavContainer.js:

```
import { bindActionCreators } from 'redux';
import { connect } from 'react-redux';

import { push, pop } from '../actions/navigationActions';

import Nav from '../components/Nav';

const mapStateToProps = state => ({
  navigation: state.navigation
});

const mapDispatchToProps = dispatch => (
  bindActionCreators({
    push,
    pop
  }, dispatch)
);

export default connect(
  mapStateToProps,
```

```
    mapDispatchToProps
) (Nav);
```

This looks very similar to other container components we've created in previous chapters. First we import the Redux utilities needed, the push and pop action creator functions, and the presentational Nav component:

```
import { bindActionCreators } from 'redux';
import { connect } from 'react-redux';

import { push, pop } from '../actions/navigationActions';

import Nav from '../components/Nav';
```

We then create a mapStateToProps function that can extract the relevant parts of the application state, in this case the navigation state, as shown in the following code snippet:

```
const mapStateToProps = state => ({
  navigation: state.navigation
});
```

Finally, we create the mapDispatchToProps function for attaching action creators to the Redux store and export the connected presentational component:

```
const mapDispatchToProps = dispatch => (
  bindActionCreators({
    push,
    pop
  }, dispatch)
);

export default connect(
  mapStateToProps,
  mapDispatchToProps
) (Nav);
```

Now that we have created NavContainer, we can replace the Nav component in App.js with the new container component:

```
import React from 'react';
import { Provider } from 'react-redux';
import NavContainer from './containers/NavContainer';
import createStore from './createStore';

const store = createStore();

export default () => (
```

```
  <Provider store={store}>
    <NavContainer />
  </Provider>
);
```

If we run the app now, we will be able to navigate, but the top navigational bar is now missing once again.

Navigation header

The NavigationExperimental Header component is probably the most straightforward part of the API. If you are trying to implement the simple, typical navigation header that we used in the previous section, much of that is done for you via default values. The Header is of course extensible, but for our purposes we will mostly take advantage of these default values, as shown in the following code snippet.

First, in the Nav.js file we need to extract the Header component from the NavigationExperimental module:

```
const { Header, CardStack } = NavigationExperimental;
```

We'll then create a simple renderNavigationBar method that returns a Header component. This method will also need to be bound to the this context in the constructor:

```
constructor(props, context) {
  super(props, context);

  this.renderScene = this.renderScene.bind(this);
  this.renderNavigationBar = this.renderNavigationBar.bind(this);
}

renderNavigationBar(sceneProps) {
  return (
    <Header
      style={styles.navigationBar}
      onNavigateBack={this.props.pop}
      {...sceneProps}
    />
  );
}
```

Here we basically pass on all of the sceneProps to the Header component, which it can use to decide whether or not to render a back button and also to display the title. We will also pass some simple styles that need to be added to the StyleSheet:

```
const styles = StyleSheet.create({
  cardStack: {
    flex: 1
  },
  navigationBar: {
    backgroundColor: globalStyles.MUTED_COLOR
  }
});
```

Additionally, we'll need to modify the page container styles in global.js to accommodate the new navigation header:

```
pageContainer: {
  backgroundColor: BG_COLOR,
  flex: 1,
  marginTop: 0,
  paddingTop: 5,
  marginBottom: 48,
  marginHorizontal: 0,
  paddingHorizontal: 10
}
```

Finally, back in Nav.js, we'll pass this new method to the renderHeader prop of the CardStack:

```
render() {
  return (
    <CardStack
      onNavigateBack={this.props.pop}
      navigationState={this.props.navigation}
      renderScene={this.renderScene}
      renderHeader={this.renderNavigationBar}
      style={styles.cardStack}
    />
  );
}
```

Tabbed navigation

We've successfully replaced `Navigator` with `NavigationExperimental`, but we have not solved the other parts of our navigation state: the tabs on the `HomeScreen` and the modal in the `NewsFeed`. Once again, our goal here is to manage all navigation state in Redux. First, let's look at how tabbed navigation can be modeled:

```
{
  index: 0,
  routes: [
    { key: 'newsFeed' },
    { key: 'search' },
    { key: 'bookmarks' }
  ]
}
```

This looks very similar to the previous example of navigational state, but this time it starts out with all three potential routes in the `routes` array. Instead of adding and removing route objects from the `routes` array, we will simply change the `index` to navigate to another scene. For instance, if we want to navigate to the search scene, we change the `index` to 1 (the index of that scene's route object in the `routes` array):

```
{
  index: 1,
  routes: [
    { key: 'newsFeed' },
    { key: 'search' },
    { key: 'bookmarks' }
  ]
}
```

The question now is, where should this live in the Redux store? Perhaps the tabbed navigation could have its own reducer. This is possible, but conceptually we think about tabs as being nested within the `HomeScreen`. It just so happens that our navigation state can actually be a recursive structure where each route object can itself be a navigational root. We can then embed the tabbed navigation within the home route like this:

```
{
  key: 'home',
  title: 'RNNYT',
  component: HomeScreen,
  index: 0,
  routes: [
    { key: 'newsFeed' },
    { key: 'search' },
    { key: 'bookmarks' }
```

```
  ]
}
```

The first thing we'll need to do to make use of this pattern is to create a new action for tabbed navigation in the `navigationActions.js` file:

```
import {
  NAVIGATION_PUSH,
  NAVIGATION_POP,
  NAVIGATION_TAB
} from './actionTypes';

export const tab = key => ({
  type: NAVIGATION_TAB,
  payload: key
});
```

This action creator function takes the `key` string of the tab as an argument. We will also need to add this new action type to the `actionTypes.js` file:

```
export const NAVIGATION_PUSH = 'NAVIGATION_PUSH';
export const NAVIGATION_POP = 'NAVIGATION_POP';
export const NAVIGATION_TAB = 'NAVIGATION_TAB';
```

Now, we need to update the navigation reducer. First, in `navigationReducer.js`, we'll add the tabbed navigation state to the home route as discussed in the previous section:

```
const routes = {
  home: {
    key: 'home',
    title: 'RNNYT',
    component: HomeScreen,
    index: 0,
    routes: [
      { key: 'newsFeed' },
      { key: 'search' },
      { key: 'bookmarks' }
    ]
  },
  intro: {
    key: 'intro',
    title: 'Welcome',
    component: IntroScreen
  }
};
```

We'll also need the `NAVIGATION_TAB` action type to be added to the imports of `navigationReducer.js`:

```
import { NavigationExperimental } from 'react-native';
import {
  NAVIGATION_PUSH,
  NAVIGATION_POP,
  NAVIGATION_TAB
} from '../actions/actionTypes';
import HomeScreen from '../components/HomeScreen';
import IntroScreen from '../components/IntroScreen';
```

Next, we'll update the `reduce` function to listen to the `NAVIGATION_TAB` action and update the state accordingly:

```
export default (state = initialState, action = {}) => {
  if (action.type === NAVNow we can refactor the HomeScreenIGATION_PUSH) {
    return StateUtils.push(state, routes[action.payload]);
  } else if (action.type === NAVIGATION_POP) {
    return StateUtils.pop(state);
  } else if (action.type === NAVIGATION_TAB) {
    const homeState = StateUtils.get(state, 'home');
    const updatedHomeState = StateUtils.jumpTo(homeState, action.payload);
    return StateUtils.replaceAt(state, 'home', updatedHomeState);
  }
  return state;
};
```

First, we extract the `'home'` scene route object using `StateUtils`:

```
const homeState = StateUtils.get(state, 'home');
```

Then, we update the `index` of the nested tabbed navigation by using the `StateUtils` `jumpTo` method, which simply updates the index to the appropriate number based on the key passed in. The `payload` of the `action`, remember, is the key to which we are navigating:

```
const updatedHomeState = StateUtils.jumpTo(homeState, action.payload);
```

Finally, we replace the HomeScene within the parent navigational state using the `StateUtilsreplaceAt` method and return the result:

```
return StateUtils.replaceAt(state, 'home', updatedHomeState);
```

Now that we have the tabbed navigation represented in the Redux store, we need to refactor the HomeScreen to use it instead of managing the state internally. We'll do this by creating a container component that wraps the HomeScreen and connects it to the Redux store in a new file, src/containers/HomeScreenContainer.js:

```
import { NavigationExperimental } from 'react-native';
import { bindActionCreators } from 'redux';
import { connect } from 'react-redux';

import HomeScreen from '../components/HomeScreen';

import { tab } from '../actions/navigationActions';

const { StateUtils } = NavigationExperimental;

const mapStateToProps = (state) => {
  const homeState = StateUtils.get(state.navigation, 'home');
  return {
    selectedTab: homeState ? homeState.routes[homeState.index].key :
'newsFeed'
  };
};

const mapDispatchToProps = dispatch => (
  bindActionCreators({
    tab
  }, dispatch)
);

export default connect(
  mapStateToProps,
  mapDispatchToProps
)(HomeScreen);
```

In this container, we give HomeScreen access to the currently active tab in the navigational state. We do this by first extracting the home route object, once again using StateUtils:

```
const homeState = StateUtils.get(state.navigation, 'home');
```

We then get the key of the active sub-route, falling back to newsFeed if the home route can't be found, as shown in the following code snippet:

```
return {
selectedTab: homeState ? homeState.routes[homeState.index].key : 'newsFeed'
};
```

We also give the `HomeScreen` access to the new tab action creator:

```
const mapDispatchToProps = (dispatch) => {
  return bindActionCreators({
    tab
  }, dispatch);
};
```

Now we can refactor the `HomeScreen` component to use props instead of an internal state:

```
import React, { Component, PropTypes } from 'react';
import {
  TabBarIOS,
  Text,
  Alert,
  Vibration,
  StatusBar
} from 'react-native';
import NewsFeedContainer from '../containers/NewsFeedContainer';
import SearchContainer from '../containers/SearchContainer';
import * as globalStyles from '../styles/global';

// Set the status bar for iOS to light
StatusBar.setBarStyle('light-content');

export default class HomeScreen extends Component {

  showBookmarkAlert() {
    Vibration.vibrate();
    Alert.alert(
      'Coming Soon!',
      'We're hard at work on this feature, check back in the near future.',
      [
        { text: 'OK', onPress: () => console.log('User pressed OK') }
      ]
    );
  }

  render() {
    const { selectedTab, tab } = this.props;

    return (
      <TabBarIOS
        barTintColor={globalStyles.BAR_COLOR}
        tintColor={globalStyles.LINK_COLOR}
        translucent={false}
      >
        <TabBarIOS.Item
```

```
       systemIcon={'featured'}
       selected={selectedTab === 'newsFeed'}
       onPress={() => tab('newsFeed')}
     >
       <NewsFeedContainer />
     </TabBarIOS.Item>
     <TabBarIOS.Item
       systemIcon={'search'}
       selected={selectedTab === 'search'}
       onPress={() => tab('search')}
     >
       <SearchContainer />
     </TabBarIOS.Item>
     <TabBarIOS.Item
       systemIcon={'bookmarks'}
       selected={selectedTab === 'bookmarks'}
       onPress={() => this.showBookmarkAlert()}
     >
       <Text>Bookmarks</Text>
     </TabBarIOS.Item>
   </TabBarIOS>
  );
 }
}


HomeScreen.propTypes = {
  selectedTab: PropTypes.string,
  tab: PropTypes.func.isRequired
};
```

We use `props.selectedTab` to identify which tab is currently active:

```
selected={selectedTab === 'newsFeed'}
```

Then, we use the `props.tab` function to navigate to the tab in place of setting an internal state:

```
onPress={() => tab('newsFeed')}
```

Finally, we need to use the `HomeScreenContainer` component in place of the, now stateless, `HomeScreen` component in the route object in the `navigationReducer.js` file:

```
import { NavigationExperimental } from 'react-native';
import {
  NAVIGATION_PUSH,
  NAVIGATION_POP,
  NAVIGATION_TAB,
} from '../actions/actionTypes';
```

```
import HomeScreenContainer from '../containers/HomeScreenContainer';
import IntroScreen from '../components/IntroScreen';

const { StateUtils } = NavigationExperimental;

const routes = {
  home: {
    key: 'home',
    title: 'RNNYT',
    component: HomeScreenContainer,
    index: 0,
    routes: [
      { key: 'newsFeed' },
      { key: 'search' },
      { key: 'bookmarks' }
    ]
  },
  intro: {
    key: 'intro',
    title: 'Welcome',
    component: IntroScreen
  }
};
```

Adding in the modal

The last piece of the navigational puzzle is the modal used to display a news article in a
WebView. Currently, the NewsFeed component manages the modal internally in its state.
Just like the tabs, we are going to move this to internal state in the navigation portion of the
Redux store.

One approach we could take is to nest a new navigational stack inside of the newsFeed
route object. Then, we could use another CardStack component in the news feed that
displays the feed scene in addition to the modal scene. This would work, but is probably
over-engineering for this simple use case. Instead, we'll simply have a modal key in the
newsFeed route object. The value of the modal key will be the URL the modal is open to or
undefined if it isn't open.

Here is the modal state initially:

```
{
  key: 'home',
  title: 'RNNYT',
  component: HomeScreenContainer,
  index: 0,
```

```
  routes: [
    { key: 'newsFeed', modal: undefined },
    { key: 'search' },
    { key: 'bookmarks' }
  ]
}
```

And here it is when we navigate to a news item `modal`:

```
{
  key: 'home',
  title: 'RNNYT',
  component: HomeScreenContainer,
  index: 0,
  routes: [
    { key: 'newsFeed', modal: 'http://example.com' },
    { key: 'search' },
    { key: 'bookmarks' }
  ]
}
```

To get this working, we'll need to add some new actions to the `navigationActions.js` file, one for opening the `modal` and another for closing it:

```
import {
  NAVIGATION_PUSH,
  NAVIGATION_POP,
  NAVIGATION_TAB,
  NAVIGATION_OPEN_MODAL,
  NAVIGATION_CLOSE_MODAL
} from './actionTypes';

export const openModal = url => ({
  type: NAVIGATION_OPEN_MODAL,
  payload: url
});

export const closeModal = () => ({
  type: NAVIGATION_CLOSE_MODAL
});
```

Notice that the `openModal` action creator function passes along the URL that needs to be opened. Once again, we'll need to add these new action types to the `actionTypes.js` file:

```
export const NAVIGATION_OPEN_MODAL = 'NAVIGATION_OPEN_MODAL';
export const NAVIGATION_CLOSE_MODAL = 'NAVIGATION_CLOSE_MODAL';
```

Next, we need to update the navigation reducer to handle these new action types. First, we'll import the new actions in the navgationReducer.js file:

```
import { NavigationExperimental } from 'react-native';
import {
  NAVIGATION_PUSH,
  NAVIGATION_POP,
  NAVIGATION_TAB,
  NAVIGATION_OPEN_MODAL,
  NAVIGATION_CLOSE_MODAL
} from '../actions/actionTypes';
import HomeScreenContainer from '../containers/HomeScreenContainer';
import IntroScreen from '../components/IntroScreen';
```

And here is the updated reducer:

```
export default (state = initialState, action = {}) => {
  if (action.type === NAVIGATION_PUSH) {
    return StateUtils.push(state, routes[action.payload]);
  } else if (action.type === NAVIGATION_POP) {
    return StateUtils.pop(state);
  } else if (action.type === NAVIGATION_TAB) {
    const homeState = StateUtils.get(state, 'home');
    const updatedHomeState = StateUtils.jumpTo(homeState, action.payload);
    return StateUtils.replaceAt(state, 'home', updatedHomeState);
  } else if (action.type === NAVIGATION_OPEN_MODAL) {
    const homeState = StateUtils.get(state, 'home');
    const openTabState = homeState.routes[homeState.index];
    const updatedTabState = { ...openTabState, modal: action.payload };
    const updatedHomeState = StateUtils.replaceAt(homeState,
openTabState.key, updatedTabState);
    return StateUtils.replaceAt(state, 'home', updatedHomeState);
  } else if (action.type === NAVIGATION_CLOSE_MODAL) {
    const homeState = StateUtils.get(state, 'home');
    const openTabState = homeState.routes[homeState.index];
    const updatedTabState = { ...openTabState, modal: undefined };
    const updatedHomeState = StateUtils.replaceAt(homeState,
openTabState.key, updatedTabState);
    return StateUtils.replaceAt(state, 'home', updatedHomeState);
  }
  return state;
};
```

The first step for both of these new action types is to extract the state of the currently open tab route object, which is nested two levels deep in our navigation state:

```
const homeState = StateUtils.get(state, 'home');
const openTabState = homeState.routes[homeState.index];
```

To open the `modal`, we use `payload` of the `action` (the URL) and store it in the `modal` key:

```
const updatedTabState = { ...openTabState, modal: action.payload };
```

To close the `modal`, we simply set it back to `undefined`:

```
const updatedTabState = { ...openTabState, modal: undefined };
```

Finally, we replace the current open tab route with the updated version and return the result:

```
const updatedHomeState = StateUtils.replaceAt(homeState, openTabState.key,
updatedTabState);
return StateUtils.replaceAt(state, 'home', updatedHomeState);
```

The `NewsFeed` component already has a container, so all we need to do is attach this new state and the new action creators to it, and then refactor the component to use them. Here is the updated container:

```
import { NavigationExperimental } from 'react-native';
import { connect } from 'react-redux';
import { bindActionCreators } from 'redux';
import { loadNews } from '../actions/newsActions';
import { openModal, closeModal } from '../actions/navigationActions';
import NewsFeed from '../components/NewsFeed';
import { allNewsSelector } from '../selectors/newsSelectors';

const { StateUtils } = NavigationExperimental;

const mapStateToProps = (state) => {
  const homeState = StateUtils.get(state.navigation, 'home');
  const newsFeedState = homeState && StateUtils.get(homeState, 'newsFeed');
  const modal = newsFeedState && newsFeedState.modal;
  return {
    news: allNewsSelector(state),
    modal: modal || undefined
  };
};

const mapDispatchToProps = dispatch => (
  bindActionCreators({
    loadNews,
```

```
      onModalOpen: openModal,
      onModalClose: closeModal
  }, dispatch)
);
```

```
export default connect(mapStateToProps, mapDispatchToProps)(NewsFeed);
```

We need to extract the `modal` value from the navigation state in the `mapStateToProps` function of the `NewsFeedContainer`:

```
const mapStateToProps = (state) => {
  const homeState = StateUtils.get(state.navigation, 'home');
  const newsFeedState = homeState && StateUtils.get(homeState, 'newsFeed');
  const modal = newsFeedState && newsFeedState.modal;
  return {
    news: allNewsSelector(state),
    modal: modal || undefined
  };
};
```

We also need to add the open and close modal action creators to the `mapDispatchToProps` function:

```
const mapDispatchToProps = dispatch => (
  bindActionCreators({
    loadNews,
    onModalOpen: openModal,
    onModalClose: closeModal
  }, dispatch)
);
```

Finally, we'll refactor the `NewsFeed` component itself to use these new props. First, we'll update the rendering of individual news items to use the new `openModal` prop:

```
renderRow(rowData, ...rest) {
  const index = parseInt(rest[1], 10);
  return (
    <NewsItem
      onPress={() => this.props.onModalOpen(rowData.url)}
      style={styles.newsItem}
      index={index}
      {...rowData}
    />
  );
}
```

Then, we'll update the `renderModal()` method to also use the new props:

```
renderModal() {
  return (
    <Modal
      animationType="slide"
      visible={this.props.modal !== undefined}
      onRequestClose={this.props.onModalClose}
    >
      <View style={styles.modalContent}>
        <TouchableOpacity
          onPress={this.props.onModalClose}
          style={styles.closeButton}
        >
          <SmallText>Close</SmallText>
        </TouchableOpacity>
        <WebView
          scalesPageToFit
          source={{ uri: this.props.modal }}
        />
      </View>
    </Modal>
  );
}
```

To complete the `NewsFeed` refactor, we'll also need to add some new `propTypes` for the newly added action creators and `modal` state:

```
NewsFeed.propTypes = {
  news: PropTypes.arrayOf(PropTypes.object),
  listStyles: View.propTypes.style,
  loadNews: PropTypes.func,
  showLoadingSpinner: PropTypes.bool,
  modal: PropTypes.string,
  onModalOpen: PropTypes.func.isRequired,
  onModalClose: PropTypes.func.isRequired
};
```

We're almost done, but there is one last update we need to make. The `newsFeed` tab is not the only one to use a `NewsFeed` component (and thus a `modal`). The `search` tab also contains a `NewsFeed` and thus also needs the ability to open and close a `modal`. Luckily, the way we've designed the navigational reducer will support modals on any tab, so all we need to do is make a few small modifications to the `SearchContainer` and the `Search` components.

First, we'll update the `SearchContainer` to have access to the modal action creators and `modal` state, as we did for the `NewsFeed` container:

```
import { NavigationExperimental } from 'react-native';
import { connect } from 'react-redux';
import { bindActionCreators } from 'redux';
import { searchNews } from '../actions/newsActions';
import { openModal, closeModal } from '../actions/navigationActions';
import Search from '../components/Search';
import { searchNewsSelector } from '../selectors/newsSelectors';

const { StateUtils } = NavigationExperimental;

const mapStateToProps = (state) => {
  const homeState = StateUtils.get(state.navigation, 'home');
  const searchState = homeState && StateUtils.get(homeState, 'search');
  const modal = searchState && searchState.modal;
  return {
    filteredNews: searchNewsSelector(state),
    modal: modal || undefined
  };
};

const mapDispatchToProps = dispatch => (
  bindActionCreators({
    searchNews,
    onModalOpen: openModal,
    onModalClose: closeModal
  }, dispatch)
);

export default connect(mapStateToProps, mapDispatchToProps)(Search);
```

We'll then use these new props in the `Search` component:

```
import React, { Component, PropTypes } from 'react';
import {
  View,
  TextInput,
  StyleSheet
} from 'react-native';
import NewsFeed from './NewsFeed';
import * as globalStyles from '../styles/global';

export default class Search extends Component {

  constructor(props) {
    super(props);
```

```
    this.state = {
      searchText: ''
    };
    this.searchNews = this.searchNews.bind(this);
  }

  searchNews(text) {
    this.setState({ searchText: text });
    this.props.searchNews(text);
  }

  render() {
    return (
      <View style={globalStyles.COMMON_STYLES.pageContainer}>
        <View style={styles.search}>
          <TextInput
            style={styles.input}
            onChangeText={this.searchNews}
            value={this.state.searchText}
            placeholder={'Search'}
            placeholderTextColor={globalStyles.MUTED_COLOR}
          />
        </View>
        <NewsFeed
          news={this.props.filteredNews}
          listStyles={{}}
          showLoadingSpinner={false}
          modal={this.props.modal}
          onModalClose={this.props.onModalClose}
          onModalOpen={this.props.onModalOpen}
        />
      </View>
    );
  }
}

Search.propTypes = {
  filteredNews: PropTypes.arrayOf(PropTypes.object),
  searchNews: PropTypes.func.isRequired,
  modal: PropTypes.string,
  onModalOpen: PropTypes.func.isRequired,
  onModalClose: PropTypes.func.isRequired
};

const styles = StyleSheet.create({
  input: {
    height: 35,
    color: globalStyles.TEXT_COLOR,
```

```
      paddingHorizontal: 5,
      flex: 1
  },
  search: {
    borderColor: globalStyles.MUTED_COLOR,
    flexDirection: 'row',
    alignItems: 'center',
    borderRadius: 5,
    borderWidth: 1,
    marginTop: 10,
    marginBottom: 5
  }
});
```

With this, we have now completely refactored the navigation of our application. We can now go to one place, the Redux store, to identify the state of navigation. Furthermore, that navigational state can be accessed by any container component in our application.

Other advanced APIs

In the final section of this chapter, we'll delve into a few other React Native advanced APIs and see how they can help us to make our application more sophisticated and user-friendly. We cannot hope to cover every available advanced API, but this feature-based approach should help to illuminate what is possible with React Native.

Offline messages with NetInfo

Our news reader application relies, in large part, on a connection to the Internet. It needs this connection to interact with the New York Times HTTP API and get the latest news articles. If the device our application is running on does not have a connection to the Internet, it would be helpful for us to know this so that we can inform our users.

React Native has an API called `NetInfo` that allows us to do just that. `NetInfo` can tell us what the connectivity status is currently and also allows us to be informed whenever that connectivity status changes. We will use this API in the `NewsFeed` component to display a **No Connection** message when an Internet connection is unavailable.

The first step is to import the `NetInfo` module into the `NewsFeed.js` file. We'll also import the `AppText` component so we can use it to display the message:

```
import React, { PropTypes, Component } from 'react';
import {
  ListView,
  StyleSheet,
  View,
  Modal,
  TouchableOpacity,
  WebView,
  RefreshControl,
  ActivityIndicator,
  NetInfo
} from 'react-native';
import NewsItem from './NewsItem';
import SmallText from './SmallText';
import AppText from './AppText';
import * as globalStyles from '../styles/global';
```

Next, we'll initialize the component's initial state to assume that there is an Internet connection, as shown in the following code snippet:

```
constructor(props) {
  super(props);
  this.ds = new ListView.DataSource({
    rowHasChanged: (row1, row2) => row1.title !== row2.title
  });
  this.state = {
    dataSource: this.ds.cloneWithRows(props.news),
    initialLoading: true,
    modalVisible: false,
    refreshing: false,
    connected: true
  };

  this.renderRow = this.renderRow.bind(this);
  this.onModalClose = this.onModalClose.bind(this);
  this.onModalOpen = this.onModalOpen.bind(this);
  this.refresh = this.refresh.bind(this);
}
```

We'll also create a method to handle changes in connectivity, binding it to `this` in the constructor:

```
constructor(props) {
  super(props);
  this.ds = new ListView.DataSource({
```

```
    rowHasChanged: (row1, row2) => row1.title !== row2.title
  });
  this.state = {
    dataSource: this.ds.cloneWithRows(props.news),
    initialLoading: true,
    modalVisible: false,
    refreshing: false,
    connected: true
  };

  this.renderRow = this.renderRow.bind(this);
  this.onModalClose = this.onModalClose.bind(this);
  this.onModalOpen = this.onModalOpen.bind(this);
  this.refresh = this.refresh.bind(this);
  this.handleConnectivityChange = this.handleConnectivityChange.bind(this);
}
...
handleConnectivityChange(isConnected) {
  this.setState({
    connected: isConnected
  });
  if (isConnected) {
    this.refresh();
  }
}
```

In this method, we are updating the value in state and refreshing the articles if the connection has been restored. Next, we'll need to register this handler with NetInfo when the component is mounted:

```
componentWillMount() {
  NetInfo.isConnected.addEventListener('change',
this.handleConnectivityChange);
  this.refresh();
}
```

And we'll need to remove the listener when the component is unmounted:

```
componentWillUnmount() {
  NetInfo.isConnected.removeEventListener('change',
this.handleConnectivityChange);
}
```

Finally, we'll update the render method to show the user a message informing them that there is not currently a network connection, as shown in the following code snippet:

```
render() {
  const {
```

```
      listStyles = globalStyles.COMMON_STYLES.pageContainer,
      showLoadingSpinner
    } = this.props;
    const { initialLoading, refreshing, dataSource } = this.state;

    if (!this.state.connected) {
      return (
        <View style={[globalStyles.COMMON_STYLES.pageContainer,
  styles.loadingContainer]}>
          <AppText>
            No Connection
          </AppText>
        </View>
      );
    }

    return (
      (initialLoading && showLoadingSpinner
        ? (
          <View style={[listStyles, styles.loadingContainer]}>
            <ActivityIndicator
              animating
              size="small"
              {...this.props}
            />
          </View>
        ) : (
          <View style={styles.container}>
            <ListView
              refreshControl={
                <RefreshControl
                  refreshing={refreshing}
                  onRefresh={this.refresh}
                />
              }
              enableEmptySections
              dataSource={dataSource}
              renderRow={this.renderRow}
              style={listStyles}
            />
            {this.renderModal()}
          </View>
        )
      )
    );
  }
```

Now, to test this new feature, we can shut off our computer's network connection and we should see the new message display, as shown in the following screenshot:

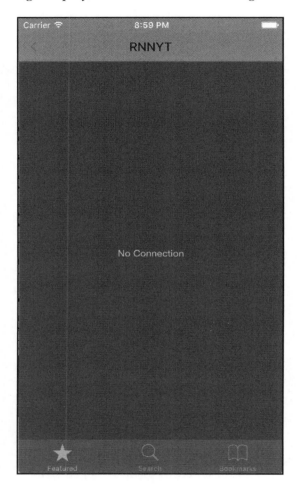

Opening the browser with linking

Currently, when the user wants to read a news article, we display it within our application using a `WebView` component. This approach works in many situations, but we may want to give the user an option to open it in their device's browser application.

The React Native `Linking` API allows us to open HTTP web URLs as well as any other URL that an installed application can handle. For instance, **mailto** links can be opened in the native mail client using the `Linking` API, as can custom URLs that have been registered to specific applications.

In this section, we will use the `Linking` API to provide an **Open in Browser** link that will allow the user to read the same article in a full browser experience. We will start this process by first importing the `Linking` API module in the `NewsFeed.js` file:

```
import React, { PropTypes, Component } from 'react';
import {
  ListView,
  StyleSheet,
  View,
  Modal,
  TouchableOpacity,
  WebView,
  RefreshControl,
  ActivityIndicator,
  NetInfo,
  Linking
} from 'react-native';
import NewsItem from './NewsItem';
import SmallText from './SmallText';
import AppText from './AppText';
import * as globalStyles from '../styles/global';
```

The `Linking` API has a static method, `openURL`, which can be used to open any URL that can be handled by an installed application. In our case, this is the browser. We'll next add a new button to our `modal` that uses this static method:

```
renderModal() {
  return (
    <Modal
      animationType="slide"
      visible={this.props.modal !== undefined}
      onRequestClose={this.props.onModalClose}
    >
      <View style={styles.modalContent}>
        <View style={styles.modalButtons}>
          <TouchableOpacity
            onPress={this.props.onModalClose}
          >
            <SmallText>Close</SmallText>
          </TouchableOpacity>
          <TouchableOpacity
            onPress={() => Linking.openURL(this.props.modal)}
```

```
      >
        <SmallText>Open in Browser</SmallText>
      </TouchableOpacity>
    </View>
    <WebView
      scalesPageToFit
      source={{ uri: this.props.modal }}
    />
  </View>
  </Modal>
  );
}
```

In order to make this display properly, we'll also need to adjust the styles, wrapping the two buttons in a flex row, as shown in the following code:

```
const styles = StyleSheet.create({
  newsItem: {
    marginBottom: 20
  },
  container: {
    flex: 1
  },
  loadingContainer: {
    alignItems: 'center',
    justifyContent: 'center'
  },
  modalContent: {
    flex: 1,
    justifyContent: 'center',
    paddingTop: 20,
    backgroundColor: globalStyles.BG_COLOR
  },
  modalButtons: {
    paddingVertical: 5,
    paddingHorizontal: 10,
    flexDirection: 'row',
    justifyContent: 'space-between'
  }
});
```

Now the modal should display a new **Open in Browser** button on the right-hand side that opens a native browser when clicked, as shown in the following screenshot:

Saving bookmarks locally with AsyncStorage

For some time now, we have had a tab set aside for bookmarked articles. It is now time to implement that feature. To do this, we will be using a React Native API called AsyncStorage. This API can be thought of as analogous to LocalStorage in the web world. It is a small key-value store that allows us to persist pieces of information about our user on their device that will remain even when the app is closed and reopened.

In this section, we'll store a list of URLs for articles that the user has bookmarked in `AsyncStorage` and load them when the application is opened. We'll start this process by creating an action creator function, `addBookmark`, in a new `src/actions/bookmarkActions.js` file:

```
import { BOOKMARK } from './actionTypes';

export const addBookmark = (url) => {
  return {
    type: BOOKMARK,
    payload: url
  };
};
```

In Redux, reducers cannot have any side-effects such as saving things in a database or, in this case, `AsyncStorage`. Whenever we need to perform such actions, the place to do it is in the action creator. With that in mind, in this same file we'll import the `AsyncStorage` module:

```
import { AsyncStorage } from 'react-native';
```

`AsyncStorage` keys and values must both be strings, so we will set the `bookmarks` key to a `JSONstringified` array containing the bookmarked URL:

```
export function bookmark(url) {
  AsyncStorage.setItem('bookmarks', JSON.stringify([url]));
  return {
    type: BOOKMARK,
    payload: url
  }
}
```

What if this is not the first bookmarked URL? In that case we will want to append the new URL to the array rather than creating a new one. For this reason, we must first read the value of the `bookmarks` key and then either append the new URL to the list or create a new list. Refer to the following code snippet:

```
export const addBookmark = (url) => {
  AsyncStorage.getItem('bookmarks').then((bookmarks) => {
    if (bookmarks) {
      const bookmarkArray = JSON.parse(bookmarks);
      return AsyncStorage.setItem('bookmarks',
JSON.stringify([...bookmarkArray, url]));
    }
    return AsyncStorage.setItem('bookmarks', JSON.stringify([url]));
  });
```

```
    return {
      type: BOOKMARK,
      payload: url
    };
};
```

Reading and writing to AsyncStorage is, as one might expect, an asynchronous operation. The getItem and setItem methods both return promises, which allows us to use the .then syntax. We also need to create an additional action creator that loads bookmarks from storage, as shown in the following code snippet:

```
import { AsyncStorage } from 'react-native';
import { BOOKMARK, LOADED_BOOKMARKS } from './actionTypes';

export const loadBookmarks = () => ({
  type: LOADED_BOOKMARKS,
  payload: AsyncStorage.getItem('bookmarks').then((bookmarks) => {
    if (bookmarks) {
      return JSON.parse(bookmarks);
    }
    return [];
  })
});
```

Here, we are getting the bookmarks item, parsing the serialized JSON if it exists, and returning an empty array if it does not. Note that the promise middleware will be responsible for resolving this payload. We'll of course need to also add these new action types to the actionTypes.js file:

```
export const BOOKMARK = 'BOOKMARK';
export const LOADED_BOOKMARKS = 'LOADED_BOOKMARKS';
```

Next, we'll create a src/reducers/bookmarkReducer.js file that manages the bookmarks section of the Redux store. In this file, we'll initialize the state as an empty array and update it when it is loaded, or a new URL is added:

```
import { BOOKMARK, LOADED_BOOKMARKS } from '../actions/actionTypes';

export default (state = [], action = {}) => {
  switch (action.type) {
    case LOADED_BOOKMARKS:
      return action.payload;
    case BOOKMARK:
      return [...state, action.payload];
    default:
      return state;
  }
```

```
};
```

We then need to register this reducer in the `createStore.js` file:

```
import { createStore, applyMiddleware, combineReducers } from 'redux';
import createLogger from 'redux-logger';
import newsFeedReducer from './reducers/newsFeedReducer';
import navigationReducer from './reducers/navigationReducer';
import searchTermReducer from './reducers/searchTermReducer';
import bookmarkReducer from './reducers/bookmarkReducer';
import promiseMiddleware from 'redux-promise';

const logger = createLogger();

export default (initialState = {}) => {
  return createStore(combineReducers({
      news: newsFeedReducer,
      searchTerm: searchTermReducer,
      navigation: navigationReducer,
      bookmarks: bookmarkReducer
    }),
    initialState,
    applyMiddleware(logger, promiseMiddleware)
  );
};
```

Lastly, we're going to create a new selector that returns only news items that are in the user's bookmarks. First, in the `newsSelector.js` file, we'll add a new `bookmarksSelector`:

```
const bookmarksSelector = state => state.bookmarks;
```

Next, we'll create a combined selector that uses both the `bookmarksSelector` and the `allNewsSelector` to return a filtered list of only bookmarked news items. We'll call this new selector `bookmarkedNewsSelector`:

```
export const bookmarkedNewsSelector = createSelector(
  [allNewsSelector, bookmarksSelector],
  (newsItems, bookmarks) => newsItems.filter(newsItem =>
bookmarks.indexOf(newsItem.url) > -1)
);
```

Now that we have the bookmark state management portion complete, we'll need to attach this to our React components. First, we'll attach the bookmark action. Remember, we created a long press handler in the NewsItem component that presents the user with a Bookmark option. We'll need to get this action into that component. To do so, we'll first connect it to NewsFeedContainer as well as SearchContainer:

```
import { addBookmark } from '../actions/bookmarkActions';

const mapDispatchToProps = dispatch => (
  bindActionCreators({
    load: loadNews,
    onModalOpen: openModal,
    onModalClose: closeModal,
    addBookmark
  }, dispatch)
);
```

We'll then have the NewsFeed component, in NewsFeed.js, pass the prop in turn down to each NewsItem component it renders:

```
renderRow(rowData, ...rest) {
  const index = parseInt(rest[1], 10);
  return (
    <NewsItem
      onPress={() => this.props.onModalOpen(rowData.url)}
      onBookmark={() => this.props.addBookmark(rowData.url)}
      style={styles.newsItem}
      index={index}
      {...rowData}
    />
  );
}
```

Also, we'll add the addBookmark function to propTypes and NewsFeed:

```
NewsFeed.propTypes = {
  news: PropTypes.arrayOf(PropTypes.object),
  listStyles: View.propTypes.style,
  load: PropTypes.func,
  showLoadingSpinner: PropTypes.bool,
  modal: PropTypes.string,
  onModalOpen: PropTypes.func.isRequired,
  onModalClose: PropTypes.func.isRequired,
  addBookmark: PropTypes.func.isRequired
};
```

Next, we'll call this prop in the `NewsItem` component, in `NewsItem.js`, if the **Bookmark** button is pressed:

```
onLongPress() {
  ActionSheetIOS.showActionSheetWithOptions({
    options: ['Bookmark', 'Cancel'],
    cancelButtonIndex: 1,
    title: this.props.title
  }, (buttonIndex) => {
    if (buttonIndex === 0) {
      this.props.onBookmark();
    }
  });
}

...

NewsItem.propTypes = {
  imageUrl: PropTypes.string,
  title: PropTypes.string.isRequired,
  description: PropTypes.string,
  date: PropTypes.string.isRequired,
  author: PropTypes.string.isRequired,
  location: PropTypes.string,
  index: PropTypes.number.isRequired,
  onPress: PropTypes.func.isRequired,
  style: View.propTypes.style,
  onBookmark: PropTypes.func.isRequired
};
```

The next step for our bookmark feature is to actually display the bookmarked articles in the bookmarks tab. To do this, we'll create a new container component that is essentially the same as `NewsFeedContainer`. The only difference with this container component is that it will use our newly created `bookmarkedNewsSelector` instead of the `allNewsSelector`. We'll also refactor the `loadNews` prop to be called, more generically, load in this container as well as `NewsFeedContainer`. This allows us to load the bookmarks when the `BookmarkContainer` component comes on screen. Here is the new container in `src/containers/BookmarksContainer.js`:

```
import { NavigationExperimental } from 'react-native';
import { connect } from 'react-redux';
import { bindActionCreators } from 'redux';
import { openModal, closeModal } from '../actions/navigationActions';
import { loadBookmarks, addBookmark } from '../actions/bookmarkActions';
import NewsFeed from '../components/NewsFeed';
import { bookmarkedNewsSelector } from '../selectors/newsSelectors';
```

```
const { StateUtils } = NavigationExperimental;

const mapStateToProps = (state) => {
  const homeState = StateUtils.get(state.navigation, 'home');
  const bookmarksState = homeState && StateUtils.get(homeState,
'bookmarks');
  const modal = bookmarksState && bookmarksState.modal;
  return {
    news: bookmarkedNewsSelector(state),
    modal: modal || undefined
  };
};

const mapDispatchToProps = dispatch => (
  bindActionCreators({
    load: loadBookmarks,
    onModalOpen: openModal,
    onModalClose: closeModal,
    addBookmark
  }, dispatch)
);

export default connect(mapStateToProps, mapDispatchToProps)(NewsFeed);
```

And the updated `NewsFeedContainer`:

```
import { NavigationExperimental } from 'react-native';
import { connect } from 'react-redux';
import { bindActionCreators } from 'redux';
import { loadNews } from '../actions/newsActions';
import { openModal, closeModal } from '../actions/navigationActions';
import { addBookmark } from '../actions/bookmarkActions';
import NewsFeed from '../components/NewsFeed';
import { allNewsSelector } from '../selectors/newsSelectors';

const { StateUtils } = NavigationExperimental;

const mapStateToProps = (state) => {
  const homeState = StateUtils.get(state.navigation, 'home');
  const newsFeedState = homeState && StateUtils.get(homeState, 'newsFeed');
  const modal = newsFeedState && newsFeedState.modal;
  return {
    news: allNewsSelector(state),
    modal: modal || undefined
  };
};

const mapDispatchToProps = dispatch => (
```

```
  bindActionCreators({
    load: loadNews,
    onModalOpen: openModal,
    onModalClose: closeModal,
    addBookmark
  }, dispatch)
);
```

```
export default connect(mapStateToProps, mapDispatchToProps)(NewsFeed);
```

We'll also need to alter the `NewsFeed` component for this updated name:

```
refresh() {
  if (this.props.load) {
    this.props.load();
  }
}
```

```
...
```

```
NewsFeed.propTypes = {
  news: PropTypes.arrayOf(PropTypes.object),
  listStyles: View.propTypes.style,
  load: PropTypes.func,
  showLoadingSpinner: PropTypes.bool,
  modal: PropTypes.string,
  onModalOpen: PropTypes.func.isRequired,
  onModalClose: PropTypes.func.isRequired,
  addBookmark: PropTypes.func.isRequired
};
```

The last step is to ensure that the `HomeScreen` component actually navigates to our new container instead of showing the alert message it has up until this point. We can do that simply by importing the new container in the `HomeScreen.ios.js` file and then refactoring the **Bookmarks** tab:

```
import React, { PropTypes } from 'react';
import {
  TabBarIOS,
  StatusBar
} from 'react-native';
import NewsFeedContainer from '../containers/NewsFeedContainer';
import SearchContainer from '../containers/SearchContainer';
import BookmarksContainer from '../containers/BookmarksContainer';
import * as globalStyles from '../styles/global';
```

```
...
```

```
<TabBarIOS.Item
  systemIcon={'bookmarks'}
  selected={this.props.selectedTab === 'bookmarks'}
  onPress={() => this.props.tab('bookmarks')}
>
  <BookmarksContainer />
</TabBarIOS.Item>
```

We now have a fully functioning bookmark tab.

 It should be noted that `AsyncStorage` is best used for simple keys and values. If you are storing complex data (even our bookmarks are pushing it), it is recommended that you use some sort of library that builds on top of `AsyncStorage` rather than interacting with it directly.

Summary

While navigation is a core concept for almost every mobile application, the waters are still a bit murky in the world of React Native. For simple applications, the Navigator API provides an easy, ready-to-use component for managing scenes. For applications that are more sophisticated, the new `NavigationExperimental` API is worth learning and applying. The statelessness of `NavigationExperimental` and its declarative API make it a much more natural fit for a React application.

In addition to navigational APIs, the React Native library comes with many other native APIs that can be used to make complex and interesting applications. In this chapter, we looked at using the `NetInfo` API to check for Internet connectivity, the `Linking` API to open articles in the native browser, and the `AsyncStorage` API to persist data locally on the device. While these APIs showcase some of the exciting things that can be done with React Native, the list here is not exhaustive. As React Native becomes more mature, even more native APIs are likely to become available.

In the next chapter, we'll enhance our application even more by immersing ourselves in React Native animation APIs and its gesture recognition system.

8

Animation and Gestures in React Native

Because React Native utilizes truly native mobile technology, it allows us to create applications that not only look native but also *feel* native. Native applications are capable of fast, 60-fps animations, and can respond to complex touch gestures such as swipe and pinch. To that end, React Native offers two complementary animation APIs–`Animated` and `LayoutAnimation`. `PanResponder` is another React Native API for handling advanced single-touch gestures or simple multi-touch gestures that can be easily paired with the `Animated` API.

In this chapter, we'll learn more about these APIs by building an *onboarding* experience for RNNYT. We'll break this process down into the following:

- Building a basic onboarding view without any animations
- Upgrading the onboarding experience using the `LayoutAnimation` API
- Further upgrading onboarding with more complex animations using the `Animated` API
- Allowing users to swipe through the onboarding views using the `PanResponder` API

Introducing LayoutAnimation and Animated

Before we delve too deeply into either animation API, let's first set out why you would use one API as opposed to the other. LayoutAnimation has a far simpler API than Animated. As a result, it's less configurable. LayoutAnimation will animate a component upon a render cycle, such as when you call setState. Animated allows you, at a much more granular level, to configure how an animation or sequences of animations is executed. Additionally, the Animated API can tie animations to user gestures, allowing users, for example, to drag an element across the screen.

Building the basic Onboarding experience

Before we dazzle our users with lots of animations, let's focus on leveraging what we've learned so far to build a basic onboarding experience. The view will have four onboarding panels, followed by a completion state. Each of the four panels will have its own message, a placeholder image (in lieu of final product photos), and a unique background color. At a high level, we'll create a root Onboarding component that manages transitioning between the different states. Additionally, we'll build a few supporting Onboarding components, and two buttons for navigating us forward and backward through the onboarding experience. Lastly, we'll create an onboarding configuration to house all the information about each onboarding state.

Getting started

First, let's build our barebones view. Inside your **RNNYT** app, add the following files inside the src/components directory:

- Onboarding.js
- OnboardingButtons.js
- OnboardingPanel.js
- Button.js
- LinkButton.js

Let's begin with a visual to understand how this experience will operate. This represents the initial onboarding state:

At the top, you see our onboarding message. After that is a placeholder image. The background color is configured for each state. We'll use a Button component as the **Next** button and a LinkButton for the **Previous** button. Based on whether you're at the beginning or end of the onboarding panels, we'll enable or disable the appropriate button.

Let's wire up our main app to include the root `Onboarding` component.

 React Native actually ships with a `ViewPagerAndroid` component that is similar to what we'll be building in this chapter. It is, however, Android only. But, more importantly, it also doesn't teach you how to write custom animations in React Native.

The first thing we'll need to do is add `Onboarding` to our navigation flow. Inside `navigationReducer.js`, start by importing the `Onboarding` component:

```
import Onboarding from '../components/Onboarding';
```

Then, update `routes` to match the following:

```
const routes = {
  home: {
    key: 'home',
    component: HomeScreenContainer,
    index: 0,
    routes: [
      { key: 'newsFeed', modal: undefined },
      { key: 'search' },
      { key: 'bookmarks' }
    ]
  },
  intro: {
    key: 'intro',
    component: IntroScreen
  },
  onboarding: {
    key: 'onboarding',
    component: Onboarding
  }
};
```

While it was fun to experiment with `NavigationExperimental` in the previous chapter, our app doesn't really need a `Header` since all your time will be spent on the home route. Because of this, I've removed all the title properties from our route objects. The next thing we should do is remove the `Header` from `Nav`.

Inside `Nav.js`, update the `render` method to match the following:

```
render() {
  return (
    <CardStack
      onNavigateBack={this.props.pop}
      navigationState={this.props.navigation}
```

```
        renderScene={this.renderScene}
        style={styles.cardStack}
    />
  );
}
```

With the `renderHeader` property removed, we can also remove all references to `Header`, `renderNavigationBar`, the `navigationBar` style, and `globalStyles` from this component.

With the navigation header gone, we'll need to make a minor adjustment to our `pageContainer` style in `style/global.js`:

```
pageContainer: {
  backgroundColor: BG_COLOR,
  flex: 1,
  marginTop: 0,
  paddingTop: 20,
  marginBottom: 48,
  marginHorizontal: 0,
  paddingHorizontal: 10
},
```

Finally, inside `IntoScreen.js`, update the `push` call of `TouchableOpacity` so it routes you to onboarding instead:

```
const IntroScreen = ({ push }) => (
  <View style={[globalStyles.COMMON_STYLES.pageContainer,
styles.container]}>
    <TouchableOpacity
      onPress={() => push('onboarding')}
    >
      <Title>React Native News Reader</Title>
      <AppText>
        Start Reading
      </AppText>
    </TouchableOpacity>
  </View>
);
```

Now that RNNYT can route its way to our `Onboarding` component, let's begin fleshing it out. Open up `Onboarding.js` and drop in these imports at the top:

```
import React, { Component } from 'react';
import {
  StyleSheet,
  View
```

```
} from 'react-native';
import OnboardingButtons from './OnboardingButtons';
import OnboardingPanel from './OnboardingPanel';
```

We haven't built OnboardingButtons or OnboardingPanel yet, but we can start by stubbing out the structure of Onboarding as shown in the following code snippet:

```
export default class Onboarding extends Component {
  render() {
    return (
      <View style={styles.container}>
        <View style={styles.container}>
          <View style={styles.panelContainer}>
            {/* active <OnboardingPanel /> goes here */}
          </View>
          <OnboardingButtons />
        </View>
      </View>
    );
  }
}

const styles = StyleSheet.create({
  container: {
    flex: 1
  },
  panelContainer: {
    flex: 1,
    flexDirection: 'row'
  }
});
```

You may have noticed I've included two identical View elements with the same styles. Currently, these are completely redundant. However, I've opted to include both to save us time on refactoring later in the chapter.

The Onboarding component's primary role is to control which onboarding panel is active. To do this, we'll add state to our component, and create a few methods that will be used to increment and decrement the currentIndex. Add these methods to Onboarding:

```
constructor(props) {
  super(props);
  this.moveNext = this.moveNext.bind(this);
  this.movePrevious = this.movePrevious.bind(this);
  this.transitionToNextPanel = this.transitionToNextPanel.bind(this);
  this.state = {
```

```
      currentIndex: 0
    };
  }

  movePrevious() {
    this.transitionToNextPanel(this.state.currentIndex - 1);
  }

  moveNext() {
    this.transitionToNextPanel(this.state.currentIndex + 1);
  }

  transitionToNextPanel(nextIndex) {
    this.setState({
      currentIndex: nextIndex
    });
  }
```

 Since currentIndex is controlling a portion of our app's navigation, I would normally advocate that it resides within the Redux state. However, to keep the example simple, I've opted to use the component state in this chapter.

Let's next create our Button component. Open up Button.js and add the following code:

```
import React, { PropTypes } from 'react';
import {
  TouchableOpacity,
  View,
  Text,
  StyleSheet
} from 'react-native';

const BORDER_COLOR = '#fff';
const BG_COLOR = 'transparent';
const TEXT_COLOR = '#fff';
const DISABLED_COLOR = `${TEXT_COLOR}5`;

const Button = ({ style, active, onPress, children, ...rest }) => (
  <TouchableOpacity
    activeOpacity={active ? 0.7 : 1}
    onPress={active ? onPress : null}
    {...rest}
    style={[styles.button, style, !active ? styles.disabledButton : {}]}
  >
    <Text style={[styles.text, !active ? styles.disabledText : {}]}>
      {children}
    </Text>
```

```
    </TouchableOpacity>
  );

Button.propTypes = {
  active: PropTypes.bool,
  style: View.propTypes.style,
  onPress: PropTypes.func,
  children: PropTypes.node
};

Button.defaultProps = {
  active: true
};
```

Before we add our styles, let's break down what's going on in this component. Again, we're leveraging JavaScript destructuring to extract the properties we're interested in. Everything else is put into an object called `rest`. The button can be disabled by setting the active prop to `false`. When `false`, we set the `onPress` handler to `null`, and add additional styles to the `TouchableOpacity` and `Text` elements to make the component look disabled. Next, add these `styles` and export the `Button`:

```
const styles = StyleSheet.create({
  button: {
    borderStyle: 'solid',
    borderColor: BORDER_COLOR,
    borderWidth: StyleSheet.hairlineWidth,
    backgroundColor: BG_COLOR,
    borderRadius: 5,
    paddingVertical: 8,
    paddingHorizontal: 15
  },
  disabledButton: {
    borderColor: DISABLED_COLOR
  },
  text: {
    color: TEXT_COLOR,
    fontWeight: 'bold'
  },
  disabledText: {
    color: DISABLED_COLOR
  }
});

export default Button;
```

Next, we'll create a `LinkButton` that simply wraps around our existing `Button` component, but also adds some additional styles:

```
import React, { PropTypes } from 'react';
import {
  View,
  StyleSheet
} from 'react-native';

import Button from './Button';

const LinkButton = ({ style, children, ...rest }) => (
  <Button
    {...rest}
    style={[styles.button, style]}
  >
    {children}
  </Button>
);

LinkButton.propTypes = {
  style: View.propTypes.style,
  children: PropTypes.node
};

const styles = StyleSheet.create({
  button: {
    borderWidth: 0
  }
});

export default LinkButton;
```

There's a new color style we'll need for a few components. Let's add it to `style/global.js` so that it's accessible to every component:

```
export const LIGHT_OVERLAY_COLOR = '#fff2';
```

With the color set and our buttons built, let's next build the component, which will house the **Previous** and **Next** buttons. Add the following to `OnboardingButtons.js`:

```
import React, { PropTypes } from 'react';
import {
  View,
  StyleSheet
} from 'react-native';
import Button from './Button';
import LinkButton from './LinkButton';
```

```
import { LIGHT_OVERLAY_COLOR } from '../styles/global';

const OnboardingButtons = ({
  totalItems,
  currentIndex,
  movePrevious,
  moveNext
}) => (
  <View style={styles.container}>
    <LinkButton onPress={movePrevious} active={currentIndex > 0}>
      Previous
    </LinkButton>
    <Button
      onPress={moveNext}
      active={currentIndex < totalItems - 1}
    >
      Next
    </Button>
  </View>
);

OnboardingButtons.propTypes = {
  totalItems: PropTypes.number.isRequired,
  currentIndex: PropTypes.number.isRequired,
  movePrevious: PropTypes.func.isRequired,
  moveNext: PropTypes.func.isRequired
};

const styles = StyleSheet.create({
  container: {
    flex: 0.25,
    flexDirection: 'row',
    alignItems: 'center',
    paddingHorizontal: 20,
    justifyContent: 'space-between',
    paddingVertical: 20,
    position: 'absolute',
    backgroundColor: LIGHT_OVERLAY_COLOR,
    bottom: 0,
    left: 0,
    right: 0
  }
});

export default OnboardingButtons;
```

We'll need our buttons in a row and docked to the bottom of the view. To achieve this, we've used absolute positioning and flexbox set to `'row'` and `'space-between'`, respectively. In order for our buttons to affect the parent Onboarding view, Onboarding needs to pass down a few props. For starters, it'll need to pass two functions-movePrevious and moveNext. These functions will update the parent Onboarding view's state.currentIndex. Also, in order for OnboardingButtons to know if we're currently on the first or last onboarding panel, we need to tell OnboardingButtons how many panels there are in total, totalItems, and which one is currently selected, currentIndex. With these pieces of information, we can set the active property of the **Previous** and **Next** buttons.

A few of our onboarding components will need to know the dimensions of our device. We can centralize this into a single file. Create a file called device.js in the config directory:

```
import { Dimensions } from 'react-native';

export const {
  width: DEVICE_WIDTH,
  height: DEVICE_HEIGHT
} = Dimensions.get('window');
```

device.js simply exports two constants-DEVICE_WIDTH and DEVICE_HEIGHT. DEVICE_WIDTH will be used to build the onboarding panel.

The onboarding panel will contain an image, text, and a custom background color. As you'd guess, we'll build that next. Add the following to OnboardingPanel.js:

```
import React, { PropTypes } from 'react';
import {
  View,
  Image,
  StyleSheet
} from 'react-native';
import AppText from './AppText';
import { LIGHT_OVERLAY_COLOR } from '../styles/global';

import {
  DEVICE_HEIGHT,
  DEVICE_WIDTH
} from '../config/device';

const MINIMUM_IMAGE_HEIGHT = 460;
const IMAGE_SIZE = 300;

const OnboardingPanel = ({ backgroundColor, message, uri, style }) => (
  <View
```

```
      style={[styles.panel, { backgroundColor }, style]}
    >
      <View style={styles.content}>
        <AppText>{message}</AppText>
      </View>
      <View style={styles.container}>
        <Image
          source={{ uri }}
          style={{ width: IMAGE_SIZE, height: IMAGE_SIZE }}
        />
      </View>
    </View>
);

OnboardingPanel.propTypes = {
  message: PropTypes.string.isRequired,
  backgroundColor: PropTypes.string.isRequired,
  uri: PropTypes.string.isRequired,
  style: View.propTypes.style
};

export default OnboardingPanel;
```

The styles for this component will require a bit of extra engineering. We need to constrain the height of the content `View` based on the available vertical screen real estate. To do this, we'll call a function that calculates this maximum height for us (styles in JavaScript FTW). Refer to the following code:

```
const calcTextContainerMaxHeight = (deviceHeight, minImageHeight) => {
  if ((deviceHeight - minImageHeight) < (deviceHeight * 0.25)) {
    return deviceHeight - minImageHeight;
  }
  return undefined;
};

const styles = StyleSheet.create({
  container: {
    flex: 1
  },
  panel: {
    flex: 1,
    justifyContent: 'center',
    alignItems: 'center',
    overflow: 'hidden',
    width: DEVICE_WIDTH
  },
  content: {
    flex: 0.25,
```

```
        justifyContent: 'flex-end',
        alignItems: 'center',
        alignSelf: 'stretch',
        padding: 20,
        marginBottom: 10,
        backgroundColor: LIGHT_OVERLAY_COLOR,
        maxHeight: calcTextContainerMaxHeight(DEVICE_HEIGHT,
    MINIMUM_IMAGE_HEIGHT)
    }
});
```

Ideally, we'd like the content area to `flex` to `0.25`. But, just to be safe, we'll call `calcTextContainerMaxHeight` to verify whether we have enough space to do so. If there's not enough space, we return a fixed maximum height.

Next, we're going to create a configuration file that houses the actual onboarding content. Add a file named `onboarding.js` to the `config` directory. We'll populate the `uri` and `message` with dummy content. Then we'll use `ACCENT_COLORS` from global styles to set a different background color for each content configuration:

```
import {
  ACCENT_COLORS,
  MUTED_COLOR,
  TEXT_COLOR
} from '../styles/global';

const placeholderImage = 'https://placeholdit.imgix.net/' +
  '~text?txtsize=24' +
  `&bg=${MUTED_COLOR.replace('#', '')}` +
  `&txtclr=${TEXT_COLOR.replace('#', '')}` +
  '&w=350&h=350&txttrack=0&txt=Placeholder+Image+';

const content = [
  'Welcome to RNNYT!',
  'With this app, you can learn all about the news!',
  'And you get to experiment with React Native!',
  'And aren\'t animations fun?!'
];

export default content.map((message, i) => ({
  message,
  color: '#fff',
  backgroundColor: ACCENT_COLORS[i % ACCENT_COLORS.length],
  uri: `${placeholderImage}${i + 1}`
}));
```

With our content ready and our components created, we're ready to piece everything together inside Onboarding. To do this, we'll need to import our onboarding configuration:

```
import onboardingContent from '../config/onboarding';
```

Because onboardingContent is just an array of objects, we can select the appropriate item by using the value of state.currentIndex. The resulting object can be passed down as props to the OnboardingPanel. Also, because we already created the methods necessary to increment and decrement state.currentIndex, we can pass these along with totalItems (onboardingContent.length) and currentIndex to OnboardingButtons:

```
render() {
  return (
    <View style={styles.container}>
      <View style={styles.container}>
        <View style={styles.panelContainer}>
          <OnboardingPanel {...onboardingContent[this.state.currentIndex]}
/>
        </View>
        <OnboardingButtons
          totalItems={onboardingContent.length}
          currentIndex={this.state.currentIndex}
          movePrevious={this.movePrevious}
          moveNext={this.moveNext}
        />
      </View>
    </View>
  );
}
```

If you refresh your app in the simulator, you'll now be able to navigate our basic onboarding experience. Take a look at the following screenshot:

Adding LayoutAnimation

With our basic onboarding experience built, let's explore React Native's `LayoutAnimation` API to apply some simple transitions as you navigate from onboarding screen to onboarding screen.

`LayoutAnimation` is a highly performant `animation` API for animating the entirety of a component and its children whenever the animated component is created or its state is updated. `LayoutAnimation` executes the animation upon the next render cycle, animating the component from its current state to its next state. Two common ways of utilizing `LayoutAnimation` are right before calling `setState` or inside the `componentWillReceiveProps` method. Before triggering the next render cycle, you simply need to call `LayoutAnimation.configureNext`, passing it the appropriate animation configuration:

```
LayoutAnimation.configureNext(animationConfiguration,
callbackCompletionMethod);
```

```
this.setState({ stateToChange: newStateValue });
```

Like many things, animation is one of those topics that is best understood through experimentation rather than documentation. With that said, let's explore how we can integrate LayoutAnimation into our onboarding experience.

To demonstrate how this works, we're going to call LayoutAnimation.configureNext inside our transitionToNextPanel method. Since moveNext and movePrevious both use this method, this is a perfect place to configure our animation. First, let's import LayoutAnimation at the top of Onboarding.js:

```
import {
  StyleSheet,
  View,
  LayoutAnimation
} from 'react-native';
```

Additionally, update transitionToNextPanel to match the following:

```
transitionToNextPanel(nextIndex) {
  LayoutAnimation.configureNext(LayoutAnimation.Presets.easeInEaseOut);
  this.setState({
    currentIndex: nextIndex
  });
}
```

This effectively tells the component, on its next render cycle, to animate using the preconfigured easeInEaseOut animation. However, this isn't quite enough for our animations to work yet. Currently, we only render one OnboardingPanel and just update its props with the currently selected onboardingContent. To get a nice, sliding transition, we should instead render all the panels and simply set the width of the invisible panels to 0. Firstly, add a style to the Onboarding style sheet:

```
hidden: {
  width: 0
}
```

Then update the render method so it renders all four OnboardingPanel elements and applies the hidden style to the inactive panels:

```
<View style={styles.panelContainer}>
  {onboardingContent.map((panel, i) => (
    <OnboardingPanel
      key={i}
      {...panel}
      style={i !== this.state.currentIndex ? styles.hidden : undefined}
```

[310]

```
        />
    ))}
  </View>
```

If you refresh your app and click either the **Next** or **Previous** button, you'll see each panel nicely transition into view. If you'd like to experiment, try out these two other preconfigured animations–**linear** and **spring**. All of the `LayoutAnimation.Presets.*` are simply that, packaged animations presets. Alternatively, you can create a customized configuration to control how elements should animate when they are created, deleted, or updated. You can also fine tune other values specific to each type of animation such as `duration` or, in the case of `spring`, `springDamping`. As an example, let's change `LayoutAnimation.configureNext` to use a very slow `spring` animation:

```
LayoutAnimation.configureNext({
  duration: 3000,
  update: {
    springDamping: 0.2,
    type: LayoutAnimation.Types.spring,
    property: LayoutAnimation.Properties.scaleXY
  }
});
```

Here, we've updated our component to use the `spring` animation, which animates the property `LayoutAnimation.Properties.scaleXY`. We've configured `springDamping` to create an exaggerated bounce effect. Lastly, we've set the duration to last `3000` milliseconds. When you test this animation, you'll find a rather exaggerated spring transition. Feel free to experiment with different configuration options until you settle on something you like. For me, I'll just stick with the original `LayoutAnimation.configureNext(LayoutAnimation.Presets.easeInEaseOut)`.

From my experience, using `LayoutAnimation` on `Text` elements can produce unexpected results. Even in our example, the `Text` doesn't always transition in lock step with the rest of the view. I have found that you can achieve more predictable results by wrapping each `Text` element in a `View`. This has been noted by others as well

`https://github.com/facebook/react-native/issues/6502`.

Adding a bit more animation

Before we wrap up this section on LayoutAnimation, let's add in one more bit of animation to close out our onboarding experience. Once the user has reached the final panel, we want them to click on a **Done** button. This will slide up one final panel before automatically transitioning them off the actual application. To do this, we'll need to add one more piece of state to our app. Update your constructor to the following:

```
constructor(props) {
  super(props);
  this.moveNext = this.moveNext.bind(this);
  this.movePrevious = this.movePrevious.bind(this);
  this.transitionToNextPanel = this.transitionToNextPanel.bind(this);
  this.moveFinal = this.moveFinal.bind(this);
  this.state = {
    currentIndex: 0,
    isDone: false
  };
}
```

The moveFinal method will use LayoutAnimation to spring open the final panel. After two seconds, Onboarding will automatically redirect you to the home (news) route. Since Onboarding is a descendent of NavigationContainer, it already has access to the push action creator:

```
moveFinal() {
  LayoutAnimation.configureNext({
    duration: 1250,
    update: {
      springDamping: 0.4,
      type: LayoutAnimation.Types.spring
    }
  });
  this.setState({ isDone: true });
  setTimeout(() => {
    this.props.push('home');
  }, 2000);
}
```

Let's be good React citizens and add prop validation to `Onboarding`:

```
import React, { Component, PropTypes } from 'react';

// omitted for clarity

Onboarding.propTypes = {
  push: PropTypes.func.isRequired
};
```

Sweet. Now we need to configure `OnboardingButtons` to dynamically hide and show the **Done** button, and call `moveFinal`. First, update the element inside `Onboarding`. Refer to the following code snippet:

```
<OnboardingButtons
  totalItems={onboardingContent.length}
  currentIndex={this.state.currentIndex}
  movePrevious={this.movePrevious}
  moveNext={this.moveNext}
  moveFinal={this.moveFinal}
/>
```

Now update `OnboardingButtons` to follow suit:

```
const OnboardingButtons = ({
  totalItems,
  currentIndex,
  movePrevious,
  moveNext,
  moveFinal
}) => (
  <View style={styles.container}>
    <LinkButton onPress={movePrevious} active={currentIndex > 0}>
      Previous
    </LinkButton>
    {currentIndex === totalItems - 1 ? (
      <Button onPress={moveFinal}>
        Done
      </Button>
    ) : (
      <Button
        onPress={moveNext}
        active={currentIndex < totalItems - 1}
      >
        Next
      </Button>
    )}
  </View>
```

```
);

OnboardingButtons.propTypes = {
  totalItems: PropTypes.number.isRequired,
  currentIndex: PropTypes.number.isRequired,
  movePrevious: PropTypes.func.isRequired,
  moveNext: PropTypes.func.isRequired,
  moveFinal: PropTypes.func.isRequired
};
```

When the user clicks **Done**, we'd like the onboarding panels to vertically collapse and a view saying **Let's read the news!** to appear. To manage this collapsible behavior, we'll create a `CollapsibleView` component.

Create a file in `src/components` called `CollapsibleView.js`:

```
import React, { PropTypes } from 'react';
import {
  StyleSheet,
  View
} from 'react-native';

const CollapsibleView = ({ children, style, hide }) => (
  <View style={[styles.container, hide ? styles.hidden : {}]}>
    <View style={[styles.absoluteContainer, style]}>
      {children}
    </View>
  </View>
);

CollapsibleView.propTypes = {
  style: View.propTypes.style,
  hide: PropTypes.bool.isRequired,
  children: PropTypes.node
};

const styles = StyleSheet.create({
  container: {
    flex: 1
  },
  absoluteContainer: {
    position: 'absolute',
    left: 0,
    right: 0,
    top: 0,
    bottom: 0
  },
  hidden: {
```

```
        height: 0,
        flex: 0
    }
});
```

```
export default CollapsibleView;
```

This component nests two `View` elements and can toggle their height when passed the `hide` prop as a Boolean. Optionally, you can pass additional style properties that are applied to the inner `View` element.

Now back in `Onboarding.js`, add these imports:

```
import AppText from './AppText';
import CollapsibleView from './CollapsibleView';
import { ACCENT_COLORS } from '../styles/global';
```

We're going to add two `CollapsibleView` elements. The first one will wrap around the onboarding panels. The second will simply contain our final message to our users before transitioning them off to the news. Each will set the `hide` property based on the `isDone` state. Once again, update the `render` method with the following:

```
render() {
  return (
    <View style={styles.container}>
      <CollapsibleView
        style={[
          styles.container
        ]}
        hide={this.state.isDone}
      >
        <View style={styles.panelContainer}>
          {onboardingContent.map((panel, i) => (
            <OnboardingPanel
              key={i}
              {...panel}
              style={i !== this.state.currentIndex ? styles.hidden :
undefined}
            />
          ))}
        </View>
        <OnboardingButtons
          totalItems={onboardingContent.length}
          currentIndex={this.state.currentIndex}
          movePrevious={this.movePrevious}
          moveNext={this.moveNext}
          moveFinal={this.moveFinal}
```

```
        />
      </CollapsibleView>
      <CollapsibleView hide={!this.state.isDone}
style={styles.doneContainer}>
          <AppText style={styles.doneText}>Let's read the news!</AppText>
      </CollapsibleView>
    </View>
  );
}
```

And, finally, add these styles to the StyleSheet in Onboarding.js:

```
doneContainer: {
  overflow: 'hidden',
  backgroundColor: ACCENT_COLORS[0],
  justifyContent: 'center',
  alignItems: 'center'
},
doneText: {
  fontSize: 20
}
```

Give the app one more run through. You'll now be able to click **Next** through each of the onboarding panels. Once you click **Done**, the message **Let's read the news!** will appear before transitioning you off to the news.

Understanding Animated

LayoutAnimation is great for transitioning views between states using simple animation logic. However, LayoutAnimation is limited in that it doesn't allow you to sequence more complex animations or potentially tie an animation to a user gesture. This is where the Animated API fills the gap. Internally, the Animated API leverages requestAnimationFrame to synchronize animations to 60 frames per second. It then updates the state via setNativeProps as a means of avoiding React's diffing algorithm, thus keeping the animations performant and smooth.

In order to use the Animated API, you need two things. First, you'll need an Animated.* component–Animated.Image, Animated.View, or Animated.Text. These special Animated.* components possess special bindings that tie them to the second thing you'll need an: Animated.Value or an Animated.ValueXY. These values are used to track animation changes across either a single-dimension Animated.Value or a two-dimension Animated.ValueXY. Unlike LayoutAnimation, you can create multiple Animated.Value objects to control many elements independently rather than being forced to animate everything together. Like earlier, this will become much clearer by walking you through an example so you can see it for yourself. So let's do exactly that.

Refactoring our Onboarding experience

With the groundwork for animation in place, we'll refactor our existing `Onboarding` component to leverage the `Animated` API. Before diving right into the code, let's diagram what it is we'll be building in this refactoring effort.

Previously, each onboarding panel was in one of two states–**expanded** or **collapsed**. The way we managed that was by comparing the item's index to `state.currentIndex`. If the onboarding panel's index did not match `state.currentIndex`, we applied `width: 0` to it via the `hidden` style. Otherwise, the panel was expanded, filling up the entire screen. In our new implementation, our panels work on a continuous horizontal scroll. Only one panel (the one that matches `state.currentIndex`) will be within the phone's visible viewport. Other panels will either be scrolled off to the left or to the right. Take a look at the following diagram:

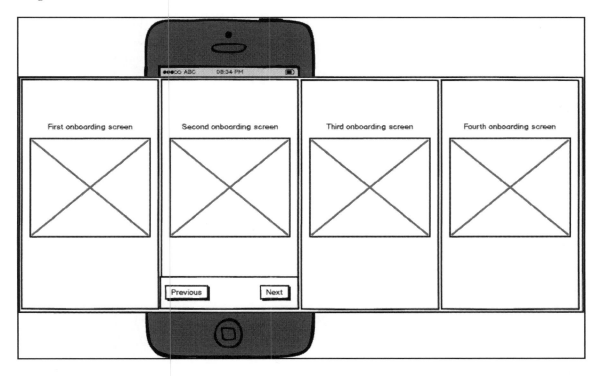

In the previous diagram, the app's `state.currentIndex` is set to 1, meaning we're looking at the second onboarding panel. On our first pass at applying the `Animated` API, we'll simply leverage the **Previous** and **Next** buttons to scroll each panel in and out of view. Once the panel has slid into view, we'll update `state.currentIndex` to match the state of our view. Later, we'll allow the user to drag the panels left or right in lieu of pressing a button. In order to set up this new implementation, let's do a bit of refactoring within our `render` method.

Adding Animated to our Onboarding experience

Before we forget, let's import the `Animated` object at the top of `Onboarding.js`:

```
import {
  StyleSheet,
  View,
  LayoutAnimation,
  Animated
} from 'react-native';
```

Like I said earlier, in order for `Animated` to do anything, we need two things–an `Animated.*` component and an `Animated.Value`. In our case, we're going to use the transform style property `translateX` to shift the position of our parent `<View style={styles.panelContainer} />` relative to the value stored in an `Animated.Value`. Put another way, if our `Animated.Value` is set to `-375`, then our panel container will have a `translateX` value of `-375`. These two values will track one to one. In order to wire this up, we'll need to make a few adjustments to our code.

For starters, in order to make the onboarding panel span four times the width of the device (see the previous diagram), we need to know how wide the device is. Import the `DEVICE_WIDTH` from `device.js`:

```
import { DEVICE_WIDTH } from '../config/device';
```

Next, inside the constructor, create a new property on state called `pan`, as an `Animated.Value` that's initialized to 0. Note that we'll be using an `Animated.Value` and not an `Animated.ValueXY` since we are only animating across a single dimension. Refer to the following code snippet:

```
this.state = {
  currentIndex: 0,
  isDone: false,
  pan: new Animated.Value(0)
};
```

The next part is interesting. We no longer need to collapse the width of the hidden panels. This is because the parent panel container will simply pan left and right such that only the active panel is within view. The others will be off screen. In order to achieve this, we'll make the panel container span four times the width of the device. Additionally, because the parent panel is now what actually animates, we need to swap it out with an `Animated.View` and apply `translateX` to it:

```
<Animated.View
  style={[
    styles.panelContainer,
    { width: DEVICE_WIDTH * onboardingContent.length },
    {
      transform: [{
        translateX: this.state.pan
      }]
    }
  ]}
>
  {onboardingContent.map((panel, i) => (
    <OnboardingPanel key={i} {...panel} />
  ))}
</Animated.View>
```

Now comes the fun part! We've got all the parts in place, we just need to make them actually do something. Let's drop in our animation code and then afterwards I'll explain what it's actually doing. Update the `transitionToNextPanel` method to the following:

```
transitionToNextPanel(nextIndex) {
  Animated.timing(this.state.pan, {
    toValue: nextIndex * DEVICE_WIDTH * -1,
    duration: 300
  }).start(() => {
    this.setState({
      currentIndex: nextIndex
    });
  });
}
```

When you refresh the app, clicking **Previous** and **Next** will nicely slide each panel in from the appropriate side.

That was a good bit of code, so let's break down what's happening. Firstly, we defined a new property on `state` called `pan` as a new `Animated.Value` and initialized it to 0. For the sake of illustration, let's assume we're using an iPhone 6, which has a `DEVICE_WIDTH` of 375. We want to transform the `translateX` property such that, when `state.currentIndex` is equal to 0, `translateX` is also 0. This means our first panel is visible. In order to show the next panel, `state.currentIndex` equals 1, we'll need to pull our onboarding panel container to the left. To achieve this, we need the `translateX` property to equal –375. To see the third panel, `translateX` needs to equal –750 (–375 * 2). To execute the animation itself, we'll use one of the many `Animated` animation methods, called `timing`. `Animated.timing` works by specifying the `Animated.Value` you wish to update (in our case, `this.state.pan`), a configuration specifying what you'd like the value to transition to (`toValue`), and how long the animation should take (`duration`). In our case, we'll calculate the `toValue` each time, based on the `nextIndex`. This will give us our desired `translateX` values of 0, –375, –750, and –1125. Calling `start` is what actually executes `Animated.timing`. You can optionally pass `start` a callback method. In our case, once the animation has completed, we'll update `this.state.currentIndex` to equal the `nextIndex` value. This way everything stays nicely in sync. The final piece of the animation equation is binding our `this.state.pan` value to `translateX`. This is achieved by adding a style object to the `Animated.View` that dynamically sets `translateX` to the value of `this.state.pan`.

In our code, we utilized `Animated.timing`, but there are two other animation options. `Animated.spring` creates a more bounce-like effect. For this, you only need to specify the `toValue`, but it also allows you to further configure it by setting the friction, tension, velocity, and bounciness. `Animated.decay` is used to slow an animation down from an initial velocity. This could be useful for simulating flicking an object so that it gradually slows down after release.

The `Animated` API also enables you to group animations in interesting ways. So far, we've only used a single `Animated.timing` that tracks against the `Animated.Value`. If you create multiple `Animated.Value` objects, you will be able to sequence one animation after another, run them in parallel, or create delays between each animation.

Take the following example:

```
Animated.stagger(200, [
    Animated.timing(this.state.animatedValue1, {
        toValue,
        duration: 500
    }),
    Animated.timing(this.state.animatedValue2, {
```

```
    toValue,
    duration: 500]
  }),
]).start()
```

 Here we've grouped two timing methods. `Animated.stagger` accepts two values–the first is the delay between each animation and the second is an ordered list of animations to execute. Alternatively, you could group the values using `Animated.sequence` or `Animated.parallel`. Both work similarly to `Animated.stagger` except they only accept a list of animations, no delay is necessary. `Animated.parallel` will fire off all animations at once. `Animated.sequence` will fire off one animation after the previous one has completed.

Interpolating Animated Values

Sometimes you may want to animate any range of numbers. Those numbers might not map exactly one to one with the value stored in an `Animated.Value`. For example, say pressing a button increments an `Animated.Value` by one on each press. Let's also say you have a `View` currently sized to 10 by 10 points. When you increment the value, the `View` will jump in size to 200 by 200 points. This is clearly not a one-to-one mapping. But, you can create this relationship between `inputs` and `outputs` via interpolation.

To illustrate this idea, let's create another component that will display the overall progress of the user's onboarding tour. There are four onboarding panels, so each time you pivot to the next, the progress bar will fill up another 25%.

`OnboardingProgress` will need two props–a reference to the `Animated.Value` (pan) of `Onboarding`, so it can interpolate progress, and the total number of panels, `totalItems`, so it can calculate how much progress has been made. We'll start by building out an inanimate version to establish structure and some styling inside `OnboardingProgress.js`:

```
import React, { PropTypes } from 'react';
import {
  View,
  Animated,
  StyleSheet
} from 'react-native';
import { DEVICE_WIDTH } from '../config/device';

const BAR_WIDTH = 250;
const COMPLETION_BAR_BORDER_COLOR = '#fff';
const COMPLETION_BAR_BG_COLOR = 'transparent';
```

```
const COMPLETION_BAR_STATUS_BG_COLOR = '#fff6';

const OnboardingProgress = ({ totalItems, pan }) => (
  <View style={styles.container}>
    <View style={styles.bar}>
      <Animated.View style={styles.status} />
    </View>
  </View>
);

OnboardingProgress.propTypes = {
  totalItems: PropTypes.number.isRequired,
  pan: PropTypes.instanceOf(Animated.Value)
};

const styles = StyleSheet.create({
  container: {
    flexDirection: 'row',
    justifyContent: 'center',
    alignItems: 'center',
    position: 'absolute',
    bottom: 100,
    left: 0,
    right: 0
  },
  bar: {
    borderRadius: 6,
    height: 10,
    borderWidth: 1,
    borderColor: COMPLETION_BAR_BORDER_COLOR,
    backgroundColor: COMPLETION_BAR_BG_COLOR,
    marginHorizontal: 20,
    width: BAR_WIDTH,
    overflow: 'hidden',
    flexDirection: 'row'
  },
  status: {
    backgroundColor: COMPLETION_BAR_STATUS_BG_COLOR,
    height: 8
  }
});

export default OnboardingProgress;
```

The progress bar will be absolutely positioned just above the button bar. The bar itself is hardcoded to 250 points wide. `Animated.View` doesn't yet have a defined width. Since we're starting on the first onboarding screen, we need it to be 25% complete, thus 62.5 points wide. When we transition to the second panel, it will animate to 125 points, and so on. The `Animated.Value` starts at 0. When it moves to the second panel, it transitions to -375. When it moves to the third panel it will be set to -750. You can think of this relationship as mapping `inputs` to `outputs`. Our input values are 0, -375, -750, and -1125. The output values are 62.5 (25%), 125 (50%), 187.5 (75%), and 250 (100%). We'll create this relationship with the `interpolate` method of our `Animated.Value`.

We'll add a function that creates this mapping dynamically, based on the number of onboarding screens, the width of our progress bar, and the overall device width. Update the `Animated.View` with the following:

```
<Animated.View
  style={[
    styles.status,
    computeCompletionBarWidth(totalItems, BAR_WIDTH, DEVICE_WIDTH, pan)
  ]}
/>
```

Then, add the `computeCompletionBarWidth` function to the `OnboardingProgress` component:

```
const computeCompletionBarWidth = (itemCount, barWidth, deviceWidth, pan)
=> {
  const inputRange = [];
  const outputRange = [];
  for (let i = itemCount - 1; i >= 0; i -= 1) {
    inputRange.push(deviceWidth * i * -1);
    outputRange.push(barWidth * ((i + 1) / itemCount));
  }

  if (outputRange.length < 2) {
    inputRange.push(inputRange[inputRange.length - 1]);
    outputRange.push(outputRange[outputRange.length - 1]);
  }

  return {
    width: pan.interpolate({
      inputRange,
      outputRange
    })
  };
};
```

This function will create input and output ranges, and return a style object that sets the width based on the interpolated mapping. The `if` block is there to ensure `inputRange` and `outputRange` have two or more values. If they don't, React Native will throw an error.

Now all that's left is adding `OnboardingProgress` to `Onboarding`:

```
import OnboardingProgress from './OnboardingProgress';
```

Then add the component between the `Animated.View` and `OnboardingButtons`:

```
<OnboardingProgress
  totalItems={onboardingContent.length}
  pan={this.state.pan}
/>
```

Now, when you run the app, you'll see the progress bar move as we transition from screen to screen. Take a look at the following screenshot:

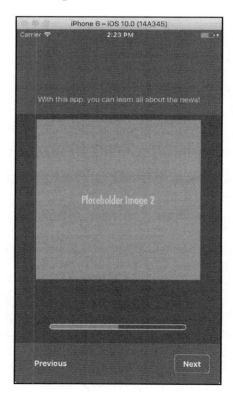

Using PanResponder with the Animated API

To round out our animation chapter, we'll explore one more very powerful way to leverage animation. PanResponder is a React Native API for tracking simple gestures. We can use PanResponder to track the user dragging their finger across the screen as a way to transition from panel to panel. As usual, we'll begin by importing PanResponder at the top of our file:

```
import {
  StyleSheet,
  View,
  LayoutAnimation,
  Animated,
  PanResponder
} from 'react-native';
```

PanResponder needs to track the value of state.pan as it updates. We'll do this by adding a componentWillMount lifecycle method. Here, we'll listen to changes in state.pan by utilizing the addListener method. We'll also add a componentWillUnmount method to remove the listener once the component is unmounted:

```
componentWillMount() {
  this.dragPosition = 0;
  this.panListener = this.state.pan.addListener((value) => {
    this.dragPosition = value.value;
  });
}

componentWillUnmount() {
  this.state.pan.removeListener(this.panListener);
}
```

As state.pan updates, the addListener callback is called with the updated value. We'll then store that value on the property dragPosition (this will come in handy a little later on). Now, in order to use PanResponder, we'll use PanResponder.create to create a number of PanResponder-specific lifecycle methods. The resulting object containing all these lifecycle methods will be stored on another property of Onboarding. Doing so will allow us to easily apply all of these methods to the element in which we want to track the user gesture.

Before we create the actual implementation, let's review the relevant PanResponder lifecycle methods we'll be using. The first one is called onMoveShouldSetPanResponder. This method simply needs to return true in order for the remaining methods to execute. onPanResponderGrant is the next in the series. It will only be called once per drag. It will initialize our Animated.Value and an offset value that corresponds to wherever the user's finger is at that moment. onPanResponderMove will follow suit after onPanResponderGrant. Unlike onPanResponderGrant, onPanResponderMove is called continuously as the drag event occurs. Each callback of onPanResponderMove receives two arguments, a synthetic touch event represented as a nativeEvent object, along with a gestureState. Each object has useful properties related to the touch event. In particular, gestureState carries a property called dx that stores the accumulated drag distance across the x axis since the touch gesture started. Once the user has lifted their finger from the device, PanResponder calls the onPanResponderRelease callback. It too receives the same nativeEvent and gestureState objects as arguments. This method is where we'll place all our business logic to simply answer the necessary questions: What do we want our view to do now that the user has finished touching the screen? Did they drag far enough? Did they drag fast enough? Did they release the touch event on the correct side of the screen? These are all questions we can answer and respond to in the onPanResponderRelease callback.

For these basics of how lifecycle operates for PanResponder, let's add them to our code and then we can review what it's actually doing. Add the following to the componentWillMount method:

```
this.panResponder = PanResponder.create({
  onMoveShouldSetPanResponder: () => true,
  onPanResponderGrant: () => {
    this.state.pan.setOffset(this.dragPosition);
    this.state.pan.setValue(0);
  },

  onPanResponderMove: (e, gestureState) => {
    this.state.pan.setValue(gestureState.dx);
  },

  onPanResponderRelease: (e) => {
    const movedLeft = e.nativeEvent.pageX < (DEVICE_WIDTH / 2);
    this.state.pan.flattenOffset();
    this.transitionToNextPanel(movedLeft
      ? this.state.currentIndex + 1
      : this.state.currentIndex - 1
    );
  }
});
```

As stated earlier, onMoveShouldSetPanResponder simply needs to return true. The onPanResponderGrant callback is then called only once per touch event. We're using it to update the offset with the current value of dragPosition and initialize state.pan to 0. Then, as long as the user continues to touch the screen, onPanResponderMove continually updates this.state.pan with the accumulated drag distance stored in gestureState.dx. Once the user releases their finger from the screen, the onPanResponderRelease callback will be called. Here, we need to determine which way the user has dragged. We can capture the point at which the user released their finger from the screen along the *x* axis by accessing e.nativeEvent.pageX. In our simple implementation, we'll assume that, if the value is less than half the device's width, that means the user dragged to the left. Otherwise, the user must have dragged to the right. Now that we know which way the user has dragged, we'll call flattenOffset. This will merge the offset value with the base value and reset our offset. And, finally, we'll call our existing method, transitionToNextPanel, with one of two values. If we swiped to the left, we need to increment state.currentIndex by one. If we swiped right, we'll decrement it by one. Now, the last piece of the puzzle is to apply these methods to our Animated.View. Refer to the following code snippet:

```
<Animated.View
  {...this.panResponder.panHandlers}
  style={[
    styles.panelContainer,
    { width: DEVICE_WIDTH * onboardingContent.length },
    {
      transform: [{
        translateX: this.state.pan
      }]
    }
  ]}
>
  /* Contents omitted for clarity */
</Animated.View>
```

This will take all the lifecycle methods we created and apply them to the Animated.View. Refresh your simulator and give it a spin by dragging across the screen.

Touching up PanResponder

If you spent a few moments playing around with the app, you may have noticed one or two flaws in our design. For starters, the user is able to swipe right on the first onboarding panel and swipe left on the final one. Either case will put the app into an undesired state. To avoid this, we need to add some additional logic to the onPanResponderRelease method to detect if the user is trying to swipe outside the permitted bounds:

```
onPanResponderRelease: (e) => {
  const movedLeft = e.nativeEvent.pageX < (DEVICE_WIDTH / 2);
  let updateState = false;
  let toValue = movedLeft
    ? DEVICE_WIDTH * (this.state.currentIndex + 1) * -1
    : DEVICE_WIDTH * (this.state.currentIndex - 1) * -1;

  if (toValue > 0) {
    toValue = 0;
  } else if (toValue < ((DEVICE_WIDTH * onboardingContent.length) -
DEVICE_WIDTH) * -1) {
    toValue = ((DEVICE_WIDTH * onboardingContent.length) - DEVICE_WIDTH) *
-1;
  } else {
    updateState = true;
  }

  this.state.pan.flattenOffset();

  if (updateState) {
    this.transitionToNextPanel(movedLeft
      ? this.state.currentIndex + 1
      : this.state.currentIndex - 1
    );
  } else {
    Animated.spring(this.state.pan, {
      velocity: 0.5,
      tensions: 0.2,
      friction: 2,
      toValue
    }).start();
  }
}
```

We've added two variables `updateState` and `toValue`. `updateState` will track whether or not we should execute the call to `transitionToNextPanel`. In order to know this, we need to calculate what the next state would be. This is where `toValue` comes in. 0 is the largest value possible. If `toValue` is greater than 0, we force the next state to 0. If the value is less than −1125, we force it to −1125. Otherwise, we call `transitionToNextPanel`. If we don't call `transitionToNextPanel`, we'll use `Animated.spring` to spring back to `toValue`.

The only piece that's left is a little bit of design polish. In the event the user tries to swipe outside the bounds of our panel list, the background color in the outlying area should match that of the active panel. We can achieve this by setting the `backgroundColor` of our main content area to match the active panel:

```
<CollapsibleView
  style={[
    styles.container,
    { backgroundColor:
onboardingContent[this.state.currentIndex].backgroundColor }
  ]}
  hide={this.state.isDone}
>
...
```

And there we have it. We've fixed our bugs and implemented a pretty impressive onboarding experience!

Summary

In this chapter we have experimented with many forms of animation. `LayoutAnimation` is great for composing simple animations, particularly when animating the size and layout of multiple elements at once. In contrast, the `Animated` API allows for much finer-tuned, precise animations. Additionally, you can pair the `Animated` API with `PanResponder` to animate elements in response to user touch interactions.

With the majority of our app built, it's time we explored a new domain of React Native. In the next chapter, we'll configure our environments for testing on an Android emulator, and refactor our RNNYT app to work across iOS and Android.

9
Refactoring for Android

With a solid footing in the React Native ecosystem, we've been able to build a very credible iOS application. But, as we stated back in `Chapter 2`, *Saying Hello World in React Native*, React Native is about more than just iOS. React Native allows us to easily build apps for both iOS and Android platforms. What you're about to learn is just how easy that is to accomplish.

The goal of this chapter is twofold. Firstly, similar to `Chapter 2`, *Saying Hello World in React Native*, where we configured our environments for building and testing on the iOS simulator, we'll need to do the same for Android. Once we've configured our computers for React Native Android development, we'll update our RNNYT app so that it can run on both platforms. What you will discover as we work through this process is that most of our code runs out of the box without any modification. There are just a few components and styles we'll need to refactor to make the experience feel native to each platform.

With that said, here's the rundown of what we'll be doing in this chapter:

- Installing and configuring all the necessary software required to run React Native apps in an Android emulator
- Reviewing how to branch our code such that we can tailor solutions to each specific platform
- Creating a customized Android `HomeScreen` component
- Refactoring our remaining components and styles to work across iOS and Android

Installing the necessary tools

If you have spent any time reading the official React Native documentation, you may have found it to be great in some areas and less great in others. Up until relatively recently, I personally found the React Native Android setup documentation to be challenging. Thankfully, as of version 0.25.0, the React Native community has really stepped up. If you head over to the React Native **Getting Started** page (`https://facebook.github.io/react -native/docs/getting-started.html`), you'll find excellent documentation that walks you through the process. The Android setup section of this chapter will closely follow the directions outlined on the official React Native setup docs. When appropriate, I'll add a bit more context, but feel free to refer to the React Native docs as they'll always be the most current.

Many of the tools required for Android development were already addressed in `Chapter 2`, *Saying Hello World in React Native*. In this chapter, the main parts you'll need to focus on are installing the **Java Development Kit (JDK)**, **Android Studio**, and configuring some environment variables. Later, we'll use the Android emulator that comes as an optional install with Android Studio. Alternatively, GenyMotion also allows you to emulate many popular Android devices and offers a more robust suite of tools, which are particularly tailored towards automated testing. However, these advanced features are not available with the free offering from GenyMotion, but may be worth exploring depending on your needs. Since we're already planning on installing Android Studio, we'll just stick with its emulator.

Installing the Java Development Kit

The JDK is a suite of software tools required for developing Java applications. Android Studio requires JDK 1.8 or higher to be installed. It's possible you already have a version of the JDK installed on your machine. Let's check by running the following command from your terminal:

```
javac -version
```

If you see a version that meets our requirements, you can skip ahead in the chapter to the *Installing Android Studio* section. If not, we'll walk through how to install it. Refer to the following screenshot:

To use the "javac" command-line tool you need to install a JDK.

Click "More Info..." to visit the Java Developer Kit download website.

More Info...   OK

To install JDK 1.8, visit `http://www.oracle.com/technetwork/java/javase/downloads/jdk8-downloads-2133151.html` in your web browser. Scroll down the page a short way and you'll find a few download options. Select the **radio** button to accept the license agreement and then click the link that corresponds with Mac OS X (macOS). Refer to the following screenshot:

Java SE Development Kit 8u91

You must accept the Oracle Binary Code License Agreement for Java SE to download this software.

◯ Accept License Agreement   ⬤ Decline License Agreement

Product / File Description	File Size	Download
Linux ARM 32 Hard Float ABI	77.72 MB	jdk-8u91-linux-arm32-vfp-hflt.tar.gz
Linux ARM 64 Hard Float ABI	74.69 MB	jdk-8u91-linux-arm64-vfp-hflt.tar.gz
Linux x86	154.74 MB	jdk-8u91-linux-i586.rpm
Linux x86	174.92 MB	jdk-8u91-linux-i586.tar.gz
Linux x64	152.74 MB	jdk-8u91-linux-x64.rpm
Linux x64	172.97 MB	jdk-8u91-linux-x64.tar.gz
Mac OS X	227.29 MB	jdk-8u91-macosx-x64.dmg
Solaris SPARC 64-bit (SVR4 package)	139.59 MB	jdk-8u91-solaris-sparcv9.tar.Z
Solaris SPARC 64-bit	98.95 MB	jdk-8u91-solaris-sparcv9.tar.gz
Solaris x64 (SVR4 package)	140.29 MB	jdk-8u91-solaris-x64.tar.Z
Solaris x64	96.78 MB	jdk-8u91-solaris-x64.tar.gz
Windows x86	182.11 MB	jdk-8u91-windows-i586.exe
Windows x64	187.41 MB	jdk-8u91-windows-x64.exe

Note: The previous screenshot may be out of date by the time you read this. Feel free to grab the latest version available from the download site.

After you've run the installer, verify the JDK version with `javac -version`. Don't worry if it doesn't match exactly with the screenshot. So long as it matches 1.8.x, you've got what's needed. Refer to the following screenshot:

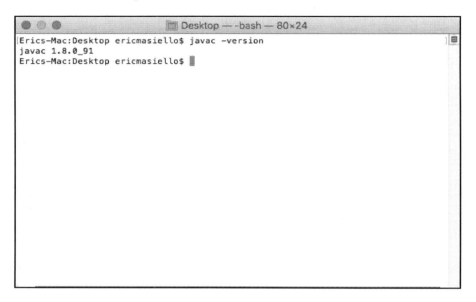

Installing Android Studio

Android Studio is an integrated development environment tailored for Android development. After we've completed the initial setup process, you won't actually need to run Android Studio for any day-to-day React Native development. For the purposes of this chapter, we're really just installing it for all the software and tools that are bundled with it.

The React Native documentation recommends installing Android Studio 2.0 or greater. You can download it from `http://developer.android.com/sdk/index.html`. Once it has completed downloading, open the DMG and drag Android Studio into your `Applications` folder. The first time you run it, Android Studio may ask you if you'd like to import your previous settings. I chose the default **I do not have a previous version of Studio...** option, but choose whichever is appropriate for you. After making your selection, Android Studio will walk you through the setup wizard. When you get to the step titled **Install Type**, select **Custom**.

Select whichever UI theme you prefer. When you get to the step entitled **SDK Components Setup**, make sure both **Performance** and **Android Virtual Device** are checked. The **Performance** piece is used for speeding up emulation. The second is the Android emulator we'll use for testing. Refer to the following screenshot:

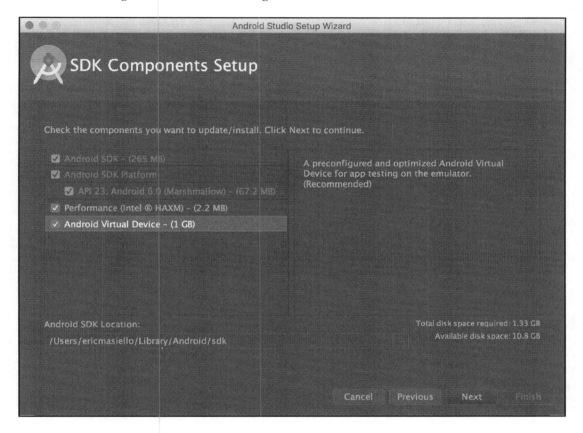

Once you click **Next**, you can complete the wizard with the default selections. The next step will download everything we've configured up to this point. Once it's complete, click **Finish**.

Configuring Android Studio

Okay, part one is done. Now we're onto part two. From the Android Studio welcome screen, select **SDK Manager** from the **Configure** menu in the lower-right corner, as shown in the following screenshot:

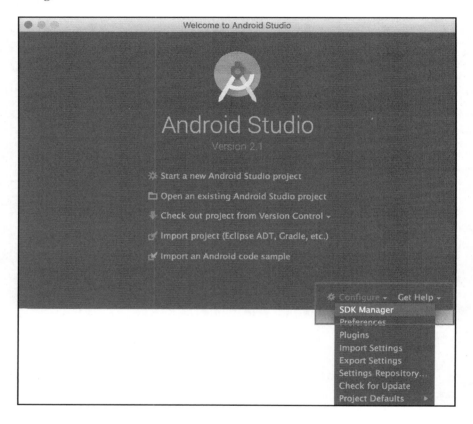

Here, we'll need to install a few more items. With the **SDK Platforms** tab selected, select **Show Package Details** in the lower-right corner. Under **Android 6.0 (Marshmallow)**, ensure the following items are checked:

- **Google APIs**
- **Intel x86 Atom System Image**
- **Intel x86 Atom_64 System Image**
- **Google APIs Intel x86 Atom System Image**
- **Google APIs Intel x86 Atom_64 System Image**

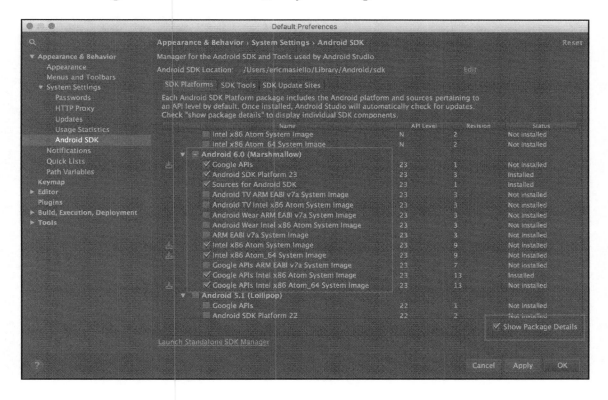

Next, select the **SDK Tools** tab and select **Show Package Details** again from the lower-right corner. In the main view, under **Android SDK Build Tools**, ensure **Android SDK Build-Tools 23.0.1** is selected. Then click **OK**. Refer to the following screenshot:

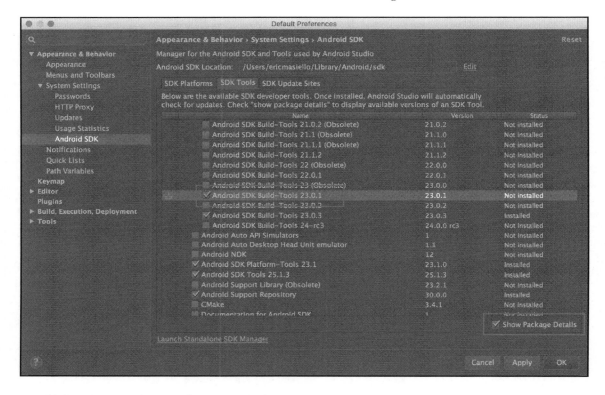

You'll then be asked to confirm you'd like to install these tools. Click **OK**, accept the terms and conditions, and complete the installation process.

Configuring ANDROID_HOME and your PATH

Once the download completes, you'll have all the necessary tools installed. The last thing you need to do is define the ANDROID_HOME environment variable. This is needed to tell your system where it can find the Android SDK. Additionally, we'll add the Android tools path to our PATH so we can use commands such as android avd and adb devices. To begin, run the following from the Terminal:

```
open ~/.bash_profile
```

If you see the error `.bash_profile does not exist,` you'll need to create one. To do that, simply type:

```
touch ~/.bash_profile.
```

Add the following lines to your `bash_profile`:

```
export ANDROID_HOME=~/Library/Android/sdk
PATH="~/Library/Android/sdk/tools:~/Library/Android/sdk/platform-
tools:${PATH}"
export PATH
```

Save the file and close it. Back in the Terminal, type:

```
source ~/.bash_profile
```

This will ensure the contents of the `.bash_profile` have been executed. To verify, type:

```
echo $ANDROID_HOME
```

You should see something similar to `/Users/your-username/Library/Android/sdk`.

Verifying that the CPU/ABIs are installed

Setting up all the necessary Android development dependencies is a bit of a chore. Personally, I've run into issues where everything required to run the Android emulator still isn't installed. To verify that you have everything, run the following from your Terminal:

```
android
```

This will open the Android SDK Manager. Scroll down to **Android 6.0 (API 23)**. Looking in the rightmost column, ensure that **SDK Platform**, **Intel x86 Atom 64 System Image**, and **Intel x86 Atom System Image** are installed. If not, don't fret. Check the three boxes and click the **Install 3 packages...** button.

Starting the Android emulator

Running the Android emulator is a bit different from how we run the iOS simulator. Initially, we'll need to create an **Android Virtual Device (AVD)** by running the following command:

```
android avd
```

This will launch the AVD Manager. Select **Device Definitions**. You're welcome to create an AVD from whichever device you'd like. I chose the **Nexus S** device. Once you've found one you like, click **Create AVD** on the right.

You'll need to fill in a few of the form fields before you're able to proceed. Select a **Target**, **CPU/ABI**, **Skin**, **Front Camera**, and **Back Camera** option. For **Skin**, be sure to select a **Skin** with dynamic hardware controls. This will expose buttons such as the **Menu** and **Home** buttons to you. Then click **OK**. Refer to the following screenshot:

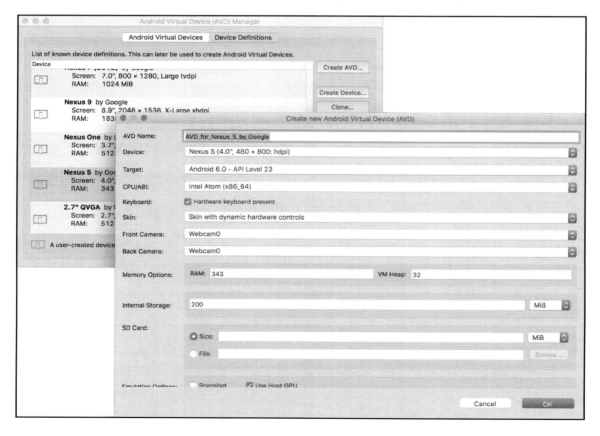

Click on the **Android Virtual Devices** tab and you'll now see your new AVD listed. Select your device and click **Start...**. Refer to the following screenshot:

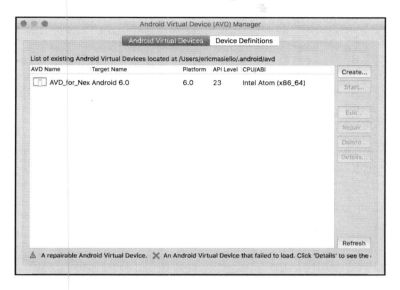

Once the AVD has launched, you're all set to run your React Native app in Android.

 Instead of first launching the AVD Manager, you can use `emulator` to launch your emulator directly by name by using the following command:

```
emulator -avd AVD_for_Nexus_S_by_Google
```

 The value `avd_for_Nexus_S_by_Google` needs to match the name of your AVD in the AVD Manager.

Adding Android support to RNNYT

With all the necessary tools installed, we can actually begin to experiment with some code in an Android emulator. Open up our RNNYT project and make sure you have your Android emulator running.

From your project's root directory, launch RNNYT in the Android emulator by running the command:

```
react-native run-android
```

With any luck, you'll see the **Welcome to React Native** screen.

Running adb devices will display a list of all attached Android devices. This list will include emulators and any physical hardware connected, with developer options enabled.

Before we dive into any refactoring, let's briefly orient ourselves to the Android emulator. The keyboard shortcut *Command + R* won't work for us anymore. If you want to refresh the screen, you'll need to either double tap the *R* key on your keyboard or launch the menu. There're a few ways to do this. The most obvious way is to click the **Menu** button visible under the section labeled **Hardware Buttons**. If keyboard shortcuts are more your thing, you can do the same by pressing *Command + M* on your keyboard. Refer to the following screenshot:

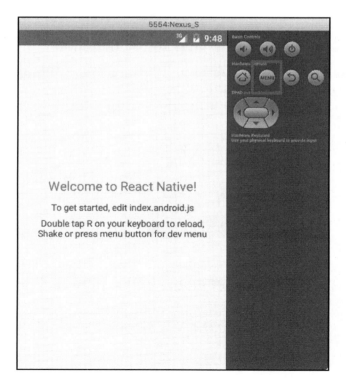

From there, you can trigger the remote debugger, hot reloading, manual reloading, and other debugging tools.

Branching platform logic

As you've most likely noticed by now, React Native allows you to optionally add a
`.ios.js` or `.android.js` extension to any file name. If you omit the platform-specific extension, React Native assumes that the file is *universal* and will be used by either platform. This is probably best explained with some examples. Imagine our project includes the following files:

- `Home.js`
- `MyComponent.js`
- `MyComponent.android.js`

Among other things, `Home.js` includes the following code:

```
import MyComponent from './MyComponent';
```

If the code is run on Android, it will use `MyComponent.android.js`. However, when the code runs on iOS, the packager is unable to find `MyComponent.ios.js` and will fall back to `MyComponent.js`.

Now look at our next example:

- `Home.js`
- `MyComponent.js`
- `MyComponent.ios.js`
- `MyComponent.android.js`

Here, iOS would ignore `MyComponent.js` and utilize `MyComponent.ios.js`. And, once again, Android would use `MyComponent.android.js`. Admittedly, this is a contrived example since `MyComponent.js` would effectively go unused. However, it illustrates the point that platform-specific files will always be favored over non-platform-specific files. If your code is meant to be universal, just use the traditional `.js` extension. There is one exception to all of this. The root project files `index.ios.js` and `index.android.js` must maintain their platform extensions. Even if the contents of each of these files are identical, you cannot create a universal `index.js` file.

This capability illustrates one of the ways you can tailor your code to a specific platform. But what if you don't want to branch an entire file? What if you only need to branch a small piece of logic within a file? Thankfully, React Native supports that too. In this case, both platforms can use the same JavaScript file, but utilize the Platform API to branch the code:

```
import { Platform } from 'react-native';

if (Platform.OS === 'android') {
  // Do something specific for Android
} else if (Platform.OS === 'ios') {
  // Handle iOS
}
```

The Platform API also includes a few other useful methods and properties. Platform.Version exposes the underlying Android version. Sadly, this only works for Android. Platform.Version on iOS will simply return undefined. Finally, Platform.select is a method you can use to toggle platform-specific code. Here's an example:

```
const backgroundStyle = Platform.select({
  ios: {
    backgroundColor: 'green'
  },
  android: {
    backgroundColor: 'red'
  }
});

const styles = StyleSheet.create({
  container: {
    flex: 1,
    padding: 20,
    ...backgroundStyle
  }
});
```

Here, Platform.select expects an object with keys that match the platform. Those keys can map to any value. In the previous code sample, the keys map to an object that defines platform-specific background colors. It then uses the spread operator to merge the background color with the rest of the styles inside the container.

Refactoring RNNYT for Android

Thankfully, we've already moved as much code as possible outside of `index.ios.js`. Therefore, we can duplicate the contents of `index.ios.js` into `index.android.js`. Take a look at the following code snippet:

```
import {
  AppRegistry
} from 'react-native';
import App from './src/App';

AppRegistry.registerComponent('RNNYT', () => App);
```

If you happen to refresh your app in the Android emulator, you'll probably see the error `Requiring unknown module "../components/HomeScreen"`. Given our discussion of platform-specific file extensions, this shouldn't come as any surprise. The `HomeScreen` component is housed inside `HomeScreen.ios.js`. Let's create a different version of `HomeScreen` that's customized for Android inside `HomeScreen.android.js`. Just to recap, `HomeScreen` is responsible for toggling between our three primary components– `NewsFeedContainer`, `SearchContainer`, and `BookmarksContainer`. We accomplished this with the iOS specific component `TabBarIOS`. For Android, we'll need to do something else. But, before we get into that, let's just get a basic component running that simply renders the `NewsFeedContainer`. Even though this component doesn't need to be a class-based component yet, we'll set it up as such since we'll be adding methods to it shortly. Take a look at the following code snippet:

```
// HomeScreen.android.js
import React, { Component, PropTypes } from 'react';
import NewsFeedContainer from '../containers/NewsFeedContainer';

export default class HomeScreen extends Component {
  render() {
    return <NewsFeedContainer />;
  }
}

HomeScreen.propTypes = {
  selectedTab: PropTypes.string,
  tab: PropTypes.func.isRequired
};
```

Aside from some styling issues within the `NewsFeed`, this simplified version of `HomeScreen` gets us back in the game. The list of news items will render and allow us to press on them to see the detailed article. However, we added an `onLongPress` event handler inside of `NewsItem`, which uses the `ActionSheetIOS` API. For Android, we'll use the `ToastAndroid` and `Vibration` APIs to inform users they've bookmarked a news article.

Import `ToastAndroid`, `Platform`, and `Vibration` at the top of `NewsItem.js`:

```
import {
  View,
  TouchableOpacity,
  StyleSheet,
  ActionSheetIOS,
  ToastAndroid,
  Platform,
  Vibration
} from 'react-native';
```

Then, inside the `onLongPress` method, we'll utilize `Platform.select` to branch the logic between Android and iOS solutions:

```
onLongPress() {
  const platformMsgFn = Platform.select({
    android: () => {
      ToastAndroid.show(
        `"${this.props.title}" has been bookmarked!`,
        ToastAndroid.LONG
      );
      Vibration.vibrate();
      this.props.onBookmark();
    },
    ios: () => (
      ActionSheetIOS.showActionSheetWithOptions({
        options: ['Bookmark', 'Cancel'],
        cancelButtonIndex: 1,
        title: this.props.title
      }, (buttonIndex) => {
        if (buttonIndex === 0) {
          this.props.onBookmark();
        }
      })
    )
  });

  platformMsgFn();
}
```

I've refactored this code using `Platform.select` to return an anonymous function based on the platform. The resulting function is stored as `platformMsgFn` and is then executed. In the case of Android, the anonymous function executes `ToastAndroid.show`, passing it a message and a constant specifying how long the toast should remain visible (this can be either `ToastAndroid.SHORT` or `ToastAndroid.LONG`). Next, we call `Vibration.vibrate` and save our bookmark using the `onBookmark` action creator.

Fixing Android vibration

If you run the app inside the Android emulator and attempt to long press one of the news articles, you'll be greeted with a very unfriendly error `Requires VIBRATE permissions`. *What's that about?* you ask. Well, Android requires that we give it explicit permissions to utilize vibration notifications. Thankfully, this is pretty simple. Open up `android/app/src/main/AndroidManifest.xml`. Within the manifest tag, add the following:

```
<uses-permission android:name="android.permission.VIBRATE"/>
```

We'll need to rebuild the app in order for the permission to take effect. From your Terminal, simply rerun:

```
react-native run-android
```

Now, if you try to bookmark an article, you'll see everything works as expected (the vibration itself will only work with actual hardware). Refer to the following screenshot:

With that behind us, let's get back to our Android `HomeScreen` component. React Native offers two components for Android that solve our navigation dilemma. One option is `ToolbarAndroid`. This component locks a fixed header at the top of your app that can contain a logo, a navigation icon (for example, a hamburger menu), a title, and a subtitle. This would work; however, I've found this component doesn't offer many options for styling. Instead, we're going to use the fairly vanilla `DrawerLayoutAndroid`. This component adds an off-screen drawer that can be toggled by swiping your finger (or, in the case of the emulator, your mouse cursor) to the right from the left edge of the device. The drawer typically contains navigation items, but could also display a logo or any other information.

Using DrawerLayoutAndroid

What I like about `DrawerLayoutAndroid` is that there isn't a lot to it. As stated earlier, it's just a component that can slide in from off-screen to display our navigation options. Beyond that, we control all the logic to display the selected view. Thankfully, this won't be too challenging. To begin, add these imports to `HomeScreen.android.js`:

```
import {
  DrawerLayoutAndroid,
  View,
  StyleSheet
} from 'react-native';
import SearchContainer from '../containers/SearchContainer';
import BookmarksContainer from '../containers/BookmarksContainer';
import AppText from './AppText';
import * as globalStyles from '../styles/global';
```

Let's also configure some styles that we'll need shortly:

```
const styles = StyleSheet.create({
  container: {
    backgroundColor: globalStyles.BG_COLOR,
    flex: 1
  },
  drawer: {
    backgroundColor: globalStyles.BG_COLOR,
    flex: 1,
    padding: 10
  },
  drawerItem: {
    fontSize: 20,
    marginBottom: 5
  },
  menuButton: {
```

```
      marginHorizontal: 10,
      marginTop: 10,
      color: globalStyles.LINK_COLOR
    }
  });
```

Next, add this navigation configuration before the `HomeScreen` component:

```
const navConfig = {
  order: ['newsFeed', 'search', 'bookmarks'],
  newsFeed: {
    title: 'News',
    view: <NewsFeedContainer />,
    tab: 'newsFeed'
  },
  search: {
    title: 'Search',
    view: <SearchContainer />,
    tab: 'search'
  },
  bookmarks: {
    title: 'Bookmarks',
    view: <BookmarksContainer />,
    tab: 'bookmarks'
  }
};
```

This configuration will be used to dynamically set the active view.

Within the render method, we're going to wrap the active container element with `DrawerLayoutAndroid`. `DrawerLayoutAndroid` accepts several props. We're just going to focus on a few key ones. `renderNavigationView` is a prop that expects a function that returns the drawer's view contents. The `drawerWidth` prop sets the width of the drawer, and `drawerPosition` configures the drawer to slide in from either the left or right side. Finally, `drawerBackgroundColor` acts as an overlay sitting between the open drawer and the remainder of the application. We'll start by filling in the completed `render` method and then we'll add in the missing pieces afterward:

```
render() {
  return (
    <DrawerLayoutAndroid
      drawerWidth={310}
      drawerPosition={DrawerLayoutAndroid.positions.Left}
      drawerBackgroundColor="rgba(0,0,0,0.5)"
      renderNavigationView={this.renderDrawer}
    >
      <View style={styles.container}>
```

```
      <AppText
        style={styles.menuButton}
        onPress={this.showNav}
      >Menu</AppText>
      {navConfig[this.props.selectedTab].view}
    </View>
  </DrawerLayoutAndroid>
 );
}
```

Inside DrawerLayoutAndroid, we've added an AppText element. At the moment, it has an onPress handler pointing to a yet-to-be-defined method. Once it's implemented, it will provide an alternative means of opening the drawer for users unfamiliar with Android's drawer swipe gesture. The renderNavigationView prop is calling out to a method we'll define next:

```
constructor(props) {
  super(props);
  this.renderDrawer = this.renderDrawer.bind(this);
}

renderDrawer() {
  return (
    <View style={styles.drawer}>
      {navConfig.order.map(key => (
        <AppText
          key={key}
          style={styles.drawerItem}
          onPress={() => this.props.tab(navConfig[key].tab)}
        >
          {navConfig[key].title}
        </AppText>
      ))}
    </View>
  );
}
```

renderDrawer does exactly that it returns a View that contains our three navigation options, News, Search, and Bookmarks. Pressing on any of them will call the tab action creator. Once the active tab is updated in the Redux state, the correct container will render inside the DrawerLayoutAndroid:

```
{navConfig[this.props.selectedTab].view}
```

This gets us a lot closer to where we'd like to be. However, we still have a few problems. For one, the **Menu** button doesn't do anything. Also, you need to manually swipe away the drawer after selecting **News**, **Search**, or **Bookmarks**. Thankfully, DrawerLayoutAndroid has openDrawer and closeDrawer methods. We just need some way of hooking them into our DrawerLayoutAndroid element so we can execute them. This is one of those cases where we'll want to use a React ref (reference). If you've used ref in React before, you may have seen something like <Component ref="myRefName" />. Here, the ref is set to a string and can be referenced in other parts of the component with this.refs.myRefName. However, the string value approach is considered legacy. So, we'll use the ref callback value. Add the following ref callback:

```
<DrawerLayoutAndroid
  ref={(c) => { this.drawer = c; }}
  //...
```

Once the DrawerLayoutAndroid element has mounted, the ref callback will execute, saving the component c to this.drawer. Next, update the onPress handler inside renderDrawer to close the drawer after the user selects an option:

```
onPress={() => {
  this.props.tab(navConfig[key].tab);
  this.drawer.closeDrawer();
}}
```

Now we can write that showNav method we've been neglecting, allowing us to open the drawer by clicking the **Menu** button:

```
showNav() {
  this.drawer.openDrawer();
}
```

Since showNav references this, we'll need to bind it in the constructor:

```
this.showNav = this.showNav.bind(this);
```

Customizing Android styling

Functionally, our app is working well on Android. Visually, however, it could use some tuning. When we defined many of our global styles back in earlier chapters, we were only taking iOS into account. We'll need to tweak a few things to make the design work nicely on both platforms.

Let's start by fixing our global styles. Through my own experimentation, I've found that, when it comes to styling view container elements, Android tends to work better with margin and iOS with padding. With that said, we're going to create two new style files in the `src/styles` directory `platform.android.js` and `platform.ios.js`.

We'll start with `platform.ios.js`. Inside this file, we'll place all the styles that are specific to iOS:

```
export default {
  PAGE_CONTAINER_STYLE: {
    paddingTop: 20,
    paddingHorizontal: 10,
    marginBottom: 48
  },
  TEXT_STYLE: {
    fontFamily: 'Helvetica Neue'
  }
};
```

Now we'll do the same for Android inside `platform.android.js`:

```
export default {
  PAGE_CONTAINER_STYLE: {
    marginTop: 10,
    marginHorizontal: 10
  },
  TEXT_STYLE: {
    fontFamily: 'sans-serif'
  }
};
```

Next, open up `global.js` and import the platform module at the top, then destructure the values into PAGE_CONTAINER_STYLE and TEXT_STYLE:

```
import platformStyles from './platform';

const { PAGE_CONTAINER_STYLE, TEXT_STYLE } = platformStyles;
```

Thanks to our use of platform file extensions, our code will automatically use the correct styles. Now we just need to apply them. To do this, update COMMON_STYLES:

```
export const COMMON_STYLES = StyleSheet.create({
  pageContainer: {
    backgroundColor: BG_COLOR,
    flex: 1,
    ...PAGE_CONTAINER_STYLE
  },
```

```
text: {
  color: TEXT_COLOR,
  ...TEXT_STYLE
}
});
```

Take a look at the following screenshot:

With everything looking nice on our primary news feed, let's switch over to the Search component. I feel there's a bit too much margin above the search box on Android. Plus, there's this unsightly dark line that Android adds by default to TextInputs. Let's touch up the Search component by importing Platform at the top of Search.js, and update the search style's marginTop to the following:

```
marginTop: Platform.OS === 'ios' ? 10 : 0,
```

While we're at it, let's update the input style so Android adds some paddingBottom:

```
paddingBottom: Platform.OS === 'android' ? 8 : 0
```

`TextInput` has several props that are platform specific allowing us to tune the styling and user experience. In order to remove the underline visible on Android, set the `underlineColorAndroid` prop to `transparent`. We can also change the Android keyboard's return key text by setting the `returnKeyLabel` prop. Thankfully, iOS will just ignore these so we don't need to add any platform branching logic. On the iOS side, we can change the keyboard's default theme to dark, using the `keyboardAppearance` prop, to match our app's aesthetic:

```
<TextInput
  style={styles.input}
  onChangeText={this.searchNews}
  value={this.state.searchText}
  placeholder="Search"
  placeholderTextColor={globalStyles.MUTED_COLOR}
  underlineColorAndroid="transparent"
  returnKeyLabel="Search"
  keyboardAppearance="dark"
/>
```

In the process of fixing up our global styles, we actually introduced a bug into our `IntroScreen`. If you visit the `IntroScreen` now on Android, you'll find an unsightly white border around the top, left, and right sides. This was introduced from the margin values we applied globally. There's also one other minor issue. We call the iOS-only `setBarStyle` method of `StatusBar`. We can fix the latter issue by once again importing `Platform` from React Native and then wrapping our call to `setBarStyle` with a simple `if` statement:

```
if (Platform.OS === 'ios') {
  StatusBar.setBarStyle('light-content');
}
```

And, finally, since neither platform actually needs a margin applied to the `IntroScreen`, we'll override the global `pageContainer` styles to reset the affected margin properties:

```
container: {
  marginTop: 0,
  marginBottom: 0,
  marginHorizontal: 0,
  justifyContent: 'center',
  alignItems: 'center'
}
```

Enabling LayoutAnimation

There's one final edit we need to make to our Onboarding component. If you click through the onboarding experience, you'll notice everything animates as expected until you reach the final transition. Pressing **Done** is intended to trigger an animation using LayoutAnimation (as opposed to using the Animated API). As is, LayoutAnimation doesn't throw any errors, but it also doesn't animate whatsoever. It just appears.

In order to use LayoutAnimation on Android, we need to explicitly opt into experimental layout animation by using the UIManager. UIManager is yet another API we'll import from the React Native library.

Inside of Onboarding.js, import the UIManager:

```
import {
  StyleSheet,
  View,
  LayoutAnimation,
  Animated,
  PanResponder,
  UIManager
} from 'react-native';
```

You'll need to exercise caution since the setLayoutAnimationEnabledExperimental method isn't available on iOS. That said, we need to first verify if the method is present. If so, we'll call it inside the Onboarding constructor:

```
constructor(props) {
  super(props);
  this.moveNext = this.moveNext.bind(this);
  this.movePrevious = this.movePrevious.bind(this);
  this.transitionToNextPanel = this.transitionToNextPanel.bind(this);
  this.moveFinal = this.moveFinal.bind(this);
  this.state = {
    currentIndex: 0,
    isDone: false,
    pan: new Animated.Value(0)
  };
  if (UIManager.setLayoutAnimationEnabledExperimental) {
    UIManager.setLayoutAnimationEnabledExperimental(true);
  }
}
```

With this change in place, the Onboarding component will behave exactly as it does on iOS.

Summary

This chapter focused on making our app run in a way that feels native to each platform. While there are minor differences between React Native on iOS and Android, the required updates were minimal and were added mostly to cater for the platform's unique interface patterns. React Native's `Android` API offers several other Android-specific components and APIs that are worth exploring. For example, the Android operating system is designed to work with a back button. `BackAndroid` lets you create event listeners within your React Native app to add custom behavior when users click the Android back button. There are also additional Android UI components you may wish to experiment with, including `DatePickerAndroid`, `ProgressBarAndroid`, `TimePickerAndroid`, and `ToolbarAndroid`.

With our cross-platform app complete, it's now time to step outside of our JavaScript-only comfort zone and into native modules. In the next chapter, we'll explore how to create React Native bindings that expose customized platform native code to our JavaScript code.

10
Using and Writing Native Modules

The React Native library has grown over time to encompass the majority of the native application programming interfaces that we need to build sophisticated applications for mobile devices. As we've seen, we can access numerous native user interface components that are available on all devices, such as list views, images, and text, as well as platform-specific UI components, such as the tab bar on iOS. We've also used some of the many available native APIs, such as those used for alerting and animation.

There will be, however, occasions where the components and APIs that exist in the React Native library are not sufficient. Luckily, React Native provides an extensible framework for writing custom native modules in platform-specific code and making them available in our application's JavaScript. The ability to create native modules is one of the most powerful parts of the React Native library because it means that there is no application that can't be created, no matter how complicated or what native APIs it needs.

Currently, custom native modules are needed to do complex things such as playing videos and audio, or using an OAuth provider for authenticating users. To add this functionality to our application, we have two options: find an open source module that fulfills our requirements and bring it into the project as a dependency or we can build our own.

In this chapter, we will:

- Start building a profile page for our RNNYT application
- Learn how to incorporate open source native modules into our application
- Learn how to build our own native modules for both iOS and Android

A couple of disclaimers are necessary before we get started. Native modules are written in a platform's native language, which means Objective-C on iOS (Swift is also possible with some additional work, but we will use Objective-C in this book) and Java on Android. A full introduction to those platforms and languages is outside the scope of this book, so a basic understanding of these languages is a prerequisite for this chapter. Also, it is worth mentioning that the modules developed in this chapter are not robust modules that should be used in production applications. Instead, they are simple modules used for a narrow use case to demonstrate the process and mechanisms of building one.

Using native modules

In React Native, we manage dependencies to our project in much the same way as other web or Node applications, that is, using npm, the Node Package Manager. Many of the dependencies we use will contain only React Native JavaScript code, but some will have native code as well. The installation process for dependencies containing native code differs slightly from that of pure JS dependencies.

Installing native modules

In order to build out our new profile page and to make our application a bit more aesthetically pleasing, we'll use an icon library called `react-native-vector-icons`. The first thing we will need to do is simply install the library with `npm` like we would any other dependency:

```
npm install --save react-native-vector-icons
```

This library contains native modules, so we are not done yet. Most libraries that contain native modules will provide one or more additional install steps. The end goal of the installation is to link the native code from the dependency to the platform-specific code of the main project. This can be done in one of a few ways.

The first installation option that most native module libraries will provide is a *manual* installation. This method is cumbersome and involves updating several project configuration files as well as native code files.

The second option that may be offered is to use a platform-specific package manager in addition to npm. On iOS, this probably means CocoaPods, and on Android, Gradle. These tools work well for the job and, compared to the manual option, is much less painful. However, it also adds two additional package managers and configurations to the project.

If these two options don't sound exactly ideal, you're in luck. A tool was developed to reduce some of the friction involved in using native dependencies called **rnmp** (**react native package manager**). Because it is much easier, most libraries are moving toward this option. In fact, it is so common and useful that rnpm was eventually merged into the React Native command line client library, which means it should already be installed.

Now we can use the React Native command line client to link the native files from the `react-native-vector-icons` library to our project:

```
react-native link react-native-vector-icons
```

We've now downloaded the dependency using `npm` and then linked the native code files, so we are all set to begin using icons in our project. We could also combine those two steps into a single command:

```
react-native install react-native-vector-icons
```

Using the library

The `react-native-vector-icons` library gives us a few components that we can use within our project. The `Icon` component can be used to simply display icons anywhere in our project. We will also use the `Icon.TabBarItemIOS` component that comes with the library that can be used in place of the React Native component `TabBarIOS.Item` and gives us access to a more robust collection of icons.

Profile page

The first thing we need to do is make a `Profile` component that can be used to display the profile page. We'll put this new component in a file called `src/components/Profile.js`:

```javascript
import React, { Component } from 'react';
import {
  View,
  StyleSheet
} from 'react-native';
import Title from './Title';
import AppText from './AppText';
```

```
import * as globalStyles from '../styles/global';

export default class Profile extends Component {

  render() {
    return (
      <View style={[globalStyles.COMMON_STYLES.pageContainer,
styles.container]}>
        <Title>Username</Title>
        <AppText>Your Name</AppText>
      </View>
    );
  }

}

const styles = StyleSheet.create({
  container: {
    justifyContent: 'center',
    alignItems: 'center'
  }
});
```

So far, this looks very similar to other components we've made. First import `React`, `react-native` and other application modules we need:

```
import React, { Component } from 'react';
import {
  View,
  StyleSheet
} from 'react-native';
import Title from './Title';
import AppText from './AppText';
import * as globalStyles from '../styles/global';
```

We then create a class for the `Profile` component and define its `render()` method. Note that this component in its current state could easily be a functional component, but we're making it a class so that we can add more sophisticated behavior later on:

```
export default class Profile extends Component {

  render() {
    return (
      <View style={[globalStyles.COMMON_STYLES.pageContainer,
styles.container]}>
        <Title>Username</Title>
        <AppText>Your Name</AppText>
      </View>
```

```
    );
  }

}
```

Finally, we add some styles in a `StyleSheet` to make the page look better:

```
const styles = StyleSheet.create({
  container: {
    justifyContent: 'center',
    alignItems: 'center'
  }
});
```

Now, we're going to use the `react-native-vector-icons` library to add an avatar image as a placeholder for the user's profile picture. The first step here is to import the `Icon` component. When we import this component, we have to specify which icon font library we want to use. For our project, we'll use the `EvilIcons` icon font library:

```
import React, { Component } from 'react';
import {
  View,
  StyleSheet
} from 'react-native';
import Icon from 'react-native-vector-icons/EvilIcons';
import Title from './Title';
import AppText from './AppText';
import * as globalStyles from '../styles/global';
```

Next, we'll add some additional styles to the components `StyleSheet` for the avatar icon:

```
const styles = StyleSheet.create({
  container: {
    justifyContent: 'center',
    alignItems: 'center'
  },
  avatarIcon: {
    color: globalStyles.HEADER_TEXT_COLOR,
    fontSize: 200
  }
});
```

Finally, we'll add an `Icon` in the `Profile` component's `render()` method. We'll use the new styles and choose the icon named `user`:

```
render() {
  return (
    <View style={[[globalStyles.COMMON_STYLES.pageContainer,
```

```
styles.container]}>
      <Icon
        name="user"
        style={styles.avatarIcon}
      />
      <Title>Username</Title>
      <AppText>Your Name</AppText>
    </View>
  );
}
```

Now that we have a working profile page, we need to make it accessible from within the application. We'll do this by adding it in the `HomeScreen.ios.js` and `HomeScreen.android.js` files.

Adding the profile to the iOS home screen

On our iOS home screen, we'll need to add an additional tab for the profile page. We'll also swap out the React Native `TabBarIOS.Item` components with the `Icon.TabBarItemIOS` component from the icon library:

```
import React, { PropTypes } from 'react';
import {
  TabBarIOS,
  StatusBar
} from 'react-native';
import Icon from 'react-native-vector-icons/EvilIcons';
import NewsFeedContainer from '../containers/NewsFeedContainer';
import SearchContainer from '../containers/SearchContainer';
import BookmarksContainer from '../containers/BookmarksContainer';
import Profile from './Profile';
import * as globalStyles from '../styles/global';

//Set the status bar for iOS to light
StatusBar.setBarStyle('light-content');

const HomeScreen = ({ selectedTab, tab }) => (
  <TabBarIOS
    barTintColor={globalStyles.BAR_COLOR}
    tintColor={globalStyles.LINK_COLOR}
    translucent={false}
  >
    <Icon.TabBarItemIOS
      iconName={'star'}
      title={'News'}
      selected={selectedTab === 'newsFeed'}
```

```
          onPress={() => tab('newsFeed')}
      >
          <NewsFeedContainer/>
      </Icon.TabBarItemIOS>
      <Icon.TabBarItemIOS
          iconName={'search'}
          title={'Search'}
          selected={selectedTab === 'search'}
          onPress={() => tab('search')}
      >
          <SearchContainer/>
      </Icon.TabBarItemIOS>
      <Icon.TabBarItemIOS
          iconName={'paperclip'}
          title={'Bookmarks'}
          selected={selectedTab === 'bookmarks'}
          onPress={() => tab('bookmarks')}
      >
          <BookmarksContainer />
      </Icon.TabBarItemIOS>
      <Icon.TabBarItemIOS
          iconName={'user'}
          title={'Profile'}
          selected={selectedTab === 'profile'}
          onPress={() => tab('profile')}
      >
          <Profile />
      </Icon.TabBarItemIOS>
    </TabBarIOS>
  );

HomeScreen.propTypes = {
    selectedTab: PropTypes.string,
    tab: PropTypes.func.isRequired
};

export default HomeScreen;
```

First, we add an import statement for our new Profile component as well as one for the Icon component:

```
import React, { PropTypes } from 'react';
import {
  TabBarIOS,
  StatusBar
} from 'react-native';
import Icon from 'react-native-vector-icons/EvilIcons';
import NewsFeedContainer from '../containers/NewsFeedContainer';
```

```
import SearchContainer from '../containers/SearchContainer';
import BookmarksContainer from '../containers/BookmarksContainer';
import Profile from './Profile';
import * as globalStyles from '../styles/global';
```

Next, we'll change each of the tab bar items to use `Icon.TabBarItemIOS`. This component needs two new props, one called `iconName`, which tells the component which icon to render, and one called `title`, which specifies the text that should be shown below the tab:

```
<Icon.TabBarItemIOS
  iconName={'star'}
  title={'News'}
  selected={selectedTab === 'newsFeed'}
  onPress={() => tab('newsFeed')}
>
  <NewsFeedContainer />
</Icon.TabBarItemIOS>
```

Notice that we've changed the name of the first tab to use the more appropriate **News** title. We can do this because now that we aren't using system icons, we have complete control over the text displayed.

Finally, we need to add a new tab for the profile page that follows the same pattern as our other tabs. For this tab, we'll use the same `user` icon that we used for the avatar:

```
<Icon.TabBarItemIOS
  iconName={'user'}
  title={'Profile'}
  selected={selectedTab === 'profile'}
  onPress={() => tab('profile')}
>
  <Profile />
</Icon.TabBarItemIOS>
```

In order to make it selectable, we'll also need to add a new profile tab to the available routes in the `navigationReducer.js` file:

```
const routes = {
  home: {
    key: 'home',
    component: HomeScreenContainer,
    index: 0,
    routes: [
      { key: 'newsFeed', modal: undefined },
      { key: 'search' },
      { key: 'bookmarks' },
      { key: 'profile' }
```

```
      ]
    },
    intro: {
      key: 'intro',
      component: IntroScreen
    },
    onboarding: {
      key: 'onboarding',
      component: Onboarding
    }
};
```

We should now be able to open the application in iOS and see our new, much more attractive, tab bar icons as well as the profile page as shown in the following screenshot:

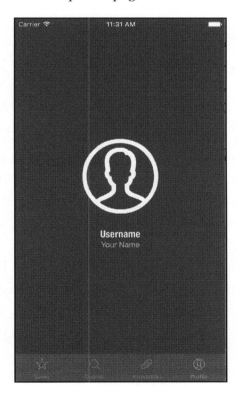

Adding the profile to the Android home screen

We will also need to update our Android home screen, which uses a drawer layout instead of a tab bar to account for the new profile page:

```
import React, { Component, PropTypes } from 'react';
import {
  DrawerLayoutAndroid,
  View,
  StyleSheet
} from 'react-native';
import NewsFeedContainer from '../containers/NewsFeedContainer';
import SearchContainer from '../containers/SearchContainer';
import BookmarksContainer from '../containers/BookmarksContainer';
import Profile from './Profile';
import AppText from './AppText';
import * as globalStyles from '../styles/global';

const navConfig = {
  order: ['newsFeed', 'search', 'bookmarks', 'profile'],
  newsFeed: {
    title: 'News',
    view: <NewsFeedContainer />,
    tab: 'newsFeed'
  },
  search: {
    title: 'Search',
    view: <SearchContainer />,
    tab: 'search'
  },
  bookmarks: {
    title: 'Bookmarks',
    view: <BookmarksContainer />,
    tab: 'bookmarks'
  },
  profile: {
    title: 'Profile',
    view: <Profile />,
    tab: 'profile'
  }
};

export default class HomeScreen extends Component {
  constructor(props) {
    super(props);
    this.renderDrawer = this.renderDrawer.bind(this);
    this.showNav = this.showNav.bind(this);
  }
```

```
    showNav() {
      this.drawer.openDrawer();
    }

    renderDrawer() {
      return (
        <View style={styles.drawer}>
          {navConfig.order.map(key => (
            <AppText
              key={key}
              style={styles.drawerItem}
              onPress={() => {
                this.props.tab(navConfig[key].tab);
                this.drawer.closeDrawer();
              }}
            >
              {navConfig[key].title}
            </AppText>
          ))}
        </View>
      );
    }

    render() {
      return (
        <DrawerLayoutAndroid
          ref={(c) => { this.drawer = c; }}
          drawerWidth={310}
          drawerPosition={DrawerLayoutAndroid.positions.Left}
          drawerBackgroundColor="rgba(0,0,0,0.5)"
          renderNavigationView={this.renderDrawer}
        >
          <View style={styles.container}>
            <AppText
              style={styles.menuButton}
              onPress={this.showNav}
            >Menu</AppText>
            {navConfig[this.props.selectedTab].view}
          </View>
        </DrawerLayoutAndroid>
      );
    }
}

HomeScreen.propTypes = {
  selectedTab: PropTypes.string,
  tab: PropTypes.func.isRequired
};
```

```
const styles = StyleSheet.create({
  container: {
    backgroundColor: globalStyles.BG_COLOR,
    flex: 1
  },
  drawer: {
    backgroundColor: globalStyles.BG_COLOR,
    flex: 1,
    padding: 10
  },
  drawerItem: {
    fontSize: 20,
    marginBottom: 5
  },
  menuButton: {
    marginHorizontal: 10,
    marginTop: 10,
    color: globalStyles.LINK_COLOR
  }
});
```

We first import the `Profile` component:

```
import React, { Component, PropTypes } from 'react';
import {
  DrawerLayoutAndroid,
  View,
  StyleSheet
} from 'react-native';
import NewsFeedContainer from '../containers/NewsFeedContainer';
import SearchContainer from '../containers/SearchContainer';
import BookmarksContainer from '../containers/BookmarksContainer';
import Profile from './Profile';
import AppText from './AppText';
import * as globalStyles from '../styles/global';
```

We then need to add the profile to the `navConfig` object in order to add it to the drawer's menu:

```
const navConfig = {
  order: ['newsFeed', 'search', 'bookmarks', 'profile'],
  newsFeed: {
    title: 'News',
    view: <NewsFeedContainer />,
    tab: 'newsFeed'
  },
  search: {
    title: 'Search',
```

```
      view: <SearchContainer />,
      tab: 'search'
    },
    bookmarks: {
      title: 'Bookmarks',
      view: <BookmarksContainer />,
      tab: 'bookmarks'
    },
    profile: {
      title: 'Profile',
      view: <Profile />,
      tab: 'profile'
    }
  };
```

Note that we have to add a new `profile` key to this object in addition to the string `'profile'` to the array describing the order of the menu options. Once we've added these things, our Android application should have the new profile page in its drawer menu:

We've now successfully incorporated an open source native module into both the iOS and Android versions of our application. Next, we'll develop our profile page further and write our own native modules.

Writing native modules

If we cannot find an open source module to meet our application's needs, we may need to write our own. For instance, we might need to write our own native module if we require some very specific behavior or if we have code from previously developed native applications that we want to incorporate into a React Native project.

We are going to create native modules-one for iOS and one for Android-that allow the user to select an image from their device's media library when the avatar icon is pressed on the profile page. As we develop these modules, we'll look at exposing both native methods and constants. We will also look at several different methods of communicating between JavaScript and native code, including callbacks, promises, and events.

Native modules in iOS

As we mentioned at the beginning of this chapter, in order to follow along in this section, you will need some basic Objective-C knowledge. When writing native modules for iOS, we will also work in **Xcode** because this will automatically add our native files to the project. This chapter also won't go into much detail about using Xcode, but luckily we do not need many of its features. To open the project in Xcode, find the `RNNYT.xcodeproj` file within the `ios` directory and double-click on it; this should open in Xcode by default.

In Objective-C, each module needs two files. The first is the `header` file and has a `.h` extension. The `header` file describes the general interface of the module (how other Objective-C code can interact with the module). The second is an `implementation` file, which uses a .m extension and implements the interface described in the header file. We are creating a native module that lets us interact with the device's image library, so we'll name the module `ImageLibraryManager` and create two files for the module within the `ios/RNNYT` directory: `ImageLibraryManager.h` and `ImageLibraryManager.m`.

Setting up the module

To add new files, right-click on the **RNNYT** folder in the left sidebar and click on **New File...**, as shown in the following screenshot:

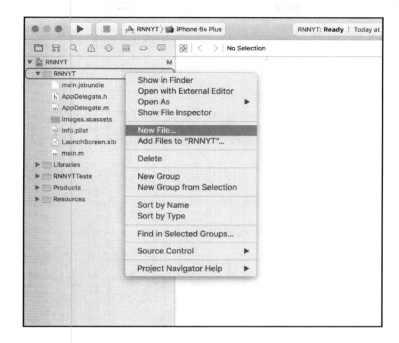

Select the **Header File** file type, as shown in the next screenshot:

Finally, give the file a name and ensure it is in the appropriate folder in the filesystem.

Xcode project structure and filesystem location are actually independent, but for our sanity, we will keep them the same.

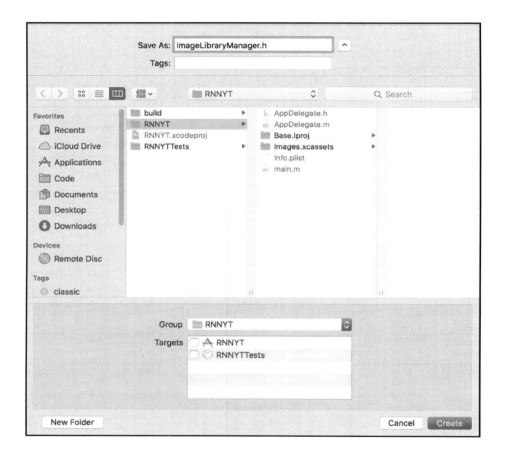

Repeat this process for the implementation file, choosing Objective-C File as the file type. Then, give the file the appropriate name and select the **Empty File** template, as shown in the following screenshot:

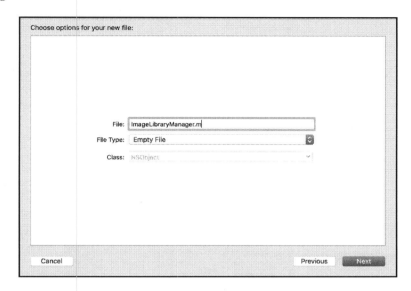

Once again, ensure we are placing this file within the `ios/RNNYT/` directory on the filesystem, as shown in the next screenshot:

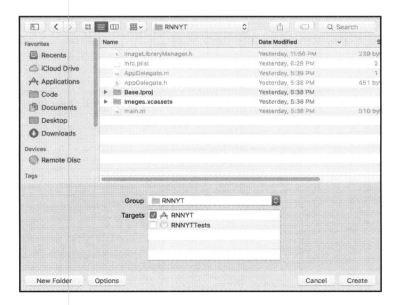

Xcode will have probably filled in some boilerplate code into the header file that we created, but we'll start replacing that content:

```
#import "RCTBridgeModule.h"

@interface ImageLibraryManager : NSObject <RCTBridgeModule>
@end
```

Our header file imports the `RCTBridgeModule` (React Bridge Module) interface:

```
#import "RCTBridgeModule.h"
```

We then describe the interface for the `ImageLibraryManager` as a class that extends from the `NSObject` base class and implements the React Native Bridge protocol. All React Native native modules for iOS need to implement this protocol:

```
@interface ImageLibraryManager : NSObject <RCTBridgeModule>
@end
```

We also need to replace the code in the `ImageLibraryManager.m` implementation file:

```
#import "ImageLibraryManager.h"

@implementation ImageLibraryManager

RCT_EXPORT_MODULE();

@end
```

Here we need to first import the header file:

```
#import "ImageLibraryManager.h"
```

Next, we need to create the implementation of the class described in the header file. In order for this class to function properly as a React Native module, we also need to add the `RCT_EXPORT_MODULE` macro:

```
@implementation ImageLibraryManager

RCT_EXPORT_MODULE();

@end
```

Finally, as of iOS 10, if an application will access the user's media library, it needs to provide an explanation for this in the **Info.plist** file. To do this, select the **Info.plist** file on the left-hand side in Xcode. Then, add this new value by selecting **Privacy – Photo Library Usage Description** and providing a brief explanation, as shown in the following screenshot:

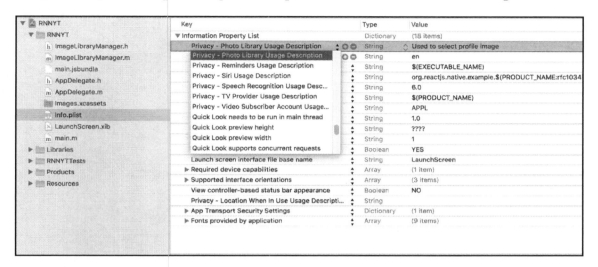

We've now added all of the boilerplate necessary to start writing a native module. With this code, we've created a module that can be accessed in JavaScript. To access it, in the `Profile.js` file, we have to import `NativeModules` from the `react-native` package, which will now contain our new module:

```
import React, { Component } from 'react';
import {
  View,
  StyleSheet,
  NativeModules
} from 'react-native';
import Icon from 'react-native-vector-icons/EvilIcons';
import Title from './Title';
import AppText from './AppText';
import * as globalStyles from '../styles/global';

const { ImageLibraryManager } = NativeModules;
```

Currently, the `ImageLibraryManager` module exists, but has no functionality within it. Throughout the rest of this section, we'll start adding both constant properties and methods to the module to make it more useful.

Exporting methods

Just like we can export an entire module by using the RCT_EXPORT_MODULE macro, we can export a method of that module by using the RCT_EXPORT_METHOD macro. We pass the method we wish to export as an argument to this macro. Since we are creating this module to allow the user to select an image from their image library, we'll call the method selectImage:

```
RCT_EXPORT_METHOD(selectImage)
{
  // Code here
}
```

We'll also import the RCTLog so that we can test calling the newly exposed method:

```
#import "ImageLibraryManager.h"

#import "RCTLog.h"

@implementation ImageLibraryManager

RCT_EXPORT_MODULE();

RCT_EXPORT_METHOD(selectImage)
{
  RCTLogInfo(@"Selecting image...");
}

@end
```

Finally, we can now call this method from JavaScript when the user presses on the avatar icon:

```
import React, { Component } from 'react';
import {
  View,
  StyleSheet,
  TouchableOpacity,
  NativeModules
} from 'react-native';
import Icon from 'react-native-vector-icons/EvilIcons';
import Title from './Title';
import AppText from './AppText';
import * as globalStyles from '../styles/global';

const { ImageLibraryManager } = NativeModules;
```

```
export default class Profile extends Component {

  render() {
    return (
      <View style={[globalStyles.COMMON_STYLES.pageContainer,
styles.container]}>
        <TouchableOpacity
          onPress={() => ImageLibraryManager.selectImage()}
        >
          <Icon
            name="user"
            style={styles.avatarIcon}
          />
        </TouchableOpacity>
        <Title>Username</Title>
        <AppText>Your Name</AppText>
      </View>
    );
  }

}

const styles = StyleSheet.create({
  container: {
    justifyContent: 'center',
    alignItems: 'center'
  },
  avatarIcon: {
    color: globalStyles.HEADER_TEXT_COLOR,
    fontSize: 200
  }
});
```

We first import the `TouchableOpacity` component to add a press listener to the avatar icon:

```
import React, { Component } from 'react';
import {
  View,
  StyleSheet,
  TouchableOpacity,
  NativeModules
} from 'react-native';
import Icon from 'react-native-vector-icons/EvilIcons';
import Title from './Title';
import AppText from './AppText';
import * as globalStyles from '../styles/global';
```

We then wrap the `Icon` component in the `TouchableOpacity` and here we can call the new `selectImage` method when it is pressed:

```
<TouchableOpacity
  onPress={() => ImageLibraryManager.selectImage()}
>
  <Icon
    name="user"
    style={styles.avatarIcon}
  />
</TouchableOpacity>
```

Now, when we rebuild the project and press the avatar, we should see the message **Selecting image...** in the Chrome console. Another important note when working with native modules is that, whenever the native code changes, you will have to rebuild for that platform (in this case `react-native run-ios`); a JavaScript refresh is not sufficient.

We now need to implement the native behavior. We'll be making use of a native iOS class `UIImagePickerController` and thus will need to import `UIKit` in the header file:

```
#import "RCTBridgeModule.h"
#import <UIKit/UIKit.h>

@interface ImageLibraryManager : NSObject <RCTBridgeModule>
@end
```

We can now complete the implementation of this module's `selectImage` method in the implementation file:

```
#import "ImageLibraryManager.h"

#import "RCTLog.h"

@import MobileCoreServices;

@implementation ImageLibraryManager

RCT_EXPORT_MODULE();

RCT_EXPORT_METHOD(selectImage)
{
  RCTLogInfo(@"Selecting image...");

  UIImagePickerController *picker = [[UIImagePickerController alloc]
init];
  picker.sourceType = UIImagePickerControllerSourceTypePhotoLibrary;
  picker.mediaTypes = @[(NSString *)kUTTypeImage];
```

```
  picker.modalPresentationStyle = UIModalPresentationCurrentContext;
  picker.delegate = self;
  UIViewController *root = [[[[UIApplication sharedApplication] delegate]
window] rootViewController];
  [root presentViewController:picker animated:YES completion:nil];
}

- (void)imagePickerController:(UIImagePickerController *)picker
didFinishPickingMediaWithInfo:(NSDictionary *)info
{
  NSString *fileName = [[[NSUUID UUID] UUIDString]
stringByAppendingString:@".jpg"];
  NSString *path = [[NSTemporaryDirectory()stringByStandardizingPath]
stringByAppendingPathComponent:fileName];
  UIImage *image = [info
objectForKey:UIImagePickerControllerOriginalImage];
  NSData *data = UIImageJPEGRepresentation(image, 0);
  [data writeToFile:path atomically:YES];
  NSURL *fileURL = [NSURL fileURLWithPath:path];
  NSString *filePath = [fileURL absoluteString];

  RCTLog(@"%@", filePath);

  [picker dismissViewControllerAnimated:YES completion:nil];
}

@end
```

There is a lot happening here, so let's break it down. The first thing we do in the
`selectImage` method is create a new `UIImagePickerController` instance:

```
UIImagePickerController *picker = [[UIImagePickerController alloc]  init];
```

Next we set some properties on the `picker` to tell the image picker how to display it and
what types of media can be selected:

```
picker.sourceType = UIImagePickerControllerSourceTypePhotoLibrary;
picker.mediaTypes = @[(NSString *)kUTTypeImage];
picker.modalPresentationStyle = UIModalPresentationCurrentContext;
```

The kUTTypeImage constant comes from the MobileCoreServices library, so that will have to be imported:

```
@import MobileCoreServices;
```

Next, we set the delegate for the picker instance. In Objective-C, a delegate is an instance of a class that implements a specific protocol. This allows certain functionality (for instance, what to do when the image is selected) to be delegated to another object of our choosing. For this example, we'll make the ImageLibraryManager instance itself (self) the delegate:

```
picker.delegate = self;
```

We then find the root view controller that is currently active:

```
UIViewController *root = [[[[UIApplication sharedApplication]  delegate]
window] rootViewController];
```

We'll use that view controller to open up our image picker instance:

```
[root presentViewController:picker animated:YES completion:nil];
```

That completes the selectImage method. However, for the delegation portion to actually work, we need to do two things. First, we need to update the header file to ensure that our ImageLibraryManager class implements the appropriate protocols, in addition to the RCTBridgeModule that it previously implemented:

```
#import "RCTBridgeModule.h"
#import <UIKit/UIKit.h>

@interface ImageLibraryManager : NSObject <RCTBridgeModule,
UINavigationControllerDelegate, UIImagePickerControllerDelegate>
@end
```

As we can see, two protocols are needed to be a delegate for the UIImagePickerController: UINavigationControllerDelegate and UIImagePickerControllerDelegate.

Second, we need to add the implementation of these protocols, which is a method that is called when the image picking has been completed by the user, named imagePickerController:didFinishPickingMediaWithInfo:

```
- (void)imagePickerController:(UIImagePickerController *)picker
didFinishPickingMediaWithInfo:(NSDictionary *)info
{
  NSString *fileName = [[[NSUUID UUID] UUIDString]
stringByAppendingString:@".jpg"];
```

```
   NSString *path =   [[NSTemporaryDirectory() stringByStandardizingPath]
stringByAppendingPathComponent:fileName];
   UIImage *image = [info
objectForKey:UIImagePickerControllerOriginalImage];
   NSData *data = UIImageJPEGRepresentation(image, 0);
   [data writeToFile:path atomically:YES];
   NSURL *fileURL = [NSURL fileURLWithPath:path];
   NSString *filePath = [fileURL absoluteString];

   RCTLog(@"%@", filePath);

   [picker dismissViewControllerAnimated:YES completion:nil];
}
```

We first have to do a number of things to extract the selected image and get a temporary file path to it:

```
NSString *fileName = [[[NSUUID UUID] UUIDString]
stringByAppendingString:@".jpg"];
NSString *path =   [[NSTemporaryDirectory() stringByStandardizingPath]
stringByAppendingPathComponent:fileName];
UIImage *image = [info  objectForKey:UIImagePickerControllerOriginalImage];
NSData *data = UIImageJPEGRepresentation(image, 0);
[data writeToFile:path atomically:YES];
NSURL *fileURL = [NSURL fileURLWithPath:path];
NSString *filePath = [fileURL absoluteString];
```

For now, we'll log the extracted file path so that we can see what is happening in the Chrome JavaScript console:

```
RCTLog(@"%@", filePath);
```

Finally, we close the image `picker` so that the user is returned to the profile page:

```
[picker dismissViewControllerAnimated:YES completion:nil];
```

Now, when we rebuild our iOS application, we can open the image `picker` by pressing on the profile page's avatar icon. When we select the image, the image `picker` will close and we'll see the file path logged in the console.

We now have a working native module. However, we don't yet have a way to communicate the result of the image selection back to our JavaScript. There are a few ways that we could potentially tackle this and we will examine each.

Communicating with callbacks

In JavaScript, callback functions are a common and traditional way to handle communication for asynchronous tasks. At a high level, a callback function is one that is called when an asynchronous task completes and is often passed the result of that asynchronous task. We can use callback functions when calling native module methods, which are necessarily asynchronous.

The first step here is to add a callback function as a parameter to the exposed native method. We use React Native's RCTResponseSenderBlock type to represent the callback function in Objective-C:

```
RCT_EXPORT_METHOD(selectImage:(RCTResponseSenderBlock)callback)
```

We aren't actually going to call the callback function until the user selects the image, which happens in the delegate method, so we need to store the callback function in an instance variable that can be accessed in either method. First, we'll declare the property on the class:

```
@interface ImageLibraryManager ()

@property (nonatomic, strong) RCTResponseSenderBlock callback;

@end
```

Next, in the selectImage method, we'll assign the callback function passed to the instance variable:

```
RCTLogInfo(@"Selecting image...");
self.callback = callback;
```

Finally, we'll call the callback function when we have the selected image's temporary file path:

```
RCTLog(@"%@", filePath);
self.callback(@[filePath]);
```

The RCTResponseSenderBlock callback takes an array of arguments that will be passed to the JavaScript callback function. When accepting arguments from JavaScript or calling JavaScript callback functions, we need to ensure that the data we pass in is serializable as JSON data (so that it can be interpreted by both languages). An NSString value, such as the filePath, is serializable, so this should work without issue.

The final step is to actually pass in a callback function from the `Profile.js` JavaScript file. We'll first reorganize the component by adding an `onSelectImage` method and binding the `this` context in the component's constructor:

```
constructor(props) {
  super(props);
  this.state = {};
  this.onSelectImage = this.onSelectImage.bind(this);
}

onSelectImage() {
  ImageLibraryManager.selectImage();
}
```

We'll call this new function when the avatar icon is pressed:

```
<TouchableOpacity
  onPress={this.onSelectImagePromise}
>
  <Icon
    name="user"
    style={styles.avatarIcon}
  />
</TouchableOpacity>
```

Now, let's pass in a `callback` function to the `selectImage` native method. Our callback will add the selected URL to the state of the component:

```
onSelectImage() {
  ImageLibraryManager.selectImage((url) => {
    this.setState({
      profileImageUrl: url
    });
  });
}
```

Finally, we'll use this URL to display the selected image in place of the avatar icon when it has been selected. To do this, we'll first need to add the `Image` component to our import statements:

```
import React, { Component } from 'react';
import {
  View,
  StyleSheet,
  TouchableOpacity,
  NativeModules,
  Image
```

```
} from 'react-native';
import Icon from 'react-native-vector-icons/EvilIcons';
import Title from './Title';
import AppText from './AppText';
import * as globalStyles from '../styles/global';
```

We'll also add some styles for the profile image to the `StyleSheet`:

```
const styles = StyleSheet.create({
  container: {
    justifyContent: 'center',
    alignItems: 'center'
  },
  avatarIcon: {
    color: globalStyles.HEADER_TEXT_COLOR,
    fontSize: 200
  },
  profileImage: {
    width: 150,
    height: 150,
    borderRadius: 75
  }
});
```

Then, we'll create a helper function that is responsible for rendering the profile image if it has been selected:

```
renderProfileImage() {
  if (this.state.profileImageUrl) {
    return (
      <Image
        source={{ uri: this.state.profileImageUrl }}
        style={styles.profileImage}
      />
    );
  }
  return (
    <Icon
      name="user"
      style={styles.avatarIcon}
    />
  );
}
```

Finally, we need to update the main `render()` method to use the new helper function instead of rendering the `Icon` component directly:

```
render() {
  return (
    <View style={[globalStyles.COMMON_STYLES.pageContainer,
styles.container]}>
      <TouchableOpacity
        onPress={this.onSelectImage}
      >
        {this.renderProfileImage()}
      </TouchableOpacity>
      <Title>Username</Title>
      <AppText>Your Name</AppText>
    </View>
  );
}
```

We should now be able to select an image from the image library and see it appear within the profile page in place of the avatar icon. This is now a complete and functional integration with a native module, but in the next two sections, we'll examine two other communication methods that can be used as an alternative to callback functions.

 It is important to point out at this point that we are not persisting this image selection in any way. If we wanted to make this a fully functioning profile, we'd need some way to store the user's selection, which is outside of the scope of this chapter.

Communicating with promises

Just like callbacks, promises in JavaScript are used to handle responses to asynchronous tasks. We can write a second JavaScript method that uses the promise syntax instead of passing in a callback function. Then, we'll update our native module to respond to callbacks or promises.

First, we'll define an `onSelectImagePromise` method in the `Profile.js` file's `Profile` component class that functionally behaves the same as `onSelectImage`, but uses the promise syntax instead of a `callback` function:

```
onSelectImagePromise() {
  ImageLibraryManager.selectImagePromise().then((url) => {
    this.setState({
      profileImageUrl: url
    });
  });
```

```
}
```

We will also need to bind the `this` context in the constructor:

```
constructor(props) {
  super(props);
  this.state = {};
  this.onSelectImage = this.onSelectImage.bind(this);
  this.onSelectImagePromise = this.onSelectImagePromise.bind(this);
}
```

Now, let's use the following function when the avatar icon is pressed instead of the original callback-based method:

```
<TouchableOpacity
  onPress={this.onSelectImagePromise}
>
  {this.renderProfileImage()}
</TouchableOpacity>
```

The JavaScript code is now ready to communicate through promises in lieu of a callback function, but we need to also update the native code within the `ImageLibraryManager.m` file. We'll add a new `selectImagePromise` method to the native module that takes the `resolve` and `reject` parameters instead of the `callback`. React Native will notice that the final two parameters of this method are promise related and will allow us to communicate back to JavaScript by using them:

```
RCT_EXPORT_METHOD(selectImagePromise:(RCTPromiseResolveBlock)resolve
                   rejecter:(RCTPromiseRejectBlock)reject)
{
  RCTLogInfo(@"Selecting image...");
  self.resolve = resolve;
  self.reject = reject;

  [self openPicker];
}
```

Just like the callback, we need to store the `resolve` and `reject` functions in instance variables so that they can be accessed after the user has selected the image. We create the instance variables in the private interface:

```
@interface ImageLibraryManager ()

@property (nonatomic, strong) RCTResponseSenderBlock callback;
@property (nonatomic, strong) RCTPromiseResolveBlock resolve;
@property (nonatomic, strong) RCTPromiseRejectBlock reject;
```

```
@end
```

And then we assign them in the `selectImagePromise` method:

```
self.resolve = resolve;
self.reject = reject;
```

Because the `selectImage` and `selectImagePromise` methods share much of the same code, we've broken out that functionality into a helper function called `openPicker`:

```
- (void)openPicker
{
  UIImagePickerController *picker = [[UIImagePickerController  alloc]
init];
  picker.sourceType = UIImagePickerControllerSourceTypePhotoLibrary;
  picker.mediaTypes = @[(NSString *)kUTTypeImage];
  picker.modalPresentationStyle =  UIModalPresentationCurrentContext;
  picker.delegate = self;
  UIViewController *root = [[[[UIApplication sharedApplication]  delegate]
window] rootViewController];
  [root presentViewController:picker animated:YES completion:nil];
}
```

Then we can call it in both of the exported methods:

```
[self openPicker];
```

Finally, in the delegate `imagePickerController` method, we need to determine which communication method to use. We'll do this by checking which instance variable is not `nil`:

```
RCTLog(@"%@", filePath);

if (self.callback != nil) {
    self.callback(@[filePath]);
} else if (self.resolve != nil) {
    self.resolve(filePath);
}
```

Once we rebuild, our application should now communicate using a promise instead of a `callback` function. We didn't make use of the `reject` parameter in the native module, but in a real application, this would be called in the event of an error.

Communicating with events

The final way that we can communicate from a native module to JavaScript is by using events. Events can be triggered at any time by a native module and can be listened to by any number of JavaScript components. These features make the use case for events slightly different than that for callbacks or promises.

Events are especially useful when an action is not initiated by JavaScript, but instead initiated by the native code. An example of this might be a user gesture that happens in a custom native module. Events are also a useful paradigm when more than one JavaScript component needs to be aware of the action.

For our application, we'll add events to the beginning and end of the image selection process and allow JavaScript components to listen to these events should they choose to. To do this, we'll first need to make our `ImageLibraryManager` class extend the `RCTEventEmitter` class instead of the `NSObject` class. The `RCTEventEmitter` class comes with methods for sending events over the React Native bridge:

```
#import "RCTBridgeModule.h"
#import "RCTEventEmitter.h"
#import <UIKit/UIKit.h>

@interface ImageLibraryManager : RCTEventEmitter <RCTBridgeModule,
UINavigationControllerDelegate, UIImagePickerControllerDelegate>
@end
```

Extending the `RCTEventEmitter` class requires us to implement the `supportedEvents` method that returns an array of event name strings. We'll add this method to the `ImageLibraryManager.m` implementation file:

```
- (NSArray<NSString *> *)supportedEvents {
  return @[@"ImageSelectionStarted", @"ImageSelectionEnded"];
}
```

Here we've added two supported event—one called `@"ImageSelectionStarted"` and another called `@"ImageSelectionEnded"`. Now, we'll send an event at the beginning of the `openPicker` function that indicates the image selection process has started:

```
- (void)openPicker
{
  [self sendEventWithName:@"ImageSelectionStarted" body:nil];
  UIImagePickerController *picker = [[UIImagePickerController alloc] init];
  ...
}
```

Likewise, we'll send an event when the selection completes in the
`imagePickerController` method, this time sending along the selected URL in the body of
the event:

```
-  (void)imagePickerController:(UIImagePickerController *)picker
didFinishPickingMediaWithInfo:(NSDictionary *)info
{
   ...

   [self sendEventWithName:@"ImageSelectionEnded" body:filePath];
   [picker dismissViewControllerAnimated:YES completion:nil];
}
```

When we rebuild, our native module is now sending events. However, no JavaScript
components are listening to these events. To start listening to these events (or any native
events), we'll need to import from the `react-native` package the `NativeEventEmitter`
module into `Profile.js`:

```
import React, { Component } from 'react';
import {
  View,
  StyleSheet,
  TouchableOpacity,
  NativeModules,
  Image,
  NativeEventEmitter
} from 'react-native';
import Icon from 'react-native-vector-icons/EvilIcons';
import Title from './Title';
import AppText from './AppText';
import * as globalStyles from '../styles/global';
```

We will subscribe to the image library manager's events when the component mounts, so
we'll need to add a lifecycle method to the component:

```
componentWillMount() {
  const imageLibraryEvents = new NativeEventEmitter(ImageLibraryManager);
  this.setState({
    startEventSubscription: imageLibraryEvents.addListener(
      "ImageSelectionStarted",
      () => console.log('Image Selection Started')
    ),
    endEventSubscription: imageLibraryEvents.addListener(
      "ImageSelectionEnded",
      url => console.log('Image Selection Ended', url)
    )
  });
```

```
}
```

We start by creating a new `NativeEventEmitter` object for the `ImageLibraryManager` native module:

```
const imageLibraryEvents = new  NativeEventEmitter(ImageLibraryManager);
```

When we add a listener, we need to specify both the event we want to listen to (that is, `"ImageSelectionStarted"`) and a callback function to run when the event is triggered. For the start event, our callback function is simply logging to the console:

```
imageLibraryEvents.addListener(
  "ImageSelectionStarted",
  () => console.log('Image Selection Started')
)
```

The `addListener` function returns a subscription object that can be used to remove the listener at a later point in time. We'll store this subscription in the component's state so that we can ultimately remove it when the component is unmounted:

```
this.setState({
  startEventSubscription: imageLibraryEvents.addListener(
    "ImageSelectionStarted",
    () => console.log('Image Selection Started')
  ),
  endEventSubscription: imageLibraryEvents.addListener(
    "ImageSelectionEnded",
    url => console.log('Image Selection Ended', url)
  )
});
```

Finally, we'll add a `componentWillUnmount` lifecycle method to remove the subscriptions when the component is removed from the application:

```
componentWillUnmount() {
  this.state.startEventSubscription.remove();
  this.state.endEventSubscription.remove();
}
```

Now when we run the application, we will see event messages in the JavaScript console in Chrome in addition to the console messages we left earlier. Though we aren't using these to do anything other than login at this point, they could easily be used to replace the callback and promise methods.

Exporting constants

In addition to exporting methods, we can also export constants from our native modules. For our example, we'll make the names of the events being triggering constants instead of hard-coded strings. In order to export constants, the native module must define a constantsToExport method that returns a dictionary of constants.

The first thing we'll do in our ImageLibraryManager example is define a couple of string constants at the top of the implementation file:

```
static NSString *const StartEvent = @"ImageSelectionStarted";
static NSString *const EndEvent = @"ImageSelectionEnded";
```

We'll then refactor the event triggering methods to use these constants instead of the hard-coded strings:

```
[self sendEventWithName:StartEvent body:nil];
```

Finally, we'll define the constantsToExport method that allows these constants to be exported as part of the React Native native module:

```
- (NSDictionary *)constantsToExport
{
  return @{ @"startEvent": StartEvent, @"endEvent": EndEvent };
}
```

With the constants exported, they can now be accessed as top-level keys on the JavaScript ImageLibraryManager object:

```
ImageLibraryManager.startEvent
// 'ImageSelectionStarted'
```

In our Profile component, we'll replace the hard-coded event names used when adding the event listeners:

```
componentWillMount() {
  const imageLibraryEvents = new NativeEventEmitter(ImageLibraryManager);
  this.setState({
    startEventSubscription: imageLibraryEvents.addListener(
      ImageLibraryManager.startEvent,
      () => console.log('Image Selection Started')
    ),
    endEventSubscription: imageLibraryEvents.addListener(
      ImageLibraryManager.endEvent,
      url => console.log('Image Selection Ended', url)
    )
  });
```

```
}
```

We now have a complete native module that exports both methods and constants and communicates with JavaScript through callback functions, promises, and events. However, our Android application is now broken because the native module is only defined in iOS. The next step will be to create parity on Android by porting the module to that platform.

Native modules in Android

Just like native modules for iOS are written in their native language, Objective-C, native modules for Android are written in the native Android language, Java. Once again, this chapter will not go into great detail about Java and the Android ecosystem at large, but will just focus on the interface between native Android code and React Native JavaScript code.

We will also use Android Studio to develop our Android native module as it provides the best Java development experience. Like Objective-C, Java is an object-oriented language. To create our native module, we'll be creating a new class that has the same name as the one used in the previous section. It will be contained in the `ImageLibraryManager.java` file. We will also need to create an `ImageLibraryManagerPackage.java` class that will be used to register the module.

Our goal in this section is to build an Android native module that has the exact same API as the iOS module. This will ensure that our JavaScript code in `Profile.js` does not have to be updated at all and can run the same on both platforms.

Setting up the module

To open our project in Android Studio, first open the Android Studio application and then open the `android` directory of the RNNYT application. When you do this, you should see two modules on the left-hand-side **Project** tab. We will be working in the **app** module, so let's first expand it and find the **com.rnnyt** package inside the `src/java` folder.

Currently, there should only be two classes within this package, **MainActivity** and **MainApplication**, as shown in the following screenshot:

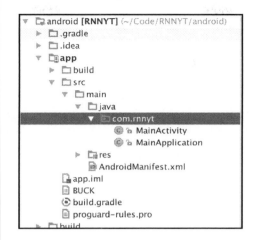

To add our new module class, right-click on the **com.rnnyt** package, and then click on **New** and then **Java Class**, as shown in the following screenshot:

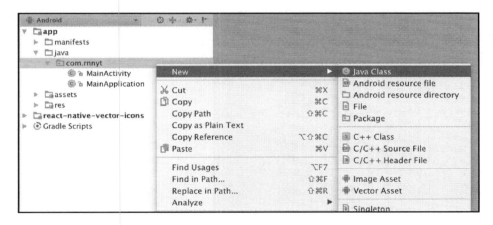

In the resulting dialog, type in the name of our new class, **ImageLibraryManager**, as shown in the following screenshot:

Repeat this process for the other **ImageLibraryManagerPackage** class.

When we create the classes, Android Studio will provide us with some boilerplate. We'll start in the `ImageLibraryManager` class:

```
package com.rnnyt;

public class ImageLibraryManager {
}
```

In order to turn this empty class into a React Native native module, we must do a few things. First, all native modules must extend the `ReactContextBaseJavaModule` class:

```
package com.rnnyt;

import com.facebook.react.bridge.ReactContextBaseJavaModule;

public class ImageLibraryManager extends  ReactContextBaseJavaModule {
}
```

The `ReactContextBaseJavaModule` class is abstract and requires us to implement a method called `getName`, which defines the name by which the module is accessed in JavaScript. We'll make ours consistent with the class name:

```
package com.rnnyt;

import com.facebook.react.bridge.ReactContextBaseJavaModule;

public class ImageLibraryManager extends ReactContextBaseJavaModule {

  @Override
  public String getName() {
    return "ImageLibraryManager";
```

```
    }

}
```

The abstract class also requires us to add a constructor that calls the super class constructor:

```
package com.rnnyt;

import com.facebook.react.bridge.ReactApplicationContext;
import com.facebook.react.bridge.ReactContextBaseJavaModule;

public class ImageLibraryManager extends  ReactContextBaseJavaModule {

  public ImageLibraryManager(ReactApplicationContext reactContext) {
    super(reactContext);
  }

    @Override
    public String getName() {
        return "ImageLibraryManager";
    }

}
```

We now need to register the module and we'll do so by editing the ImageLibraryManagerPackage class. This class needs to implement the ReactPackage interface:

```
package com.rnnyt;

import com.facebook.react.ReactPackage;

public class ImageLibraryManagerPackage implements ReactPackage {
}
```

The ReactPackage interface requires us to implement several methods:

```
package com.rnnyt;

import com.facebook.react.ReactPackage;
import com.facebook.react.bridge.JavaScriptModule;
import com.facebook.react.bridge.NativeModule;
import com.facebook.react.bridge.ReactApplicationContext;
import com.facebook.react.uimanager.ViewManager;

import java.util.List;

public class ImageLibraryManagerPackage implements ReactPackage {
```

```
  @Override
  public List<NativeModule>  createNativeModules(ReactApplicationContext
reactContext) {
     return null;
  }

  @Override
  public List<Class<? extends JavaScriptModule>> createJSModules()  {
     return null;
  }

  @Override
  public List<ViewManager>  createViewManagers(ReactApplicationContext
reactContext) {
     return null;
  }
}
```

Our only goal for this package is to register a native module so that we can return empty lists for the createViewManagers and createJSModules methods:

```
package com.rnnyt;

import com.facebook.react.ReactPackage;
import com.facebook.react.bridge.JavaScriptModule;
import com.facebook.react.bridge.NativeModule;
import com.facebook.react.bridge.ReactApplicationContext;
import com.facebook.react.uimanager.ViewManager;

import java.util.Collections;
import java.util.List;

public class ImageLibraryManagerPackage implements ReactPackage {
  @Override
  public List<NativeModule> createNativeModules(ReactApplicationContext
reactContext) {
     return null;
  }

  @Override
  public List<Class<? extends JavaScriptModule>> createJSModules() {
     return Collections.emptyList();
  }

  @Override
  public List<ViewManager> createViewManagers(ReactApplicationContext
reactContext) {
     return Collections.emptyList();
```

```
    }
}
```

However, for the `createNativeModules` method, we will need to return a list containing an instance of our `ImageLibraryManager` class:

```
package com.rnnyt;

import com.facebook.react.ReactPackage;
import com.facebook.react.bridge.JavaScriptModule;
import com.facebook.react.bridge.NativeModule;
import com.facebook.react.bridge.ReactApplicationContext;
import com.facebook.react.uimanager.ViewManager;

import java.util.ArrayList;
import java.util.Collections;
import java.util.List;

public class ImageLibraryManagerPackage implements ReactPackage {
  @Override
  public List<NativeModule>  createNativeModules(ReactApplicationContext
reactContext) {
    List<NativeModule> nativeModules = new ArrayList<>();
    nativeModules.add(new ImageLibraryManager(reactContext));
    return nativeModules;
  }

  @Override
  public List<Class<? extends JavaScriptModule>> createJSModules()  {
    return Collections.emptyList();
  }

  @Override
  public List<ViewManager>  createViewManagers(ReactApplicationContext
reactContext) {
    return Collections.emptyList();
  }
}
```

Our final step in the registration process is to update the `MainApplication` class to add an instance of our `ImageLibraryManagerPackage` to the list of application packages:

```
@Override
protected List<ReactPackage> getPackages() {
  return Arrays.<ReactPackage>asList(
      new MainReactPackage(),
      new ImageLibraryManagerPackage()
  );
```

```
}
```

We have now gone through the setup process for an Android native module. This process could be repeated anytime we need to construct a native module. We are now ready to start developing the image picker for Android.

Exporting methods

To export a method in an Android module, we simply add an `@ReactMethod` annotation to any public method within the module class, `ImageLibraryManager`. We're going to start with the `selectImage` method that allows a user to select an image from their image library:

```
@ReactMethod
public void selectImage() {
  Activity currentActivity = getCurrentActivity();

  Intent libraryIntent = new Intent(Intent.ACTION_PICK,
android.provider.MediaStore.Images.Media.EXTERNAL_CONTENT_URI);

  currentActivity.startActivityForResult(libraryIntent, 1);
}
```

In this method, we start by getting the currently visible Android `Activity`:

```
Activity currentActivity = getCurrentActivity();
```

Next, we create an `Intent` instance that indicates we want to open the media library in order to select an image:

```
Intent libraryIntent = new Intent(Intent.ACTION_PICK,
android.provider.MediaStore.Images.Media.EXTERNAL_CONTENT_URI);
```

Finally, we send this intent to the current `Activity` to open the media library:

```
currentActivity.startActivityForResult(libraryIntent, 1);
```

Now that we've opened the `Activity` media library, we need our class to be able to listen to when the image selection has been completed. To do this, we need our class to implement the `ActivityEventListener` interface:

```
public class ImageLibraryManager extends ReactContextBaseJavaModule
  implements ActivityEventListener {
```

This interface requires us to implement two methods. The first, `onActivityResult`, is the method we are primarily concerned with; it will be called when the image selection has completed. Here we will extract the image URL that was selected. The second, `onNewIntent`, we won't use, so we'll leave this method empty:

```
@Override
public void onActivityResult(Activity activity, int requestCode, int
resultCode, Intent data) {
  String filePath = data.getDataString();
}

@Override
public void onNewIntent(Intent intent) {

}
```

Finally, now that the `ImageLibraryManager` class implements the `ActivityEventListener` interface, we need to update the constructor to set the instance as an activity listener. This is similar to the iOS delegate pattern that we used in the previous section:

```
public ImageLibraryManager(ReactApplicationContext reactContext) {
  super(reactContext);
  reactContext.addActivityEventListener(this);
}
```

We now have the basic method set up for our Android native module. The next step is to communicate the result of this selection back to JavaScript.

Communicating with callbacks

Like we saw in the iOS module, the first strategy we can use to communicate with JavaScript is by accepting a callback function into the native method. The first step in this process is to add a `Callback` as a parameter to the `selectImage` method. The `Callback` class is contained in the `com.facebook.react.bridge` package:

```
@ReactMethod
public void selectImage(Callback callback) {
```

We will call the callback function when the user has finished selecting the image, so once again, we will need to store the callback in an instance variable. In Android classes, instance variables are typically prefixed with the m character. First, we create the field at the top of the class:

```
private Callback mCallback;
```

Then we assign the value within the selectImage method:

```
@ReactMethod
public void selectImage(Callback callback) {
  mCallback = callback;
```

Now we can invoke that callback function when the selection has completed:

```
@Override
public void onActivityResult(int requestCode, int resultCode, Intent data)
{
  String filePath = data.getDataString();
  mCallback.invoke(filePath);
}
```

The arguments passed to invoke need to be JSON serializable as they will be passed to the JavaScript callback. Now, we have a selectImage method in our Android native module that conforms exactly to the API of its iOS counterpart.

Communicating with promises

We can also use promises in the Android native module to communicate back to JavaScript. In Objective-C, to use a promise, you must add two parameters to the method: a resolver and a rejector. In Java, you only need a single parameter: a com.facebook.react.bridge.Promise. We'll create a new method selectImagePromise method that has this promise parameter:

```
@ReactMethod
public void selectImagePromise(Promise promise) {

}
```

Just like we stored the callback function in an instance variable, we will also store the promise in a new instance variable called `mPromise`:

```
private Promise mPromise;

...

@ReactMethod
public void pickImagePromise(Promise promise) {
    mPromise = promise;
}
```

Since the rest of the behavior for `selectImagePromise` is the same as the callback version, `selectImage`, we'll abstract that logic into an `openPicker` helper function:

```
@ReactMethod
public void selectImage(Callback callback) {
  mCallback = callback;
  openPicker();
}

@ReactMethod
public void selectImagePromise(Promise promise) {
  mPromise = promise;
  openPicker();
}

private void openPicker() {
  Activity currentActivity = getCurrentActivity();

  Intent libraryIntent = new Intent(Intent.ACTION_PICK,
android.provider.MediaStore.Images.Media.EXTERNAL_CONTENT_URI);

  currentActivity.startActivityForResult(libraryIntent, 1);
}
```

Finally, in the `onActivityResult` method, we need to check if the promise or callback instance variables have been set before calling them:

```
@Override
public void onActivityResult(Activity activity, int requestCode,  int
resultCode, Intent data) {
    String filePath = data.getDataString();

  if (mCallback != null) {
    mCallback.invoke(filePath);
  } else if (mPromise != null) {
    mPromise.resolve(filePath);
```

```
      }
   }
```

Since our JavaScript Profile component uses this `selectImagePromise` method in its current form, we are close to being able to use this Android native module. However, our module isn't quite at parity yet as there is one more method of communication remains.

Communicating with events

The final way to communicate back to JavaScript is by sending events through the device event emitter. We use the `ReactContext` to emit these events, so the first thing we need to do is store a reference to the context in an instance variable:

```
private Callback mCallback;
private Promise mPromise;
private ReactContext mReactContext;

public ImageLibraryManager(ReactApplicationContext reactContext) {
   super(reactContext);

   reactContext.addActivityEventListener(this);

   mReactContext = reactContext;
}
```

We'll emit the start event in the `openPicker` method using the stored context:

```
private void openPicker() {
   mReactContext
      .getJSModule(DeviceEventManagerModule.RCTDeviceEventEmitter.class)
      .emit("ImageSelectionStarted", null);

   Activity currentActivity = getCurrentActivity();

   Intent libraryIntent = new Intent(Intent.ACTION_PICK,
   android.provider.MediaStore.Images.Media.EXTERNAL_CONTENT_URI);

   currentActivity.startActivityForResult(libraryIntent, 1);
}
```

In this line of code, we get the device event emitter from the react context and then use it to emit an event. The first argument passed to `emit` is the name of the event and the second is a data object. Since there is no additional data that we need to send for this event, we have left the second argument `null`:

```
mReactContext
.getJSModule(DeviceEventManagerModule.RCTDeviceEventEmitter.class)
.emit("ImageSelectionStarted", null);
```

We also need to emit an event after the image selection has completed. This time we will send the image's `filePath` along with the event:

```
@Override
public void onActivityResult(Activity activity, int requestCode, int
resultCode, Intent data) {
  String filePath = data.getDataString();

  if (mCallback != null) {
    mCallback.invoke(filePath);
  } else if (mPromise != null) {
    mPromise.resolve(filePath);
  }

  mReactContext
  .getJSModule(DeviceEventManagerModule.RCTDeviceEventEmitter.class)
  .emit("ImageSelectionEnded", filePath);
}
```

Our native Android module will now emit an event just before the image library opens and another right when it ends.

Exporting constants

Before these will start working again in our React Native application, we will have to also export the names of the events as constants. In order to do this, we'll first create constants within the Java class:

```
private static final String START_EVENT = "ImageSelectionStarted";
private static final String END_EVENT = "ImageSelectionEnded";
```

We can now replace hard-coded strings in the class with these constants:

```
mReactContext
.getJSModule(DeviceEventManagerModule.RCTDeviceEventEmitter.class)
.emit(START_EVENT, null);
...
mReactContext
.getJSModule(DeviceEventManagerModule.RCTDeviceEventEmitter.class)
.emit(END_EVENT, filePath);
```

Finally, we can export these constants to JavaScript by implementing a method called getConstants that returns a map of constants:

```
@Nullable
@Override
public Map<String, Object> getConstants() {
  Map<String, Object> constants = new HashMap<>();
  constants.put("startEvent", START_EVENT);
  constants.put("endEvent", END_EVENT);
  return constants;
}
```

We've now completed our Android native module. Not only does it behave in the same way as the iOS module, but it also has the same application programming interface. This means that, in JavaScript, we can write code that is not platform aware. Let's take a look at the ImageLibraryManager in its entirety:

```
package com.rnnyt;

import android.app.Activity;
import android.content.Intent;

import com.facebook.react.bridge.ActivityEventListener;
import com.facebook.react.bridge.Callback;
import com.facebook.react.bridge.Promise;
import com.facebook.react.bridge.ReactApplicationContext;
import com.facebook.react.bridge.ReactContext;
import com.facebook.react.bridge.ReactContextBaseJavaModule;
import com.facebook.react.bridge.ReactMethod;
import com.facebook.react.modules.core.DeviceEventManagerModule;

import java.util.HashMap;
import java.util.Map;

import javax.annotation.Nullable;

public class ImageLibraryManager extends  ReactContextBaseJavaModule
implements ActivityEventListener {
```

```java
private static final String START_EVENT =  "ImageSelectionStarted";
private static final String END_EVENT = "ImageSelectionEnded";

private Callback mCallback;
private Promise mPromise;
private ReactContext mReactContext;

public ImageLibraryManager(ReactApplicationContext reactContext) {
  super(reactContext);

  reactContext.addActivityEventListener(this);

  mReactContext = reactContext;
}

@Override
public String getName() {
  return "ImageLibraryManager";
}

@Nullable
@Override
public Map<String, Object> getConstants() {
  Map<String, Object> constants = new HashMap<>();
  constants.put("startEvent", START_EVENT);
  constants.put("endEvent", END_EVENT);
  return constants;
}

@ReactMethod
public void selectImage(Callback callback) {
  mCallback = callback;
  openPicker();
}

@ReactMethod
public void selectImagePromise(Promise promise) {
  mPromise = promise;
  openPicker();
}

private void openPicker() {
  mReactContext
  .getJSModule(DeviceEventManagerModule.RCTDeviceEventEmitter.class)
  .emit(START_EVENT, null);

  Activity currentActivity = getCurrentActivity();
```

```
    Intent libraryIntent = new Intent(Intent.ACTION_PICK,
    android.provider.MediaStore.Images.Media.EXTERNAL_CONTENT_URI);

    currentActivity.startActivityForResult(libraryIntent, 1);
  }

  @Override
  public void onActivityResult(Activity activity, int requestCode, int
resultCode, Intent data) {
    String filePath = data.getDataString();
    if (mCallback != null) {
      mCallback.invoke(filePath);
    } else if (mPromise != null) {
      mPromise.resolve(filePath);
    }

    mReactContext
    .getJSModule(DeviceEventManagerModule.RCTDeviceEventEmitter.class)
    .emit(END_EVENT, filePath);
  }

  @Override
  public void onNewIntent(Intent intent) {

  }
}
```

Summary

Though React Native gives us access to many native visual components and APIs, there are some situations where we need direct access to the native code. To do this, we can either find an open source module that has been written to solve our problem or we can write our own. Writing native modules requires knowledge of the native ecosystem and language.

It is important to note that the native module we developed in this chapter is not production ready. If we were writing this module for production, we would need to add sufficient error handling and configuration options. Luckily, there are open source alternatives that we can use to select images and videos from the native media library.

In the next chapter, we'll take our application and begin preparing it for production. Specifically, we'll look at testing React Native applications, running them on real devices, performance optimizations, and deploying them to app stores.

11
Preparing for Production

Now that we have a completely functional, cross-platform application written using React Native, we need to start thinking about getting it into the hands of users. Our ultimate goal is to get an application into each platform's App Store, but there are several steps along the way. In this chapter, we'll take our application from *feature-complete* to *production-ready*. While most of the high-level steps mirror those for a completely native application, the details we'll focus on are those that are specific to React Native.

Through the context of the RNNYT application, this chapter will cover a plethora of practical matters including:

- Unit and component-testing React Native JavaScript code using Jest
- Performance analysis and optimization of React Native applications
- Running on a physical device
- Deploying React Native applications to the Apple App Store and the Google Play Store

Testing

In software development, there are several different kinds of testing. Each variety of testing serves a different purpose. **Unit testing** is used to ensure the accuracy of a single unit of computation. **Component testing** is a method of testing that ensures that the individual units work in concert when combined into a component, for instance, a React Native UI component.

In the React community, the primary tool for application testing is a library called **Jest**. Jest is an open source testing library, also created by Facebook, that builds on the functionality of a popular testing framework called **Jasmine**. Jest adds functionality to Jasmine to both make testing of JavaScript applications more robust and to add methods for testing React (and React Native) components.

Using Jest is so common among React Native developers, in fact, that it is now automatically installed and configured when an application is initialized (using `react-native init`). Looking in the `package.json` file for our RNNYT project will reveal Jest configuration that we do not need to change, but is helpful to know about. First, we see that `jest` is installed as a `devDependency` in addition to a few other Jest-related Node modules. Refer to the following code snippet:

```
"devDependencies": {
  "babel-jest": "16.0.0",
  "babel-preset-react-native": "1.9.0",
  "eslint-config-ericmasiello": "^0.5.0",
  "jest": "16.0.1",
  "jest-react-native": "16.0.0",
  "react-test-renderer": "15.3.2"
}
```

In the `scripts` section, we see that the test script simply runs `jest`, which will discover and run all test files throughout our project:

```
"scripts": {
  "start": "node node_modules/react-native/local-cli/cli.js start",
  "lint": "eslint . .eslintrc.js --ext [js,jsx] --cache",
  "test": "jest"
}
```

This means that, whenever we want to run our Jest `test` suite, we can simply type into the terminal:

```
npm test
```

Finally, we notice a section in the `package.json` file specifically for configuring Jest; it tells the test suite to use a `jest-react-native` preset for compiling and running tests:

```
"jest": {
  "preset": "jest-react-native"
}
```

By default, Jest will not be able to load platform-specific files that we've used in our application (those ending in `.ios.js` or `.android.js`), so we'll add an array to the Jest configuration of acceptable `moduleFileExtensions`:

```
"jest": {
  "preset": "jest-react-native",
  "moduleFileExtensions": [
    "js",
    "json",
    "es6",
    "ios.js",
    "android.js"
  ]
}
```

Jest works by scanning project directories for folders with the name __tests__ and running each file inside those folders as a test suite or part of a test suite. You'll notice that the root of our project already has a __tests__ folder and inside are two test files, `index.android.js` and `index.ios.js`. If we were to run `npm test` from the terminal, these tests would fail. We'll delete these two files and create tests that are specific to our application in their stead.

Unit testing

To learn about the basics of Jest, we're going to start off by writing a test for a utility function that is simply JavaScript (as opposed to a React Native component). To do this, we'll create a new `test` suite file `dataTransformations.test.js` inside a new __tests__/src/util/ directory (notice we are replicating the main project's directory structure within the __tests__ directory).

In this test suite, we're going to write one simple test for the `reshapeNewsData` function. This test will take mock data, shaped like that from the NYT API, pass it through the function, and compare the result to an expected result. The test data is rather large, so rather than putting it directly into our test file, we'll create a `testData.json` file in the same directory and place it there:

```
[{
  "section": "U.S.",
  "subsection": "Technology",
  "title": "React Native Expands to New Platforms",
  "abstract": "React Native, the framework for building mobile applications
with web technologies, is expanding to new platforms.",
  "url": "http://example.com/react-native-expands",
```

```
    "byline": "By JACOB FRIEDMANN",
    "item_type": "Article",
    "updated_date": "2016-09-10T11:48:04-04:00",
    "created_date": "2016-09-10T11:48:03-04:00",
    "published_date": "2016-09-10T05:00:00-04:00",
    "material_type_facet": "",
    "kicker": "",
    "des_facet": [
      "React Native",
      "Mobile Applications"
    ],
    "org_facet": [
      "Facebook"
    ],
    "per_facet": [],
    "geo_facet": [],
    "multimedia": [
      {
        "url": "https://example.com/image.jpg",
        "format": "thumbLarge",
        "height": 150,
        "width": 150,
        "type": "image",
        "subtype": "photo"
      }
    ]
}]
```

In order to read this file, we'll use the Node `fs` module from within the
`dataTransformations.test.js` file. We'll also import the function being tested,
`reshapeNewsData`:

```
import { reshapeNewsData } from '../../../src/util/dataTransformations';
import fs from 'fs';

const testData = JSON.parse(fs.readFileSync(__dirname + '/testData.json'));
```

We create Jest tests by using a series of globally defined functions, such as `describe`, `it`,
and `expect`, that allow us to write tests that almost read like English. If you've used
Jasmine, the testing library that Jest is built on top of, these functions will look familiar.
Refer to the following code snippet:

```
describe('dataTransformations util', () => {

  describe('reshapeNewsData function', () => {

    it('should correctly transform NYT news objects', () => {
```

```
        const transformedData = reshapeNewsData(testData);

      expect(transformedData).toEqual([
        {
          description: 'React Native, the framework for building mobile
applications with web technologies, is expanding to new platforms.',
          author: 'JACOB FRIEDMANN',
          location: '',
          imageUrl: 'https://example.com/image.jpg',
          date: 'Sep 10th 2016',
          title: 'React Native Expands to New Platforms',
          url: 'http://example.com/react-native-expands'
        }
      ]);
    });

  });

});
```

Here we use the `describe` function to organize our test suite by creating a group and then a subgroup of tests. Not only does this help to organize the test file, but it will also make the output more readable. Refer to the following code snippet:

```
describe('dataTransformations util', () => {

  describe('reshapeNewsData function', () => {

  });

});
```

The global `it` function defines a single test. The string passed to `it` is a description of what the test is meant to assert, as shown in the following code snippet:

```
it('should correctly transform NYT news objects', () => {
});
```

Finally, we will run the function we're testing on the mock test data and then use the global `expect` function to assert that the output is what we, for lack of a better term, *expect* it to be:

```
const transformedData = reshapeNewsData(testData);

expect(transformedData).toEqual([
  {
    description: 'React Native, the framework for building mobile
applications with web technologies, is expanding to new platforms.',
```

```
    author: 'JACOB FRIEDMANN',
    location: '',
    imageUrl: 'https://example.com/image.jpg',
    date: 'Sep 10th 2016',
    title: 'React Native Expands to New Platforms',
    url: 'http://example.com/react-native-expands'
  }
]);
```

Now that we have a complete, albeit simple, test suite, we can run it from the terminal:

```
npm test
> RNNYT@0.0.1 test /Users/jacobfriedmann/Code/RNNYT
> jest

PASS  src/util/__tests__/dataTransformations.test.js
  dataTransformations util
    reshapeNewsData function
      ☐ should correctly transform NYT news objects (7ms)
Test Summary
    Ran all tests.
    1 test passed (1 total in 1 test suite, run time 2.13s)
```

Component testing

Next, we'll create a component test for a React Native component that we developed for this project. We're going to test the `NewsItem` component using what Jest calls **snapshot testing**. Snapshot testing first creates a base *snapshot* of a component, given some props. This snapshot is a string representation of the rendered component. Jest then compares future snapshots to the base snapshot; if the snapshots are equal, the test passes. The underlying assumption in these tests is that the component starts in a valid state and future changes to the code base should leave the rendered output of the component unchanged.

To get started, we'll first create a new test suite file `NewsItem.test.js` in a folder called `__tests__/src/components`. Following is the snapshot that we will create in this file:

```
import 'react-native';
import React from 'react';
import NewsItem from '../../../src/components/NewsItem';
import renderer from 'react-test-renderer';

const noop = () => {};

const testData = {
  description: 'React Native, the framework for building mobile
```

```
applications with web technologies, is expanding to new platforms.',
  author: 'JACOB FRIEDMANN',
  location: '',
  imageUrl: 'https://example.com/image.jpg',
  date: 'Sep 10th 2016',
  title: 'React Native Expands to New Platforms',
  url: 'http://example.com/react-native-expands',
  onPress: noop,
  onBookmark: noop
};

describe('NewsItem component', () => {

  it('should render correctly', () => {
    const renderedComponent = renderer.create(
      <NewsItem
        index={0}
        {...testData}
      />
    ).toJSON();
    expect(renderedComponent).toMatchSnapshot();
  });

});
```

First, we'll need to import our component, React, React Native, and the Jest React renderer, which gives Jest the ability to create the component `snapshots`:

```
import 'react-native';
import React from 'react';
import NewsItem from '../NewsItem';
import renderer from 'react-test-renderer';
```

 The `react-native` package must be imported prior to the `react-test-renderer` package in order to function properly.

We will also need some test data to use as props for the `NewsItem` component. Additionally, we define a `noop` (a function that does nothing) constant that can be used for function type props in the component:

```
const noop = () => {};

const testData = {
  description: 'React Native, the framework for building mobile
applications with web technologies, is expanding to new platforms.',
```

```
    author: 'JACOB FRIEDMANN',
    location: '',
    imageUrl: 'https://example.com/image.jpg',
    date: 'Sep 10th 2016',
    title: 'React Native Expands to New Platforms',
    url: 'http://example.com/react-native-expands',
    onPress: noop,
    onBookmark: noop
};
```

Now we'll use the global `describe` and `it` functions to set the stage for our new test:

```
describe('NewsItem component', () => {

  it('should render correctly', () => {
  });

});
```

The test itself is relatively simple. First we render the component with the mock props to a JSON string and then we check to make sure the rendered string matches the base `snapshot`:

```
const renderedComponent = renderer.create(
  <NewsItem
    index={0}
    {...testData}
  />
).toJSON();
expect(renderedComponent).toMatchSnapshot();
```

The first time this test runs, it will generate the base snapshot in a `__snapshots__` directory and automatically pass. On subsequent runs, it will compare the generated snapshot to the one created on the first run. If we were ever to change how the component is rendered, the test would fail. If, however, this change is intentional, we can update the base snapshot by running the following command (`u` for update):

```
npm test -- -u
```

Now that we have a simple component snapshot test, we could expand on it by creating other tests within the suite that pass different props into the component. A robust test suite would include these tests for each component in the project.

Performance

When we refer to the performance of a mobile application, especially one that is not written in the native language, what we are most often talking about is framerate. It is generally accepted that the human eye can process up to 60 still frames per second (fps). When a series of images is displayed at or above this upper limit, we perceive it as motion instead of discreet images. With this in mind, our goal when optimizing the performance of an application is to ensure that the framerate never or rarely dips below 60 fps.

The practical implications of this requirement are that any blocking computation must complete within 16.67 milliseconds (1,000 milliseconds per 60 fps). Whenever we do something computationally expensive, for instance, rendering a new scene with many child components, there is a risk that the task will not complete in the allotted time. When this happens, we will *drop a frame* and the user will experience jitteriness or unresponsiveness as a result.

In React Native, this picture is further complicated by the fact that there are two threads behind UI rendering. First, there is the main UI thread. This thread is running the native code that is part of the React Native core library and is directly responsible for rendering UI components. The second thread, on iOS, is the **JavaScriptCore (JSC)** thread that runs all of the code that we write in JavaScript. The JSC thread does not itself render UI elements, but it is often responsible for driving rendering by telling the main thread what components to render and what properties they should have.

 In this chapter, we will look at performance analysis and optimization from the point of view of a React Native iOS application. However, these techniques and optimizations will work on either platform.

Both of these two threads have their own framerate that could potentially impact the perceived performance of the application. Generally speaking, drops in framerate in React Native applications can usually be attributed to one of two things:

- Occasionally, we write JavaScript that is not performant, causing the JSC thread's framerate to drop. This, in turn, causes the main thread to appear to drop frames as it awaits instruction from the slow JSC thread.
- While the languages themselves, JavaScript and Objective-C/Java, are independently very fast and capable of maintaining the framerate, communication between them over the React Native Bridge is not especially rapid. If this communication happens too often, carrying too much data, or at inopportune times, it can significantly impact the performance of both threads.

Performance optimization in React Native comes down to first using a suite of tools provided by the framework to locate performance bottlenecks and then using optimization techniques from the world of React and React Native to mitigate them.

In this section, we'll imagine that we have been away from our RNNYT application for some time and, upon returning, we realize that there are some serious performance issues with the application introduced by other developers. We'll put the aforementioned tools and techniques to use and try to restore the application's framerate to its former glory.

 If you wish to follow along, this chapter comes with two bundles of code: application preoptimizations (where we start from) and application post optimization (where we are going).

Problematic ListView

The first thing we noticed when using the application is that the news feed, which was once smooth as we scrolled through articles displayed in a React Native ListView component, is now jittery. It turns out ListViews, especially ones that contain many rows, are a common source of performance problems in React Native applications. Let us first verify that what we think we're seeing (a drop in the framerate as we scroll) is indeed occurring.

Using Perf Monitor

The first tool we'll look at is the React Native **Perf Monitor**. This tool can be used within the application to monitor key metrics during runtime. It can be used to get a high-level view of the overall application performance as well as to narrow down the source of performance problems.

To open Perf Monitor, first open the developer menu by pressing command + D in the simulator or, if on a real device, shaking it. In the menu, select the **Show Perf Monitor** option, as shown in the following screenshot:

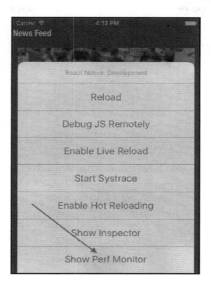

Once we do this, we should see the small Perf Monitor modal on screen. It generally sits in the upper left-hand corner of the screen, but it can be dragged to any location where it is least obstructive, as shown in the following screenshot:

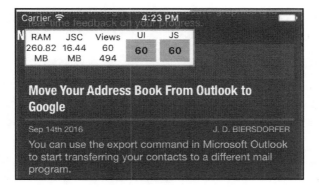

Inside this modal, we see several different metrics that help us get a feel for how the application is performing. Let's examine these one by one.

The first number on the left is the total **RAM (Random Access Memory)** being used by the application. This is an important number to watch because, if it becomes too large, the operating system will take things into its own hands and kill our application. A snapshot of this number can be used to know generally if your application is consuming too much memory. Even more important is to ensure that this number does not increase without bounds over time, which would be a sign of a memory leak.

The next number, labeled **JSC**, is the amount of memory allocated to the `JavaScriptCore` thread specifically. This number is included within the total RAM number, but is useful to us because it is directly within our control as React Native developers.

Next, there are two numbers under the **Views** label. The bottom number is the total number of native views currently on the heap (in memory). The top number is the subset of those total views that are actually visible on the screen for the user to see.

Finally, probably the two most important numbers are the ones labeled **UI** and **JS** on the far right. These numbers represent the framerate for the previous second for the main UI thread and the JavaScript thread, respectively. The numbers are also overlaid onto a graph of these framerates over time, which can help us to identify dips in framerate as they relate to specific interactions (that is, scrolling).

If you click or press on the Perf Monitor modal, it will expand to reveal more metrics. These are also helpful, but we will rely on them less often when doing performance analysis, as shown in the following screenshot:

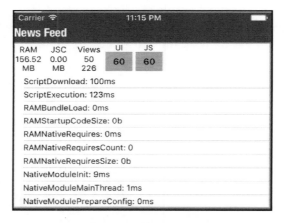

If your Perf Monitor is missing metrics for JavaScript, namely the JSC memory allocation and the JS framerate, it is probably because you are debugging the application remotely. When debugging remotely, the JavaScript actually runs in your Chrome browser's V8 JavaScript engine instead of the JavaScriptCore engine inside the device or simulator. In order to see JavaScript performance metrics, we need to disable remote debugging in the developer menu and allow the JavaScript to run in the JavaScriptCore engine.

With the Perf Monitor open, let's scroll down the news feed. What we see when we do this is that, as we expected, the JavaScript framerate plummets every time we scroll up and down. Refer to the following screenshot:

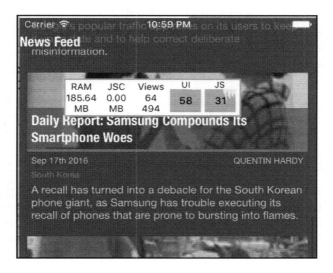

Now we know that we aren't crazy and there is indeed a performance issue in the application. We also know that the issue is originating in the JavaScript thread. However, this by itself is not enough to tell us where to look for problems. For this, we'll need some more information.

Analyzing a Systrace

Next we'll use the **Systrace** tool that also ships with React Native and to dive deeper. The Systrace tool monitors the execution of marked functions such as React's calls to `render` components and other lifecycle functions, as well as common functions in native code. This information can be visualized in what some call a **flame graph**, which shows function execution over time by thread.

 Once again, the Systrace tool relies on the fact that the JavaScript code is running within the JavaScriptCore engine and not Chrome's V8. This means we must first disable remote JavaScript debugging in the developer menu before starting to trace; otherwise, we will not see JavaScript execution, though we will see other threads.

To start tracing, we'll open the Developer menu and select **Start Systrace**, as shown in the following screenshot:

Once we start tracing, we'll scroll down the news feed again. We don't need to do it for very long to collect useful information, so after a few seconds open the Developer menu and select **Stop Systrace**. When we do this, we'll likely see a modal warning that the Systrace could not be converted to HTML and recommending we install a tool called `trace2html`. Refer to the following screenshot:

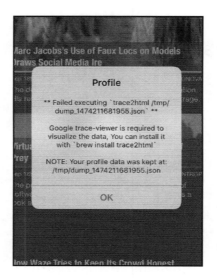

At the time of this writing, `trace2html` is broken, so installing it with Homebrew would be fruitless. However, we're in luck because Chrome provides us with a simple utility to visualize the JSON file created and stored in the `/tmp` directory.

The first step is to open the Chrome browser and navigate in the address bar to `chrome://tracing`. When we arrive at this page, we'll see a mostly empty dashboard. In the upper left-hand corner, there is a button labeled **Load**, as shown in the following screenshot:

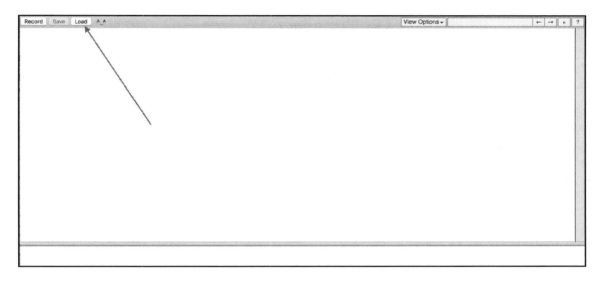

We'll use this to load the JSON file stored in the /tmp folder into the tracing utility, and when we do, several things show up in the dashboard, as shown in the following screenshot:

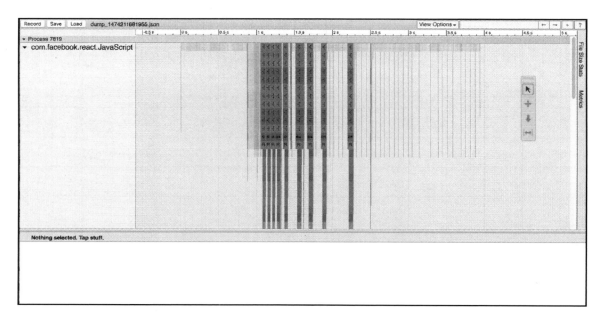

There is a lot going on here, so let's try to break it down. On the left-hand side, we can see that activity is grouped by the thread that it is running on. The top thread is likely **com.facebook.react.JavaScript**, which, as it happens, is the JavaScript thread we know is misbehaving. If we scroll down or collapse that thread, we can see below it several other threads including the main UI thread, which is simply labeled main. Refer to the following screenshot:

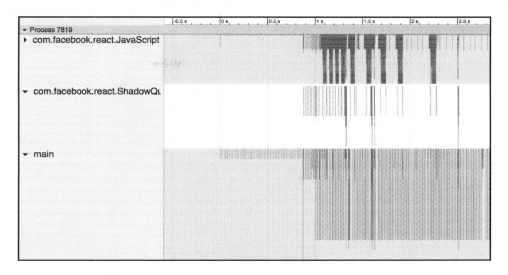

The top *x*-axis is displaying the time. We can see that the bulk of the activity is happening within about a second. We can probably assume that this is when we were actually doing the scrolling. Each horizontal band in the graph represents a function call. From this zoom level, it is impossible to make any sense of the graph, so we'll need to zoom in using the w key (or the zoom tool). Take a look at the following screenshot:

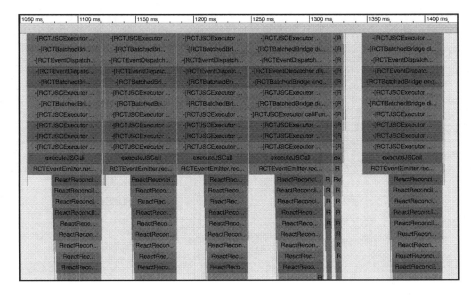

Functions are placed below the functions that call them. Each *flame* or stack of functions here is a top-level function call (in this case `RCTJSCExecutor executeBlockOnJavaScriptQueue`) cascading down into many other functions. What matters then for rendering performance is that the top-level bands do not exceed 16.6 milliseconds, at least not often, the time limit mandated by a 60 fps framerate.

Looking at this, even naively, we can see by the repeated shapes that there is some sort of repetitive event happening. We can measure one of these events using the measurement tool to see how long each event is taking. When we can do this, we can see that even one of the smaller stacks has a duration of over 60 milliseconds, which would cause at least three dropped frames. Refer to the following screenshot:

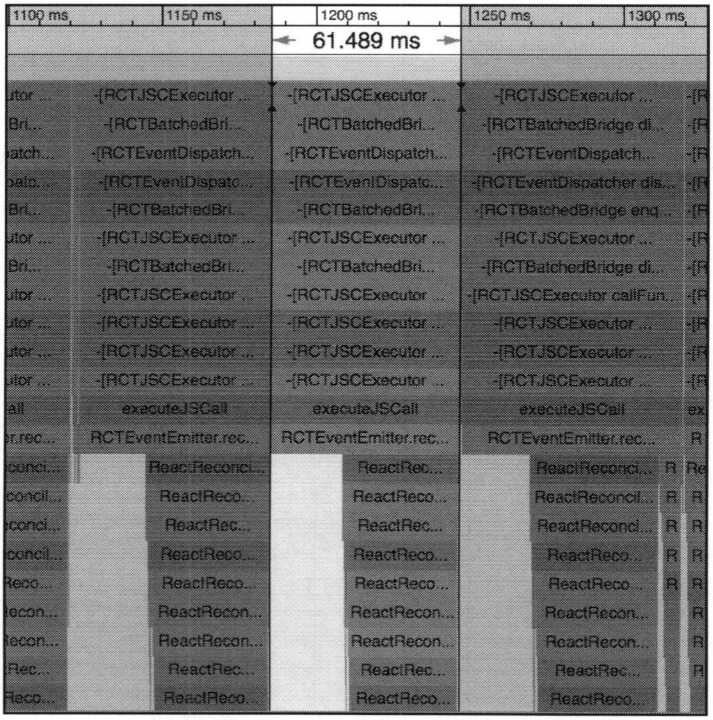

It is still difficult to tell what is happening here, but when we zoom in a little further, the picture becomes a little clearer, as shown in the following screenshot:

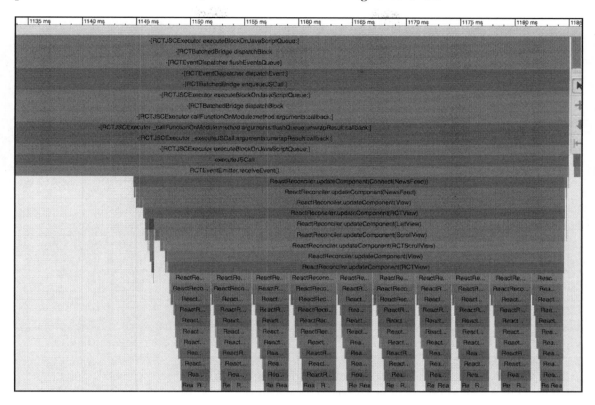

What we see when we zoom in is that React is doing a bunch of repetitive rendering of components as we're scrolling. Near the top of this section, we can see the `NewsFeed` component being updated. If we follow this down, the smaller stacks are the individual `NewsItems` being updated. As we can see, all of this component updating and rerendering is expensive, but is it necessary?

The content and appearance of the news feed are not obviously changing as we scroll down. If this is the case, then we are wasting a lot of time rendering views that are not changing. We need to determine if all this rendering is necessary or if we are wasting precious time.

The React Perf Library

Next, we're going to turn to a tool from the world of React proper. The React `Perf` library will measure all component renders and tell us which of those renders were *wasted*. Wasted renders are renders that occurred even though the output (UI) did not change. We can improve the performance of a React application by reducing the number of wasted renders.

To get started with the React Perf library, we'll first need to install the library as a dependency for our project using npm by using the following command:

```
npm install --save react-addons-perf
```

The easiest way to work with the `Perf` library is to expose it as a global variable. To do this, we'll import it into the `App.js` file and store it in the window global namespace:

```
import React from 'react';
import Perf from 'react-addons-perf';
import { Provider } from 'react-redux';
import HomeScreen from './components/HomeScreen';
import createStore from './createStore';

window.Perf = Perf;
```

Now, we'll enable remote debugging in the Developer menu so that we can access the `Perf` library from the Chrome JavaScript console. Oddly, when we first try to access the global `Perf` variable we created, we notice that it isn't defined. This is because the application code is actually running in a service worker thread inside Chrome, rather than on the Chrome tab's main thread. To get access to the scope of the service worker, we can switch to the **debuggerWorker.js** thread in the upper left-hand corner. Take a look at the following screenshot:

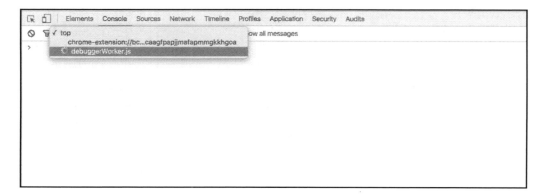

We are now ready to start monitoring rendering performance. To do this, we'll type the following command into the Chrome console:

```
Perf.start()
```

Then, we'll once again scroll down the news feed and, when finished, will type the following into the Chrome console:

```
Perf.stop()
Perf.printWasted()
```

This second command will print out a big colorful table into the console, describing the rendering activity that took place during monitoring, as shown in the following screenshot:

(index)	Owner > Component	Inclusive wasted time (ms) ▼	Instance count	Render count
0	"NewsItem > View"	1861	84	1344
1	"HomeScreen > Connect(NewsFeed)"	1093	1	16
2	"Connect(NewsFeed) > NewsFeed"	1091	1	16
3	"NewsFeed > View"	1078	1	16
4	"NewsFeed > ListView"	1073	1	17
5	"ListView > ScrollView"	1061	1	17
6	"ScrollView > View"	1050	1	17
7	"ListView > StaticRenderer"	1048	28	448
8	"StaticRenderer > NewsItem"	1030	28	448
9	"NewsItem > TouchableOpacity"	809	28	448
10	"TouchableOpacity > AnimatedComponent"	778	28	448
11	"AnimatedComponent > View"	714	28	448
12	"NewsItem > Thumbnail"	302	28	448
13	"Byline > View"	291	65	1040
14	"NewsItem > Byline"	256	28	448
15	"Thumbnail > View"	208	33	528
16	"Thumbnail > Image"	121	23	368
17	"Byline > SmallText"	95	65	1040
18	"SmallText > AppText"	91	65	1040
19	"Thumbnail > Title"	79	28	448

By default, the table will be sorted by whichever class of components (labeled in the second column **Owner > Component**) wasted the most time needlessly rerendering. We can see that there are many offenders, but at the top of the list is the NewsItem component, wasting nearly two whole seconds (!) of time on rendering when nothing has changed.

If you are perceptive, you will have also noticed that redux-logger was logging a new action as we scrolled down with a type FEED_PROGRESS. It seems pretty likely that this is the root cause of the rerendering, but it doesn't explain why components are rerendering when they don't have to. Now that we've closed in on the problem using our performance tool suite, let's look at how we can start to remedy this situation.

shouldComponentUpdate and PureRenderMixin

Way back in Chapter 1, *Building a Foundation in React*, we talked about the various lifecycle functions that each component has. One of these lifecycle functions is shouldComponentUpdate, which is called before rendering to determine whether or not a new render is necessary. By default, if this method is not overridden, it will always return true, meaning that the component will always rerender when its parent rerenders.

In the case of the NewsItem component, which we know is rerendering needlessly, we can improve upon this by implementing our own shouldComponentUpdate method. However, if we know that the component's render method is a pure function of the inputs (props and state), we can take advantage of a class called PureComponent. This gives us a relatively simple implementation of shouldComponentUpdate that can be used within any of our components that are pure (and hopefully most are).

To get started, we'll need to import PureComponent into the NewsItem component in place of the standard Component class:

```
import React, { PureComponent, PropTypes } from 'react';
import {
  View,
  TouchableOpacity,
  StyleSheet,
  ActionSheetIOS,
  ToastAndroid,
  Platform,
  Vibration
} from 'react-native';
```

Next, we'll make the NewsItem component class extend from the PureComponent class:

```
export default class NewsItem extends PureComponent {
```

And that's it! The shouldComponentUpdate method of PureComponent simply checks to see if the props and state inputs have changed and returns true, meaning the component should update if, and only if, they have. This alone should be enough to make a dent in our performance problem. To verify, let's take another look at the React Perf libraries wasted-time table after this change.

The `PureComponent` uses shallow equality to determine whether or not the `props` and `state` have changed. This is a compromise between strict equality, which would not recognize two objects as being equal even if all of their keys and values are equivalent, and deep equality, which would crawl down the object tree ensuring that all leaves are equivalent. Deep equality is potentially expensive and strict equality is not very useful when reducers generate new objects (as they should). Shallow equality meets somewhere in the middle by checking the top-level values of an object for strict equality.

Take a look at the following screenshot:

ReactPerf.js:412

(index)	Owner > Component	Inclusive wasted time (ms)	Instance count	Render count
0	"HomeScreen > Connect(NewsFeed)"	72	1	21
1	"Connect(NewsFeed) > NewsFeed"	70	1	21
2	"NewsFeed > ListView"	58	1	33
3	"NewsFeed > View"	56	1	21
4	"ListView > ScrollView"	32	1	33
5	"ScrollView > View"	14	1	33
6	"ListView > StaticRenderer"	11	28	391
7	"NewsFeed > Title"	5	1	21
8	"Title > H1"	4	1	21
9	"H1 > AppText"	4	1	21
10	"NewsFeed > ProgressViewIOS"	3	1	21
11	"AppText > Text"	0	1	21
12	"NewsFeed > RefreshControl"	0	1	21

Wow! This is a huge improvement. We could probably stop now and call it a day, but let's go a bit further and think about why all of these components are trying to render in the first place.

Minimizing the impact of state changes

As we noticed earlier, there is a new action being fired as we scroll down the news feed. This action is being used to update a new progress bar at the top of the **News Feed** and nothing else. Refer to the following screenshot:

If we look at the following code, we can see that the progress comes from the store into the news feed container, which mean the news feed, a large component with many children, is receiving new props many times during the scroll. We can minimize the impact of these changes by making the progress bar itself a container component so that it alone receives new props during the scroll process.

To do this, we make a simple UI presentational component for the progress bar in a file called `src/components/ProgressBar.ios.js`:

```
import React from 'react';
import {
  ProgressViewIOS
} from 'react-native';
import * as globalStyles from '../styles/global';

const ProgressBar = props => (
  <ProgressViewIOS
    progress={props.progress}
    progressTintColor={globalStyles.HEADER_TEXT_COLOR}
  />
);

ProgressBar.propTypes = {
  progress: React.PropTypes.number.isRequired
};

export default ProgressBar;
```

And then we create a container component that is attached to the store in a file called `src/containers/ProgressBarCointainer.js`:

```
import { connect } from 'react-redux';
import ProgressBar from '../components/ProgressBar';

const mapStateToProps = state => ({
  progress: state.progress
});

export default connect(mapStateToProps, {})(ProgressBar);
```

We then replace the `ProgressViewIOS` from the `NewsFeed` component with the new container component `ProgressBarContainer`:

```
<View style={styles.container}>
  {isIOS && <ProgressBarContainer />}
  <ListView
    refreshControl={
```

```
        <RefreshControl
          refreshing={refreshing}
          onRefresh={this.refresh}
        />
      }
      enableEmptySections
      dataSource={dataSource}
      renderRow={this.renderRow}
      style={[listStyles, styles.list]}
      onChangeVisibleRows={this.onProgress}
    />
    {this.renderModal()}
  </View>
```

With the impact of the progress changes minimized into this single, small container component, we are ready to take another Perf measurement. The following is the result:

Perf.printWasted()				
				ReactPerf.js:412
(index)	Owner > Component	Inclusive wasted time (ms)	Instance count	Render count
0	"NewsFeed > ListView"	20	1	12
1	"ListView > ScrollView"	8	1	12
2	"NewsFeed > Connect(ProgressBar)"	5	1	14
3	"Connect(ProgressBar) > ProgressBar"	3	1	14
4	"ProgressBar > ProgressViewIOS"	2	1	14
5	"ScrollView > View"	1	1	12

Once again, this relatively small change has had a pretty big impact. It is hard to imagine we can improve upon this, but we will try.

The ListView data source

As we discussed in a previous chapter, when we create a ListView, we give it a function to determine whether or not a row has changed. In many respects, this function is similar to shouldComponentUpdate in that it is used to determine whether or not a row of the list should be rerendered. If we take a look at the ListView in the NewsFeed component, we'll notice that something is awry. Take a look at the following code:

```
this.ds = new ListView.DataSource({
    rowHasChanged: (row1, row2) => true
});
```

This function has changed since we last saw it. In this state, whenever it is called, the row will be rerendered because it always returns `true` to the question: Has this row changed? It is restored to the same form in the following:

```
this.ds = new ListView.DataSource({
    rowHasChanged: (row1, row2) => row1.title !== row2.title
});
```

With this corrected, we'll once again look at the wasted-time table:

```
Perf.printWasted()
                                                                        ReactPerf.js:412
(index)   Owner > Component                 Inclusive wasted time (ms)  Instance count   Render count
0         "NewsFeed > Connect(ProgressBar)"   3                         1                15
1         "Connect(ProgressBar) > ProgressBar" 3                        1                15
2         "ProgressBar > ProgressViewIOS"     3                         1                15
```

We see another pretty large improvement and can now claim victory over wasted renders. Before we reexamine the Systrace and framerate, let's look at a few more optimizations that can be made.

Additional optimizations

With any `ListView`, we can optimize the initial rendering cost by using several properties in concert. The first one we'll add is `initialListSize`. This property tells `ListView` how many rows to render when it first appears. The default value is 10 rows, but if we know that the number of initially visible rows is fewer than that, we can reduce the initial rendering cost. It looks like three rows will be showing at a time, so we'll make this value 4 for good measure. Take a look at the following code snippet:

```
<ListView
  refreshControl={
    <RefreshControl
      refreshing={refreshing}
      onRefresh={this.refresh}
    />
  }
  enableEmptySections
  dataSource={dataSource}
  renderRow={this.renderRow}
  style={[listStyles, styles.list]}
  onChangeVisibleRows={this.onProgress}
  initialListSize={4}
/>
```

Similarly, we can use the `pageSize` property to tell `ListView` how many rows it should render per event loop. This ensures that rendering the rows in their entirety is not a blocking task that could potentially drag down the framerate. This is 1 by default, which for our application makes sense, so we will not change it.

Next, we could use the `scrollRenderAheadDistance` property to tell the `ListView` how many pixels before it reaches a row it should begin to render that row. This ensures we don't render rows that are off-screen if the user isn't moving towards them. Once again, the default (1,000 pixels) is adequate for our application.

In certain places, we can ask for views to be rasterized into bitmaps. This is most useful when a complex view is being animated or when there are several opaque views layered on top of one another. In our application, we can add this to the `Image` inside our `Thumbnail` component that has text layered on top of it. We need to be careful when doing this to monitor memory usage as rasterized `Views` are stored in memory and can get big. Refer to the following code snippet:

```
<Image
  style={[styles.image, imageStyle]}
  source={{
    uri: url
  }}
  shouldRasterizeIOS
>
  {TitleComponent}
</Image>
```

Logging to the console is also an expensive operation in React Native applications. Generally, this will be stripped out of production code, but it is also useful for us to turn logging off when doing performance testing to ensure that it is not skewing the result. We can reduce the amount of logging by turning off the `redux-logger` middleware in the store.

Running Systrace again, we can see that our work has really paid off. The timeline is much sparser, and in fact, it is more empty than not and the stacks are all much smaller than 16.67 milliseconds:

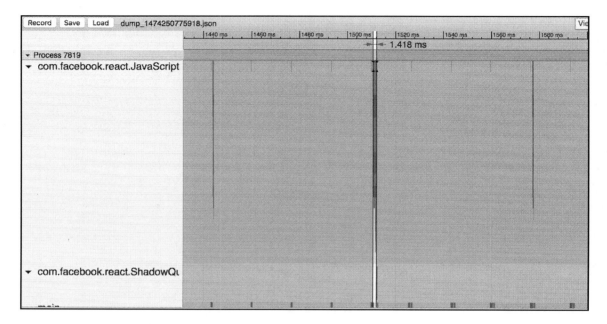

If we were to look at the Perf Monitor, we would see that we can barely make a dent in the framerate by scrolling as fast as we can.

Unresponsive touch and slow navigation

There are two other, somewhat related, common categories of performance problem in React Native applications: components that are slow to give feedback after being touched and navigational transitions that are either slow to start or clunky as they animate.

A problem has been introduced into our application that belongs to one of these categories, but at the outset we are not sure which. Now, when we click on an article in the news feed, for a brief time it seems as if nothing is happening. Eventually, the modal appears and the article loads, but by that time we've already annoyed our user.

Mitigating unresponsive touch

The first thing we'll attempt is to make the touch interaction faster and more responsive. React Native's touchable components (TouchableOpacity and TouchableHighlight) block animation until the function passed as their onPress property returns. This means that, if the onPress function is doing something computationally expensive, it could impact the feedback experience seen by the user.

A common solution for this problem is to do any expensive computation in the onPress function asynchronously. The onPress prop of the NewsItem in the NewsFeed component only calls an action, but perhaps some cascading effects are causing the delay. We'll use the requestAnimationFrame function to ensure that the action happens asynchronously and doesn't block touch animations:

```
<NewsItem
  onPress={() => {
    requestAnimationFrame(() =>
this.props.onModalOpen(rowData.url));
  }}
  onBookmark={() => this.props.addBookmark(rowData.url)}
  style={styles.newsItem}
  index={index}
  {...rowData}
/>
```

A common source of bugs and memory leaks in React applications is the use of timer functions such as requestAnimationFrame (also setTimeout, setImmediate, and setInterval). Each of these asynchronous functions might need to be cleaned up in some way when the component unmounts.

We have done some good work here, but has it made an impact? When we go back to test the performance of clicking on a news item again, we might see that the press animation is a little smoother, but there is still something keeping the modal animation from starting. To get a little more context, we can run Systrace and see what is going on. Take a look at the following screenshot:

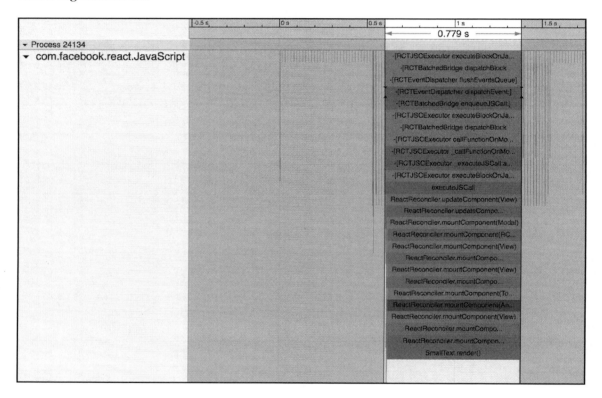

Looking at the result, there is a pretty clear problem. It appears as if there is a nearly full-second, blocking JavaScript call to the `SmallText` component's `render` method. Looking more closely at that component's `render` method reveals that someone added a function (to apply `fallColors`) that looks mightily expensive. Take a look at the following code snippet:

```
const fallColors = unformattedText => unformattedText.split('').map((c) =>
{
  const randomColors = [];
  let rand1 = 200;
  let rand2 = 100;
  let rand3 = 0;
  for (let i = 0; i < 5000000; i += 1) {
```

```
      randomColors.push(Math.floor(Math.random() * 255));
    }
    for (let j = 0; j < randomColors.length; j += 1) {
      if (randomColors[j] >= 200) {
        rand1 = randomColors[j];
      }
    }
    for (let k = 0; k < randomColors.length; k += 1) {
      if (randomColors[k] < 200 && randomColors[k] >= 100) {
        rand2 = randomColors[k];
      }
    }
    for (let l = 0; l < randomColors.length; l += 1) {
      if (randomColors[l] < 100) {
        rand3 = randomColors[l];
      }
    }
    const paddedHex1 = (`0${rand1.toString(16)}`).slice(-2);
    const paddedHex2 = (`0${rand2.toString(16)}`).slice(-2);
    const paddedHex3 = (`0${rand3.toString(16)}`).slice(-2);
    const randColor = `#${paddedHex1}${paddedHex2}${paddedHex3}`;
    return (
      <Text
        key={c}
        style={{
          color: randColor
        }}
      >
        {c}
      </Text>
    );
  });
```

Of course, we can and should fix this function to make it more efficient, but let's also look at ways of mitigating the expense if we can't do this.

 To get more precise data about which function calls are impacting performance the most, we could use the CPU Profiler tool. However, the Profiler is difficult to assemble and, at the time of writing, broken for iOS10. In most scenarios, Systrace will be enough to diagnose or narrow down the potential causes of performance issues.

Smoothing out animations with InteractionManager

Navigational animation issues are most typically related to the influx of React rendering that happens when a component is mounted. When navigating, often we are mounting an entire new scene with dozens or perhaps hundreds of child components. This process is expensive and can get in the way of smooth transition animations.

To mitigate this expense, React Native has a module called InterationManager that allows us to defer expensive rendering until after a navigational interaction is complete. We have now identified that the source of our issue is an expensive render in one component, SmallText. We'll use the InteractionManager within that component to render a simplified version of the component until after the navigation is complete.

First, we'll need to import the InteractionManager module. We'll also need to convert this component into a class-based component so that the InteractionManager can take advantage of the lifecycle methods, so we'll need to import Component from the React package as well:

```
import React, { Component, PropTypes } from 'react';
import {
  StyleSheet,
  Text,
  InteractionManager
} from 'react-native';
import AppText from './AppText';
```

Next, we'll create a constructor component that initializes some internal state. We'll create a flag in the component's state that tells us whether or not to render the expensive portions and initialize it as false, as shown in the following code snippet:

```
class SmallText extends Component {
  constructor(props) {
    super(props);

    this.state = {
      doExpensiveRender: false
    };
  }

  render() {
    const { children, useFallColors, style, ...rest } = this.props;
    let childrenFormatted = children;
    if (useFallColors) {
      childrenFormatted = fallColors(children);
    }
    return (
```

```
      <AppText style={[styles.small, style]} {...rest}>
        {childrenFormatted}
      </AppText>
    );
  }
}
```

Now, we'll modify the `render` method to only apply `fallColors` if the `doExpensiveRender` flag is true:

```
render() {
  const { children, useFallColors, style, ...rest } = this.props;
  let childrenFormatted = children;
  if (useFallColors && this.state.doExpensiveRender) {
    childrenFormatted = fallColors(children);
  }
  return (
    <AppText style={[styles.small, style]} {...rest}>
      {childrenFormatted}
    </AppText>
  );
}
```

Finally, we'll use the interaction manager to allow the expensive render after interaction animations have completed. To do this, we'll use the `componentDidMount` lifecycle method:

```
componentDidMount() {
  InteractionManager.runAfterInteractions(() => {
    this.setState({
      doExpensiveRender: true
    });
  });
}
```

Now, if we rerun our application, we'll be able to click on an article and see the modal open instantly. About a second later, `fallColors` will once again adorn the **Close** text, as shown in the following screenshot:

Performance summary

Though there are some common pitfalls and a number of typical solutions that we've discussed in this chapter, it is important to note that these solutions are not an exact prescription for creating a performant application. Every application is different and those circumstances effect how we apply optimizations.

The key takeaways from this section are knowing the categories of performance issues, general strategies for addressing them, and the tools that are available to help. It should be mentioned that each platform also has a set of native profiling tools that are enormously helpful especially if you find yourself writing a significant number of native modules.

Running on physical devices

Up to this point, we've been running our application strictly on simulated hardware. It is important that we take it one step further and run on actual mobile devices to be sure the application performs in the way that we expect. In this section, we'll discuss running React Native applications on both iOS and Android devices.

Debugging on an iOS device

Before submitting your app to the App Store, it's highly recommended that you first test your app on physical hardware. In fact, the more devices you can test on, the better. Simulators are great for rapid development testing, but they don't give you an honest sense of how the app feels in your hands. Are the touch targets large enough? Are the animations smooth on lower end hardware? Does the app feel responsive? These are all questions that are best answered with actual device testing.

Not long ago, Apple required that developers pay $99/year to join the Apple Developer Program in order test iOS apps on hardware. While you still need to pay to submit to the App Store, there is thankfully no longer a paywall for testing on devices. That said, there are a few steps required before deploying your React Native app to a personal iOS device.

The very first thing you'll need to do is ensure you're registered as an Apple developer at `https://developer.apple.com/`. Again, you don't need to pay the $99 if all you intend to do is test on your personal devices. Once you're registered, open up Xcode, go to **Xcode** | **Preferences**, and add your account credentials under the **Accounts** tab. Next, open up your React Native project's Xcode project file found under the `ios` directory. Then, follow these steps:

1. Ensure your app (for example, RNNYT) is set as the target.
2. Select the **General** tab.
3. Under **Signing**, select **[Your Name] (Personal Team)** from the **Team** drop-down menu.
4. Now change the target to the **Tests** app (for example, RNNYTTests) and follow steps 2 and 3 again.
5. Connect your personal device to your computer through a USB and ensure it's on the same Wi-Fi network as your computer.
6. From the Xcode menu, select **Product** | **Destination** and then select your device.
7. Click on **Build** and **Run** (the Play button). This will start the React Native Packager if it's not already running.

If this is your first time deploying this app to your device, you'll likely encounter an error from Xcode, which states: `Could not launch [App Name]. Verify the Developer App Certificate for your account is trusted on your device...` If you continue reading this error, it gives you specific instructions for trusting your Developer App Certificate on your device. Once you've completed these steps, click on **Build** and Run again from Xcode and the app will launch on your device. If you wish to debug the app, simply shake the device and the Developer menu will appear. From there, you're able to do all the usual debugging you're accustomed to from the iOS Simulator.

Testing your app on an iOS device using Release

This approach works great for testing, but you're unfortunately still tethered to your computer since the React Native Packager must be running on the same Wi-Fi connection as your device. Shaking your device also opens the Developer menu, which in the real world you'll want disabled. By building your app for Release, you'll be able to run your React Native app completely decoupled from your computer and the React Native Packager. The Release scheme will run all your JavaScript locally on the device and will automatically disable the Developer menu.

To configure the Release scheme from Xcode, run these steps:

1. Select **Product** | **Scheme** | **Edit Scheme**.
2. Ensure **Run** is selected on the left-hand side.
3. Set the **Build Configuration** drop-down menu to **Release**.
4. With your iOS device connected, verify it's set as the **Destination**.
5. Click on **Build** and Run.

Once the app appears on your phone, you can close your laptop and give the app a test in the real world.

Debugging on Android devices

If you intend to release your app to the Android store, it's not enough to test on iOS hardware. You'll also want to test on Android hardware. In fact, since many variations of Android hardware exist, testing on as many devices as possible is encouraged.

The first step for testing on Android hardware is to enable Developer mode on the device itself:

1. Open **Settings** | **About** | **Software Information** | **More**.
2. Tap **Build** number seven times to enable **Developer options**.

If you go back to **Settings**, you'll now see the **Developer options** listed.

Now to actually test your React Native app on your developer-enabled hardware, follow these steps:

1. Connect your Android device to your computer through a USB connection.
2. Run `adb` devices from the terminal to verify only your phone is listed. If you see other devices, be sure to terminate any running Android emulators running on your computer.
3. Run `react-native run-android` to install and run the app.

Clicking on the menu button on your Android device will toggle the Developer menu. Note that in order for you to continue debugging on Android, you'll need to keep the device connected over USB and the React Native Packager will need to be running.

> If you run into any issues while trying to debug your app on an Android device, consult the React Native docs as they have extensive documentation; for more information, refer to `https://facebook.github.io/react-native/docs/running-on-device-android.html`.

Generating a signed APK

If you wish to test your app on Android hardware in a more realistic setting, you'll need to generate an APK. An APK, or Android application package, is the actual binary you'll distribute to the Android Play Store. While there are a few steps involved in this, the React Native docs are extremely thorough and easy to follow, even for a non-Android developer. So rather than reinvent the wheel, I recommend you follow their instructions on `https://facebook.github.io/react-native/docs/signed-apk-android.html`.

Deploying our application

Now that we have a fully featured, well-tested, and performant application, it is time to get it into the hands of our users. In this section, we'll briefly go through the steps involved in getting an application into a mobile app store, focusing on the parts of the process that are specific to React Native.

Remove debugging code

No matter where we plan on distributing our application, we will want to ensure that we remove any code that is specific to debugging from our production application build. Some of this, including things such as React PropTypes, will be done for us in the React library, but occasionally we will need to do it ourselves.

One example of code that can be removed from the production build is redux-logger. This tool is very helpful when we're developing an application, but it has no business in a production application. Not only is it superfluous extra weight for our JavaScript asset, but it also impacts performance. In React Native JavaScript applications, we get access to a global Boolean variable __DEV__ that can be used to determine what environment the code is running in. We can use this variable in our createStore.js file to ensure redux-logger is not shipped to production:

```
import { createStore, applyMiddleware, combineReducers } from 'redux';
import createLogger from 'redux-logger';
import promiseMiddleware from 'redux-promise';
import newsFeedReducer from './reducers/newsFeedReducer';
import searchTermReducer from './reducers/searchTermReducer';
import navigationReducer from './reducers/navigationReducer';
import bookmarkReducer from './reducers/bookmarkReducer';
import newsFeedProgressReducer from './reducers/newsFeedProgressReducer';

const logger = createLogger();
const middleWare = global.__DEV__ ? [logger, promiseMiddleware] :
[promiseMiddleware];

export default (initialState = {}) => (
  createStore(
    combineReducers({
      news: newsFeedReducer,
      searchTerm: searchTermReducer,
      navigation: navigationReducer,
      bookmarks: bookmarkReducer,
      progress: newsFeedProgressReducer
    }),
    initialState,
    applyMiddleware(...middleWare)
  )
);
```

Likewise, we can use it to decide whether or not to expose the React `Perf` library in `App.js`:

```
import React from 'react';
import Perf from 'react-addons-perf';
import { Provider } from 'react-redux';
import NavContainer from './containers/NavContainer';
import createStore from './createStore';

if (global.__DEV__) {
  window.Perf = Perf;
}

const store = createStore();

export default () => (
  <Provider store={store}>
    <NavContainer />
  </Provider>
);
```

iOS

The iOS deployment process is notoriously lengthy. We will go through each of the steps involved from a high level and focus on parts of the process where React Native applications diverge from that of a completely native mobile application.

In order to release an application to the iOS App Store, you must be a registered Apple developer. Registration costs $99/year for an individual.

Creating provisioning profiles

In order to distribute an iOS application, you must obtain a provisioning profile for that application. To do this, navigate in a browser to `https://developer.apple.com` and log in. From here, navigate to **Certificates, Identifiers & Profiles**. Refer to the following screenshot:

From here, select **Provisioning Profiles** | **Distribution** in the side navigation:

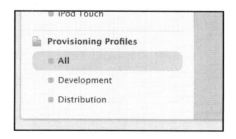

We're going to create two new profiles: one that will be used for beta testing and another that will be used for distributing to the App Store. For the first, select the **Ad Hoc** profile type. Complete the process by selecting your application ID and selecting or creating a certificate. We'll call this first profile RNNYT Beta.

The site will then prompt you to download the profile. Do this and then repeat the process for an App Store profile. Once both have been downloaded, clicking on them should open them in Xcode, making Xcode aware of your new profiles.

Registering an application in iTunes Connect

Not only do we need to register our application on the Apple developer site, but we also must register the application with iTunes Connect in order to upload it to the App Store. To do this, navigate in the browser to https://itunesconnect.apple.com. Log in here with your Apple developer ID and navigate to **My Apps**.

Once there, add a new application:

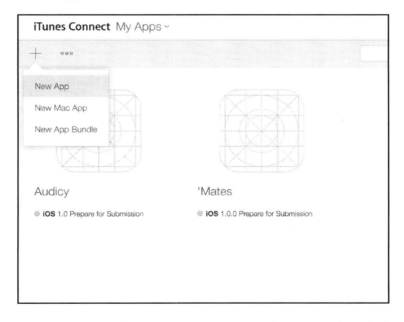

Fill out the form to create an application. Most importantly, ensure that the bundle ID matches that in XCode and that on the Apple developer website.

Adding icons and updating the launch screen

Before we can submit the application to the App Store, we'll need to update the launch screen and add icons for our application. Both of these tasks can be done from within XCode.

By clicking on the LaunchScreen.xib file in the XCode sidebar, we can visually edit the appearance of the launch screen. Apple generally recommends that this screen look similar to the first screen of your application. Take a look at the following screenshot:

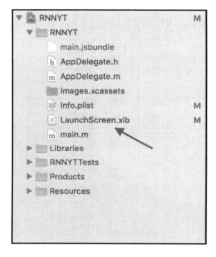

Similarly, we can add App icons by clicking on **Images.xcassets** | **AppIcon**. We will need to add images of several different sizes and resolutions. See the Apple documentation for exact icon dimensions. Refer to the following screenshot:

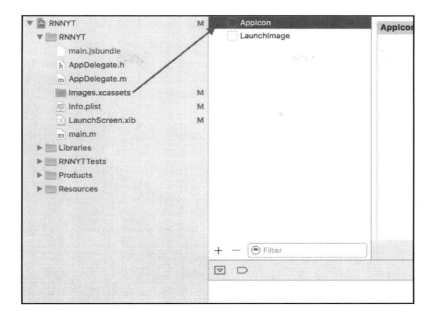

Creating an archive

Now that we have provisioning profiles and a completed application with a launch screen and app icons, we are ready to create the archive that we will deliver to Apple. Before we do, let's discuss how this works as it relates to React Native.

Normally, when we build our application during the development process, we use the XCode Debug configuration. This configuration relies on our local React Native development server to load the JavaScript asset. It also enables debugging features such as the Developer menu, performance monitoring, and remote debugging in Chrome.

When we create the archive for our application, we use the `Release` configuration. This configuration creates a static JavaScript bundle and includes it as an asset of the application. It also disables the aforementioned debugging features and sets the global JavaScript `__DEV__` variable to false. All this is handled for us by how React Native sets up our project, but it is helpful to know.

To create an archive, we must first select the **Generic iOS Device** option from the device drop-down, as shown in the following screenshot:

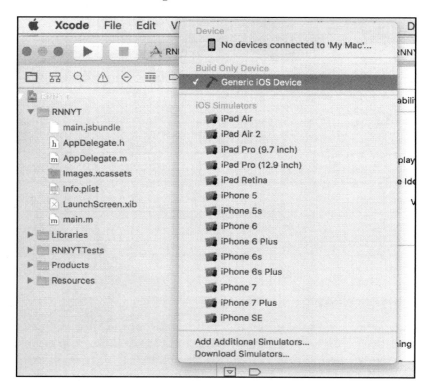

Next, in XCode, select from the top menu **Product | Archive**.

  If this is not the first time we are creating an archive for upload, we will need to also increase the version and build number under build settings.

Take a look at the following screenshot:

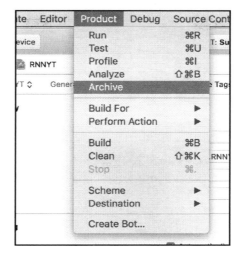

Once the Archive is complete, we should see a list of archives and a button labeled **Upload to App Store...**, as shown in the following screenshot:

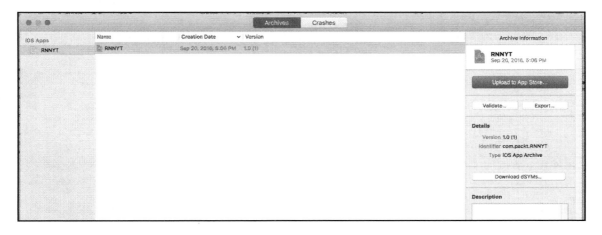

Assuming we have correctly configured our application on the Apple developer website and iTunes Connect and attached the appropriate launch icons and app icons, our archive should upload successfully.

Beta testing and release

From here, the rest of the process will happen on iTunes Connect. Plenty of documentation exists on this topic as it is, so we won't go into too much depth. TestFlight can be used to allow internal and external testers to beta-test our application before officially submitting it to the store. This is helpful because, in order to complete the submission process, our application will have to go through the Apple review process, which can take some time.

Android

The process for preparing a React Native application for the Google Play store is analogous to that of iOS, except that we can do all of it from the command line and don't need Android Studio.

Signing the application

The first thing we need to do is sign our application with a private key. This is used to ensure the authenticity of the application when it is downloaded by an Android device from the store. The first thing we will need to do is generate a private key for the application with the keytool command:

```
$ keytool -genkey -v -keystore rnnyt-release-key.keystore -alias rnnyt-key-
alias -keyalg RSA -keysize 2048 -validity 10000
```

This command will generate the rnnyt-release-key.keystore file. Which we can use to sign our application.

 This file is private and should not be committed to your repository. To do this, we'll add android/app/rnnyt-release-key.keystore to our .gitignore file. Also, we need to keep track of this file as it will be needed to make future changes to our application in the Google Play store.

Place the newly generated keystore file in the android/app directory within the project. We then need to edit our user-level Gradle configuration to use the new keystore file. To do this, we'll need to create or edit the file ~/.gradle/gradle.properties:

```
RNNYT_RELEASE_STORE_FILE=rnnyt-release-key.keystore
RNNYT_RELEASE_KEY_ALIAS=rnnyt-key-alias
RNNYT_RELEASE_STORE_PASSWORD=*YOUR_PASSWORD*
RNNYT_RELEASE_KEY_PASSWORD=*YOUR_PASSWORD*
```

Finally, we need to add these new key variables to the `android/app/build.gradle` configuration file. There are multiple `build.gradle` files in the project, so ensure you are editing the right one:

```
...
defaultConfig {
        applicationId "com.rnnyt"
        minSdkVersion 16
        targetSdkVersion 22
        versionCode 1
        versionName "1.0"
        ndk {
            abiFilters "armeabi-v7a", "x86"
        }
}
signingConfigs {
        release {
            storeFile file(RNNYT_RELEASE_STORE_FILE)
            storePassword RNNYT_RELEASE_STORE_PASSWORD
            keyAlias RNNYT_RELEASE_KEY_ALIAS
            keyPassword RNNYT_RELEASE_KEY_PASSWORD
        }
}
splits {
...
```

Now that we have the ability to sign our application, we are ready to test the release build.

Testing the release build

Before we upload an application to the Google Play store, we will want to ensure that the application continues to behave appropriately when it is built with a release configuration. To this, we simply need to add an argument to the `run-android` command:

```
react-native run-android --variant=release
```

Like the iOS release build, this will strip out development code and package the JavaScript with the applications. Once we're sure that the application works as expected when built for release, we can generate the file that we will upload to the Play Store: the APK.

Generating the APK

For Android, the deliverable for an application is the APK file. In order to create this, we will use the `gradle` build tool from the **android** directory:

```
cd android && ./gradlew assembleRelease
```

Once this completes, we will have an APK file for our project located in the directory `android/app/build/outputs/apk/app-release.apk`.

Beta-test and release

To release our application, we will need to navigate in the browser to the Google Play store developer console at `https://play.google.com/apps/publish/signup`. Here we can register for an account; this, like iOS, is not free (though much cheaper). Once in the console, it is easy to add a new application APK for alpha, beta, or production. Here we can also add metadata and assets (such as icons) to the Google Play store.

Summary

When we finish with the functionality of an application, there are still several steps before our friends, family, and customers can begin to download it from the App Store. Any production application is well tested for correctness and performance characteristics. Luckily for us, the React Native ecosystem has many tools, continuously developing and maturing, that can aid us in this process.

What draws frontend developers to React Native is that it is a framework that empowers them to make native applications with the skills they already possess. What, hopefully, keeps them there is the fact that with proper tuning it can match the performance and feel of full native applications for most use cases. The steps outlined in this chapter are important for realizing that promise.

In the next, and final, chapter, we'll take a look at other resources that can help you on your continued journey to master React Native.

12
React Native Tools and Resources

As we bring this book to a close, it's time to acknowledge how much we've accomplished. We've learned about numerous React Native APIs and how to configure our environments for building React Native apps for both iOS and Android. And more importantly, we've used this knowledge to build a fully featured, cross-platform app that uses several advanced techniques for modeling data, communicating with a remote server, animating views, and even bridging code to the underlying platform. *Phew!*

But we developers are never satisfied are we? Sadly, no. So let's spend this final chapter learning how to further improve upon the development experience and how to continue leveling up as React Native developers. Specifically, we'll look at:

- Tools that improve upon the React Native development experience
- Ways to build React Native apps for platforms other than iOS and Android
- Great online resources for React Native development

Evaluating React Native Editors, Plugins, and IDEs

I'm hard pressed to think of another topic that developers are more passionate about than their preferred code editor. Of the many options, two popular editors today are GitHub's Atom and Microsoft's Visual Studio Code (not be confused with the Visual Studio 2015). Both are cross-platform editors for Windows, macOS, and Linux and are easily extended with additional features. In this section, I'll detail my personal experience with these tools and where I have found they complement the React Native development experience.

Atom and Nuclide

Facebook has created a package for Atom known as Nuclide that *provides a first-class development environment for React Native* It features a built-in debugger similar to Chrome's DevTools, a React Native Inspector (think the **Elements** tab in Chrome DevTools), and support for the static type checker Flow.

Download Atom from `https://atom.io/` and Nuclide from `https://nuclide.io/`.

To install the Nuclide package, click on the **Atom** menu and then on **Preferences...**, and then select **Packages**. Search for Nuclide and click on **Install**. Once installed, you can actually start and stop the React Native Packager directly from Atom (though you need to launch the simulator/emulator separately) and set breakpoints in Atom itself rather than using Chrome's DevTools. Take a look at the following screenshot:

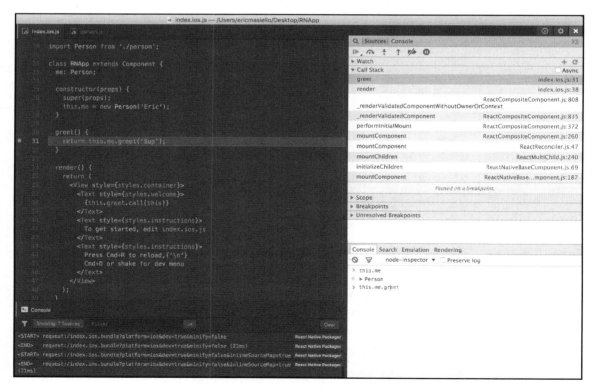

If you plan to use **Flow**, Nuclide will identify errors and display them inline. Take the following example, I've annotated the function `timesTen` such that it expects a number as a parameter and should return a number. However, you can see that there's some errors in the usage. Refer to the following code snippet:

```
/* @flow */

function timesTen(x: number): number {
    var result = x * 10;
    return 'I am not a number';
}

timesTen("Hello, world!");
```

Thankfully, the Flow integration will call out these errors in Atom for you. Refer to the following screenshot:

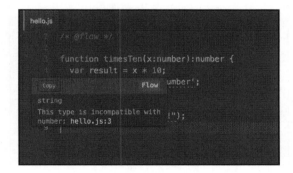

Flow integration of Nuclide exposes two other useful features. You'll see annotated autocompletion as you type. And, if you hold the Command key and click on a variable or function name, Nuclide will jump straight to the source definition, even if it's defined in a separate file. Refer to the following screenshot:

Visual Studio CodeVisual Studio Code is a first class editor for JavaScript authors. Out of the box, it's packaged with a built in debugger that can be used to debug Node applications. Additionally, VS Code comes with an integrated terminal and a git tool that nicely shows visual diffs.

> Download Visual Studio Code from `https://code.visualstudio.com/`.

The React Native Tools extensions for VS Code add some useful capabilities to the editor. For starters, you'll be able to execute the `React Native: Run-iOS` and `React Native: Run Android` commands directly from VS Code without needing to reach for a terminal, as shown in the following screenshot:

And, while a bit more involved than Atom to configure, you can use VS Code as a React Native debugger. Take a look at the following screenshot:

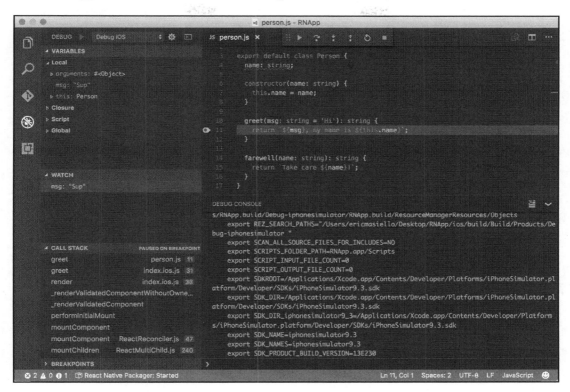

The React Native Tools extension also provides **IntelliSense** for much of the React Native API, as shown in the following screenshot:

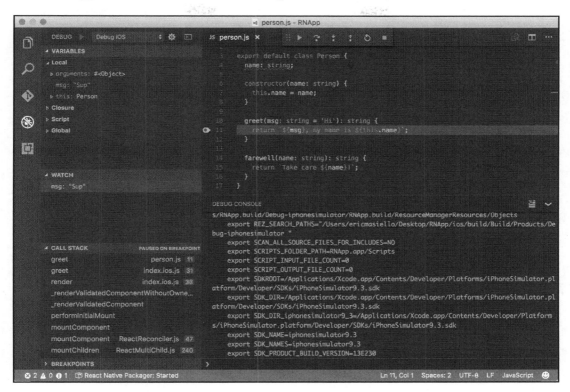

When reading through the VS Code documentation, I found it (unsurprisingly) more directed toward Windows users. So, if Windows is your thing, you may feel more at home with VS Code. As a macOS user, I slightly prefer Atom/Nuclide over VS Code. VS Code comes with more useful features out-of-the-box but that can easily be addressed by installing a few Atom packages. Plus, I found Flow support for Nuclide really useful. But don't let me dissuade you from VS Code. Both are solid editors with great React Native support. And they're both free so no harm in trying both.

Before totally switching gears, there is one more editor worth mentioning. **Deco** is an **Integrated Development Environment** (**IDE**) built specifically for React Native development. Starting up a new React Native project is super quick since Deco keeps a local copy of everything you'd get when running `react-native init`. Deco also makes creating new stateful and stateless components super easy.

Download Deco from `https://www.decosoftware.com/`.

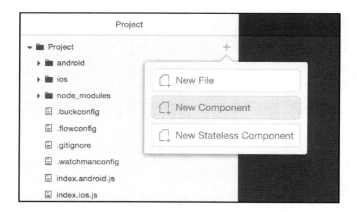

Once you create a new component using Deco, it gives you a nicely prefilled template including a place to add `propTypes` and `defaultProps` (something I often forget to do). Refer to the following screenshot:

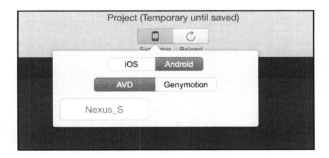

From there, you can drag and drop components from the sidebar directly into your code. Deco will auto-populate many of the props for you as well as adding the necessary import statements. Take a look at the following code snippet:

```
<Image
    style={{
        width: 300,
        height: 200,
    }}
    resizeMode={"contain"}
    source={{uri:'https://unsplash.it/600/400/?random'}}/>
```

The other nice feature Deco adds is the ability to easily launch your app from the toolbar in any installed iOS simulator or Android AVD. You don't even need to first manually open the AVD, Deco will do it all for you. Refer to the following screenshot:

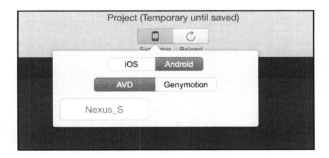

Currently, creating a new project with Deco starts you off with an outdated version of React Native (version 0.27.2 currently). If you're not concerned with using the latest version, Deco is a great way to get a React Native app up quickly. However, if you require more advanced tooling, I suggest you look at Atom with Nuclide or Visual Studio Code with the React Native Tools extension.

Taking React Native beyond iOS and Android

The development experience is one of the most highly touted features by React Native proponents. But, as we well know by now, React Native is more than just a great development experience. It's also about building cross-platform applications with a common language and, often, reusable code and components. Out of the box, the Facebook team has provided tremendous support for iOS and Android. And thanks to the community, React Native has expanded to include other promising platforms. In this section, I'll take you through a few of these React Native projects. I won't go into great technical depth, but I'll provide a high-level overview and show how to get each running.

Introducing React Native Web

React Native Web is an interesting one. It treats many React Native components you've learned about, such as `View`, `Text`, and `TextInput`, as higher-level abstractions that map to HTML elements, such as `div`, `span`, and `input`, thus allowing you to build a web app that runs in a browser from your React Native code. Now, if you're like me, your initial reaction might be–But why? We already have React for the web. It's called ... React! However, where React Native Web shines over React is in its ability to share components between your mobile app and the Web because you're still working with the same basic React Native APIs.

 Learn more about React Native Web at `https://github.com/necolas/re` `act-native-web`.

Configuring React Native Web

React Native Web can be installed into your existing React Native project just like any other npm dependency:

```
npm install --save react react-native-web
```

Depending on the version of React Native and React Native Web you've installed, you may encounter conflicting peer dependencies for React. This may require manually adjusting which version of React Native or React Native Web is installed. Sometimes, just deleting the node_modules folder and rerunning npm install does the trick.

From there, you'll need some additional tools to build the web bundle. In this example, we'll use webpack and some related tooling:

```
npm install webpack babel-loader babel-preset-react babel-preset-es2015
babel-preset-stage-1 webpack-validator webpack-merge --save
npm install webpack-dev-server --save-dev
```

Next, create a webpack.config.js file in the root of the project:

```javascript
const webpack = require('webpack');
const validator = require('webpack-validator');
const merge = require('webpack-merge');
const target = process.env.npm_lifecycle_event;
let config = {};

const commonConfig = {
  entry: {
    main: './index.web.js'
  },
  output: {
    filename: 'app.js'
  },
  resolve: {
    alias: {
      'react-native': 'react-native-web'
    }
  },
  module: {
    loaders: [
      {
        test: /\.js$/,
        exclude: /node_modules/,
        loader: 'babel',
        query: {
```

```
            presets: ['react', 'es2015', 'stage-1']
          }
        }
      ]
    }
};

switch(target) {
  case 'web:prod':
    config = merge(commonConfig, {
      devtool: 'source-map',
      plugins: [
        new webpack.DefinePlugin({
          'process.env.NODE_ENV': JSON.stringify('production')
        })
      ]
    });
    break;
  default:
    config = merge(commonConfig, {
      devtool: 'eval-source-map'
    });
    break;
}

module.exports = validator(config);
```

Add the following two entries to the scripts section of package.json:

```
"web:dev": "webpack-dev-server --inline --hot",
"web:prod": "webpack -p"
```

Next, create an index.html file in the root of the project:

```
<!DOCTYPE html>
<html>
<head>
  <title>RNNYT</title>
  <meta charset="utf-8" />
  <meta content="initial-scale=1,width=device-width" name="viewport" />
</head>
<body>
  <div id="app"></div>
  <script type="text/javascript" src="/app.js"></script>
</body>
</html>
```

And, finally, add an `index.web.js` file to the root of the project:

```javascript
import React, { Component } from 'react';
import {
  View,
  Text,
  StyleSheet,
  AppRegistry
} from 'react-native';

class App extends Component {
  render() {
    return (
      <View style={styles.container}>
        <Text style={styles.text}>Hello World!</Text>
      </View>
    );
  }
}

const styles = StyleSheet.create({
  container: {
    flex: 1,
    backgroundColor: '#efefef',
    alignItems: 'center',
    justifyContent: 'center'
  },
  text: {
    fontSize: 18
  }
});

AppRegistry.registerComponent('RNNYT', () => App);
AppRegistry.runApplication('RNNYT', { rootTag:
document.getElementById('app') });
```

To run the development build, we'll run webpack-dev-server by executing the following command:

npm run web:dev

web:prod can be substituted to create a production ready build.

While developing, you can add React Native Web specific code much like you can with iOS and Android by using `Platform.OS === 'web'` or by creating custom `*.web.js` components.

React Native Web still feels pretty early days. Not every component and API is supported, and the HTML that's generated looks a bit rough for my taste. While developing with React Native Web, I think it helps to keep the right mindset. That is, think of this as *I'm building a React Native mobile app, not a website*. Otherwise, you may find yourself reaching for web-specific solutions that aren't appropriate for the technology.

React Native plugin for Universal Windows Platform

Announced at the Facebook F8 conference in April, 2016, the React Native plugin for **Universal Windows Platform (UWP)** lets you author React Native apps for Windows 10 desktop, Windows 10 mobile, and Xbox One.

 Learn more about the React Native plugin for UWP at `https://github.co m/ReactWindows/react-native-windows`.

You'll need to be running Windows 10 in order to build UWP apps. You'll also need to follow the React Native documentation to configure your Windows environment for building React Native apps. If you're not concerned with building Android on Windows, you can skip installing Android Studio. The plugin itself also has a few additional requirements. You'll need to be running at least `npm 3.x` and to install Visual Studio 2015 Community (not be confused with Visual Studio Code). Thankfully, the Community version is free to use. The UWP plugin docs also tell you to install the Windows 10 SDK Build 10586. However, I found it's easier to do that from within Visual Studio once we've created the app so that we can save that part for later.

Configuring the React Native plugin for UWP

I won't walk you through every step of the installation. The UWP plugin docs detail the process well enough. Once you've satisfied the requirements, start by creating a new React Native project as normal:

```
react-native init RNWindows
cd RNWindows
```

Next, install and initialize the UWP plugin:

```
npm install --save-dev rnpm-plugin-windows
react-native windows
```

Running `react-native windows` will actually create a windows directory inside your project containing a Visual Studio solution file. If this is your first time installing the plugin, I recommend opening the solution (`.sln`) file with Visual Studio 2015. Visual Studio will then ask you to download several dependencies including the latest Windows 10 SDK. Once Visual Studio has installed all the dependencies, you can run the app either from within Visual Studio or by running the following command:

```
react-native run-windows
```

Take a look at the following screenshot:

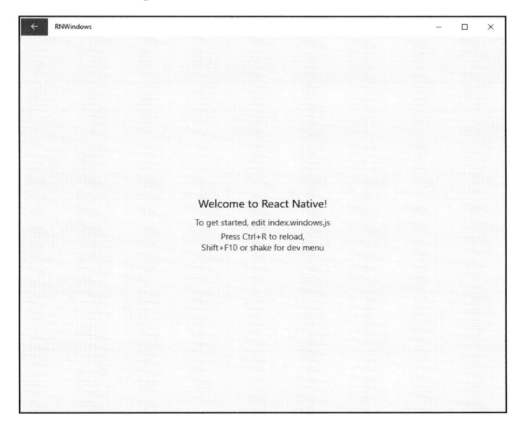

React Native macOS

Much as the name implies, React Native allows you to create macOS desktop applications using React Native. This project works a little differently than the React Native Web and the React Native plugin for UWP. As best I can tell, since React Native macOS requires its own custom CLI for creating and packaging applications, you are not able to build a macOS and mobile app from the same project.

 Learn more about React Native macOS at `https://github.com/ptmt/rea` `ct-native-macos`.

Configuring React Native macOS

Much like you did with the React Native CLI, begin by installing the custom CLI globally by using the following command:

```
npm install react-native-macos-cli -g
```

Then, use it to create a new React Native macOS app by running the following command:

```
react-native-macos init RNDesktopApp
cd RNDesktopApp
```

This will set you up with all required dependencies along with an entry point file, `index.macos.js`. There is no CLI command to spin up the app, so you'll need to open the Xcode project and manually run it. Run the following command:

```
open macos/RNDesktopApp.xcodeproj
```

The documentation is pretty limited, but there is a nice **UIExplorer** app that can be downloaded and run to give you a good feel for what's available. While on some level it's unfortunate your macOS app cannot live alongside your iOS and Android code, I cannot think of a use case that would call for this. That said, I was delighted with how easy it was to get this project up-and-running.

Summary

I think it's fair to say that React Native is moving quickly. With a new version released roughly every two weeks, I've lost count of how many versions have passed by in the course of writing this book. I'm willing to bet React Native has probably bumped up a version or two from the time you started reading this book until now. So, as much as I'd love to wrap up by saying you now know everything possible about React Native, sadly that isn't the case.

References

Let me leave you with a few valuable resources to continue your journey of learning and building apps with React Native:

- React Native AppleTV is a fork of React Native for building apps for Apple's tvOS. For more information, refer to `https://github.com/douglowder/react-native-appletv`. (Note that preliminary tvOS support has appeared in early versions of React Native 0.36.)
- React Native Ubuntu is another fork of React Native for developing React Native apps on Ubuntu for Desktop Ubuntu and Ubuntu Touch. For more information, refer to `https://github.com/CanonicalLtd/react-native`
- `JS.Coach` is a collection of the community's favorite components and plugins for all things React, React Native, Webpack, and related tools. For more information, refer to `https://js.coach/react-native`
- Exponent is described as **Rails for React Native**. It supports additional system functionality and UI components beyond what's provided by React Native. It will also let you build your apps without needing to touch Xcode or Android Studio. For more information, refer to `https://getexponent.com/`
- React Native Elements is a cross-platform UI toolkit for React Native. You can think of it as Bootstrap for React Native. For more information, refer to `https://github.com/react-native-community/react-native-elements`
- The **Use React Native** site is how I keep up with React Native releases and news in the React Native space. For more information, refer to `http://www.reactnative.com/`

- React Native Radio is fantastic podcast hosted by Nader Dabit and a panel of hosts who interview other developers contributing to the React Native community. For more information, refer to `https://devchat.tv/react-native-radio`
- React Native Newsletter is an *occasional* newsletter curated by a team of React Native enthusiasts. For more information, refer to `http://reactnative.cc/`
- And, finally, Dotan J. Nahum maintains an amazing resource titled **Awesome React Native** that includes articles, tutorials, videos, and well-tested components you can use in your next project. For more information, refer to `https://github.com/jondot/awesome-react-native`

Index